GEORGIA POLITICS IN A STATE OF CHANGE

Charles S. Bullock III
The University of Georgia

Ronald Keith Gaddie
The University of Oklahoma

Longman

Boston   Columbus   Indianapolis   New York   San Francisco
Upper Saddle River   Amsterdam   Cape Town   Dubai   London
Madrid   Milan   Munich   Paris   Montreal   Toronto   Delhi   Mexico City
Sao Paulo   Sydney   Hong Kong   Seoul   Singapore   Taipei   Tokyo

Editor-in-Chief: Eric Stano
Marketing Manager: Lindsey Prudhomme
Production Manager: Wanda Rockwell
Project Coordination, Text Design, and Electronic Page Makeup: Niraj Bhatt/Aptara®, Inc.
Cover Design Manager: Nancy Danahy
Cover Designer: Nancy Sacks
Cover Illustration/Photo: Getty Images, Inc.
Manufacturing Buyer: Wanda Rockwell
Printer and Binder: Courier Companies, Inc.
Cover Printer: Courier Companies, Inc.

Library of Congress Cataloging-in-Publication Data

Bullock, Charles S.,
  Georgia politics in a state of change / Charles S. Bullock, Ronald Keith Gaddie.
    p. cm.
  ISBN-13: 978-0-205-70685-3
  ISBN-10: 0-205-70685-1
  1. Georgia—Politics and government.   I. Gaddie, Ronald Keith.   II. Title.
  JK4341.B85 2009
  320.4758—dc22

                                                                 2009038229

1 2 3 4 5 6 7 8 9 10—DOH—12 11 10 09

Longman
is an imprint of

www.pearsonhighered.com   ISBN-13: 978-0-205-70685-3
                                 ISBN-10:   0-205-70685-1

BRIEF CONTENTS

DETAILED CONTENTS

PREFACE

POLITICS IN A STATE OF CHANGE

Georgia politics is a remarkable mix of continuity and change. If a Georgian who died half a century ago returned today, she would be stunned by the changes, such as Republican dominance in state politics; the widespread integration of African Americans into public life; and the diversification of the economy, which has made Atlanta an international business and communications center and cultural destination. A visitor from the last century would see a state where rural counties no longer control state politics, the rhetoric of segregation no longer enters public discourse, and the Cross of St. Andrew no longer dominates the state flag. Henry W. Grady's nineteenth-century dream of a New South with Atlanta as its capital would unfold before our time-displaced Georgian.

After overcoming the shock of seeing the changes, a Georgian from 50 years ago would notice that some things remained the same. Geography continues to matter. Politics still pits Atlanta against much of the rest of the state. Under the gold dome of the state Capitol, a part-time legislature functions with a minimum of staff while lobbyists continue to exert substantial influence. The governor (nearly as powerful as ever) is yet again a rural white man from below the Fall Line who previously served as a powerful state legislator. Various other institutions chug along, modernized in terms of equipment and personnel but controlled by old norms and political alliances that in some cases predate the 1908 Model-T Ford.

The challenges of politics would seem sometimes familiar, sometimes strange. Much of state and local politics everywhere is about concrete—where to pour it and from whom to buy it—and this is true of Georgia in the past and Georgia today. In Atlanta, our Georgian would discover that the business of politics is still business. Rick Allen, author of *The Secret Formula* and *Atlanta Rising*, observed once that, "Atlanta is a city first and foremost run by its Chamber of Commerce." The downtown chamber crowd is not as powerful as it was when Floyd Hunter argued in his 1953 book on Atlanta, *Community Power Structure*, that a power structure guided the city's political decisions with a hand unseen by the public, but Atlanta politics continues to be about doing business.[1] The issue of race is neither as stark nor powerful as when the Southern Christian Leadership Conference sought to integrate Georgia institutions, but the politics of the state have a racial dimension, institutionalized in the two-party system and incorporating an empowered black electorate.

But new issues have arisen. From Tybee Light to just below the shadow of Lookout Mountain in Chattanooga, Georgia is growing. The old Georgian would see that development has overrun north Georgia, aided by a highway network that make Lake Burton in distant Rabun County and Lake Oconee

---

[1]Floyd Hunter, *Community Power Structure* (Chapel Hill: University of North Carolina Press, 1953).

just north of Milledgeville relatively easy destinations from Atlanta. Urban and suburban Georgia face all of the challenges of southern California—traffic congestion, water shortages, sprawl. The social policy challenges of both urban and rural communities would seem alien to our out-of-time Georgian. Yet, at base, the debate often is set in a racial context, as political debate has been in Georgia since the eighteenth century.

This book explores Georgia's constitution, politics, and government. It is written with an eye on the present and an appreciation of history, because without an understanding of where Georgia came from, it is impossible to understand the state and its politics at the beginning of the twenty-first century. The text is organized into four broad sections, each of which contains a collection of brief chapters.

Part I traces Georgia's politics in the postbellum era, which begins with white, rural Democratic Party domination and ends with the ascendancy of suburban Republicans and a heavily African American Democratic Party. The historical foundation of rural dominion in Georgia politics is discussed, and the peculiar social institutions of Georgia that perpetrated rural, white dominion are described.

Part II explores Georgia's constitution and the institutions of state government—legislature, executive, and judiciary—that translate elections into public policy. This section also lays out the design and function of local government in Georgia.

Part III examines three agents of change in Georgia politics: the civil rights revolution and the concomitant voting rights revolution in the South; the demise of rural power and the urban ascendancy facilitated by legislative redistricting; and the impact of urbanization and suburbanization on where Georgians live, who they are, and how they relate to their governments.

Part IV explores elections, campaign finance, parties, and interest groups, and also discusses a primary focus of those activities—education policy.

We would like to thank Wendell S. Broadwell, Jr., at Georgia Perimeter College; Scott E. Buchanan at The Citadel; Tom Caiazzo at East Georgia College; Michael F. Digby at Georgia College & State University; Hyacinth C. Ezeamii at Albany State University, Georgia; Rebecca L. Sims at South Georgia College; Carl Anthony Wege at College of Coastal Georgia; and others who reviewed the material anonymously.

Charles S. Bullock III
Ronald Keith Gaddie

PART ONE

Georgia Politics
From Talmadgism to Two-Party Competition

CHAPTER 1

Georgia and the Rule of the Rustics

"The past is not dead. In fact, it's not even past."

—WILLIAM FAULKNER

On January 1, 2008, Fidel Castro, the world's longest-serving political leader, celebrated his forty-ninth anniversary as the dictator of Cuba before stepping aside in favor of his brother Raul. In 1989, Communist control over the Soviet Union ended 70 years after being established by Vladimir Lenin. Louis XIV sat on the throne of France for 72 years. The House of Stuart ruled Great Britain, off and on, for 85 years.

These regimes pale in comparison to the hegemony of the Democratic Party of Georgia, which consistently won elections beginning before the end of Reconstruction and continuing until 2003, when, after losing 50 consecutive gubernatorial elections, the Republican Party finally succeeded for the first time in six generations. Democratic control of the state legislature also ended early in the new century, and after the 2006 election, Republicans held 12 of 15 offices elected statewide.

The extended and uninterrupted dominance of Georgia gubernatorial elections by Democrats was but a part of the complete control of Georgia government enjoyed by Democrats. During most of the 130 years that Democrats held Georgia's governorship, they also held *all* statewide constitutional offices, all of the federal offices, and virtually all of the state legislative and local offices. The one-party government that V. O. Key observed in the South was nowhere more thoroughgoing than in the Peach State.[1]

To understand politics and government in Georgia is to understand the role of the past, the amazing changes that created present-day Georgia, and the new institutions and economic and social forces that confront the legacy of the past. From the past comes a politics borne out of a frontier history, agrarian economics, slavery, martial defeat, segregation, and populism. The agents of change are many, some coming from technology, external political forces, or the inevitable demands of individuals to overturn the vestiges of history that are facially unfair. Those agents of change create new political institutions and movements, which simultaneously lead the state forward but still must contend with the state's cultural heritage of the past.

THE HISTORIC PAST

The Civil War resolved political disagreements regarding slavery, the power of the states relative to the national government, and the primacy of technology and monetarism over agrarianism that defined the antebellum period. For states of the South, including Georgia, modern politics begin to take shape in the Reconstruction following the Civil War.

As in the rest of the South, Republicans briefly held power immediately after the war. In 1868, Republican businessman Rufus Bullock won the governorship, and Georgia's congressional delegation consisted of four Republicans and three Democrats. Republicans won by constructing a biracial coalition at a time when many whites could not vote because they had taken up arms in support of the Confederacy.

While white Democrats "redeemed" the southern states by the mid-1870s and ultimately eliminated most blacks from the voter rolls, Republican success ended in Georgia earlier than in most places. Between the 1868 election of Governor Bullock and that fall's presidential elections, Democrats mobilized more of their followers while intimidating black and white Republicans so that the Grand Old Party (GOP) success in the gubernatorial election did not extend to the presidential election. Ulysses Grant lost Georgia by a margin of 64 to 36 percent. The Republican tide ebbed so rapidly that Bullock could not finish out his term. Facing a threat of impeachment, he fled the state and was succeeded by Benjamin Conley, the Republican president of the Georgia Senate. The election of James Smith in 1872 launched the Democratic Party's record-setting 130 years in the governor's chair. By 1876, the state's congressional delegation included only Democrats.

---

[1]V. O. Key Jr., *Southern Politics* (New York: A. A. Knopf, 1949).

The only threat to Democratic control of the congressional delegation prior to the 1960s came from Populists in the 1890s. In 1892 and 1894, Populists contested every congressional district but scored no successes, although some members of Congress elected as Democrats, like Tom Watson, converted to the Populist cause. Watson, from the city of Thompson, was the state's leading Populist and one of the leaders of that movement nationwide. In a rare move for this period, he helped fashion a biracial coalition. That effort soon collapsed when Democrats foiled his reelection bid in a campaign fraught with controversy and scandal. Democrats allegedly brought in black voters from South Carolina, whom they marched to the polls in Augusta and forced to vote illegally. Watson lost his seat by a margin of 5,400 votes. A comeback effort in 1894 failed, and while Watson received the Populist nomination for vice president in 1896, both the movement and his career in that party never recovered.[2]

Watson's defeat proved to be even more consequential for Georgia. "The Sage," as he liked to be called, who had once led white farmers to protect a black follower who was being threatened by a mob, became one of the region's most inflammatory racial demagogues. He directed his racist venom not only at African Americans but also at any who were not white Anglo-Saxon Protestants. Late in his life, he fomented the hatred that led to the lynching of Atlanta pencil factory superintendent Leo Frank, who had been convicted of murdering a young girl employed at the factory.[3]

During the first half of the twentieth century, Republican presidential candidates struggled to get as much as a quarter of the vote in Georgia. In some instances, the Republican nominee came up spectacularly short. For example, in 1916, Charles Hughes attracted only 7 percent of the vote in his effort to deny a second term to Woodrow Wilson, who had spent part of his youth in Augusta and practiced law in Atlanta. Warren Harding's candidacy in 1920 prompted Tennessee to become the first southern state to vote Republican in a presidential election since 1876 but left Georgians unmoved. In 1932, Herbert Hoover lost his reelection bid in Georgia, taking fewer than 20,000 votes. Hoover had been the one relatively strong Republican in Georgia during this era when he took 44 percent of Georgia's vote in 1928, as some Democrats rejected their party's nominee, Al Smith, because of his Catholicism. While Hoover made the 1928 presidential election competitive in Georgia, this performance paled compared to his winning Florida, North Carolina, Tennessee, Texas, and Virginia. Even as Rim South states began to support Republican

---

[2]C. Vann Woodward, *Tom Watson: Agrarian Rebel* (Savannah, GA: Beehive Press, 1973).

[3]Contemporary fair-minded observers believe that the conviction rested more on anti-Semitism than evidence (Stephen Oney, *And the Dead Shall Rise*, 2003). When Governor John Slayton commuted Frank's death sentence to life imprisonment, Watson used his weekly newspaper, *The Jeffersonian*, to urge a lynch mob to carry out the sentence imposed by the trial judge. Watson's call was answered by some of the leading citizens of Marietta, the murdered girl's hometown.

presidential candidates in 1950s, Georgia hung back.[4] Dwight Eisenhower got less than a third of Georgia's votes in either of his presidential bids. Though weak, the performance of Republican presidential candidates actually might have seemed impressive compared to how Republicans fared in other contests during the first half of the twentieth century. From 1880 to 1962, no Republican even ran for governor. In U.S. Senate elections, only two Republicans ran from the time at which popular election of senators was introduced in 1914 until 1968. For decades, winning the Democratic nomination guaranteed winning almost every public office in the state. A consequence of such a one-party system is that all competition, debate, and political ambition is confined to that party.

BIFACTIONAL POLITICS

During part of the period when parties failed to structure, Georgia politics was not as fluid as in other states, such as Florida or Arkansas. When Key described the politics of the South in the middle of the twentieth century, Georgia was among three states that had "bifactional" politics.[5] Key observed that bifactional politics often revolved around a powerful family or individual of great personality, creating a "pro" and "anti" bloc. In Louisiana, it was the Long family versus the "Regulars" and then later the "anti-Longs."[6] Georgia had no Republican Party during the second quarter of the twentieth century, except in a couple of mountain counties, so in place of well-defined party competition, Georgia politics revolved around voters' feelings about the Talmadge family. The leader of the faction, Eugene Talmadge, had burst on the political scene in 1926 when he defeated the commissioner of agriculture. For the next 20 years, Talmadge appeared on the ballot every year except 1944.

The "ag" commissioner could fill a substantial number of patronage positions, and with the Georgia economy so heavily dependent upon agriculture, the position commanded widespread respect. Serving as agriculture commissioner only temporarily satisfied Talmadge's ambitions, so in 1932 he ran for governor. He launched this effort despite a controversial tenure as ag commissioner. He had been accused of using state funds to take family and friends to the Kentucky Derby.[7] He had also transferred state funds to a non-interest-bearing account in a bank run by a relative of his wife. Most

---

[4]Georgia, Alabama, Louisiana, Mississippi, and South Carolina are Deep South states, while Arkansas, Florida, North Carolina, Tennessee, Texas, and Virginia are Rim or Peripheral South states. See Key, *Southern Politics*.

[5]Key, *Southern Politics*.

[6]Ibid.

[7]William Anderson, *The Wild Man from Sugar Creek* (Baton Rouge: Louisiana State University Press, 1975).

significantly, he used state funds to buy 80 railroad carloads of hogs, which he shipped to Chicago, where they sold for less than he had paid. All of this was done without proper authorization.

Talmadge used the gubernatorial campaign to refine his hypnotic appeal to rural voters. Socialized to Watson's Populist message, Talmadge could identify with struggling rural farmers because even though he had a law degree from the University of Georgia, he never prospered as an attorney and had worked as a dirt farmer in south Georgia. He used Populist appeals to whip up rural voters as he warned them, "The dirt farmer of Georgia has got only three friends: Sears Roebuck, God Almighty and Gene Talmadge!" When accused of having misused his authority to purchase the carloads of swine, he confronted the allegations head on. Speaking to sweaty crowds of farmers and mechanics at county fairgrounds, he declared, "They say I stole. I did! I stole for you, the dirt farmers!" And the crowds would go wild and stream to the ballot boxes to vote for "Ol' Gene," and to be part of his "loyal hundred-thousand."

Despite opposition from urbanites and the better class of Georgians, Talmadge easily won the governorship. After winning reelection in 1934, he ran unsuccessfully for the U.S. Senate in 1936, because he was limited to two consecutive terms as governor. He lost a second Senate bid in 1938 but won a third term as governor in 1940. His one gubernatorial loss came in 1942. In 1946, dying from cirrhosis, he mounted his final gubernatorial bid.

While Talmadge led one faction, the opposition had multiple leaders. Anti-Talmadge Governor E. D. Rivers (1937–40) had two future governors, Ellis Arnall and M. E. Thompson, among his protégés. The anti-Talmadge faction ran better among urban areas and north Georgia and attracted those who had controlled Georgia's politics until Talmadge's election as governor. These voters were outraged at his extra-legal actions, such as when he used bullying tactics to achieve his policy objectives and called out the National Guard, surrounded the Capitol, and then replaced competent administrators with family and friends. Supporters of President Franklin Roosevelt also opposed Talmadge because the governor kept Georgia from participating in various grants programs set up by the New Deal.

Talmadge reclaimed the governorship in 1940 but committed what his son acknowledged to be his biggest mistake.[8] Talmadge, who never hesitated to exploit every available resource to achieve his objectives, had forced the firing of the dean of the University of Georgia's College of Education and the president of Georgia Teachers College (now Georgia Southern University). These educators incurred the governor's wrath by being insufficiently adamant in their support for racial segregation. When the University Systems Board of Regents refused to do Talmadge's bidding and fire the educators, he replaced enough board members to achieve his goal.

---

[8]Herman Talmadge with Max Royden Winchell, *Talmadge* (Atlanta: Peachtree Publishers, 1987).

As punishment for the governor's interference with education policy, the university system lost accreditation. Attorney General Ellis Arnall's promise to regain accreditation attracted 57.5 percent of the vote, and he defeated the "Wild Man from Sugar Creek."

Only in his loss to Arnall did Talmadge face a single opponent in a gubernatorial election. The structuring of the opposition took on more significance in Georgia than in other states because of a unique electoral arrangement. Success in Democratic primary contests for statewide offices and some congressional districts rested on an institutional structure similar to the Electoral College. From 1917 until 1962, the county unit system allocated counties between two and six unit votes. The eight most populous counties had six votes, while the next 30 in size got four votes each. All the remaining counties had only two votes. The candidate who got a plurality of the popular vote in a county received all of its unit votes. This arrangement encouraged candidates to concentrate on small rural counties—precisely those in which Talmadge did best—where a few voters could determine the outcome. Winning three rural counties in which only a few hundred voted could offset the need to mobilize thousands of voters in an urban county. *Time* observed in 1946 that the 1,996 voters of Chattahoochee, Quitman, and Echols counties in south Georgia offset the 125,000 voters of Fulton County under the county unit system.[9] The presence of bosses in approximately a fourth of Georgia's counties made the task of winning rural counties even easier. Some of the bosses were irrevocably committed to Talmadge, while others had equally strong commitment to the anti-Talmadge forces. A third set tried to anticipate the outcome so as to be with the winning candidate in order to get a share of the spoils distributed by the governor.[10] Since a plurality sufficed to carry a county's unit votes, Talmadge benefited when more than one candidate represented the opposition. This proved critical in 1946 when he lost the popular vote to Bell Bomber plant executive James Carmichael by 16,000 votes but won 244 county unit votes to Carmichael's 144 and E. D. Rivers' 22 votes.[11]

"THREE GOVERNORS"

Talmadge's death in 1946 before his inauguration created a constitutional crisis. The 1946 election marked the first time that Georgia elected a lieutenant

[9]"The Red Galluses," *Time* (October 15, 1946).

[10]Charles S. Bullock III, and Jessica L. McClelland, "The County Boss and Statewide Elections: A Multivariate Analysis of Georgia's Bifactional Politics," *Politics and Policy* 32 (December 2004): 740–55.

[11]See, for example, Jimmy Carter, 1993. *Turning Point: A Candidate, a State, and a Nation Come of Age* (New York: Times Books); Anderson; Scott E. Buchanan, "The Effects of the Abolition of the Georgia County Unit System on the 1962 Gubernatorial Election," *Southeastern Political Review* 25 (1997).

governor. The winner of that post, M. E. Thompson, claimed that he should succeed to the governorship. Talmadge's son also laid claim to the office. Some Talmadge supporters, recognizing the seriousness of their leader's illness, had written in Herman Talmadge's name on general election ballots. They relied on a passage in the state constitution that authorized the legislature to choose the governor from among the two leading vote getters if no candidate obtained a majority. In light of the conflicting claims, Arnall announced that he would stay on as governor.

The effort to position the younger Talmadge to succeed his father almost failed when the general election canvass showed that the leading recipient of write-in votes (Eugene Talmadge was the only name on the ballot) was the unsuccessful Democratic primary opponent Carmichael, who got 669 votes. In second place came Talmadge Bowers, a tombstone salesman from Marietta, with 637 votes. Son Herman placed third with only 617 votes. But before the election returns could be certified, the legislature found an additional 58 votes for Talmadge in a second envelope from his home county of Telfair. With Talmadge, now the leader among those receiving write-in votes, the legislature, voting along factional lines, chose him to be governor.

The anti-Talmadge forces shifted the field of battle to the courts and 63 days later, a 5-to-2 majority of the Georgia Supreme Court overturned the legislature decision and made Lieutenant Governor Thompson acting governor, authorized to serve until the 1948 election. The court may have been influenced by evidence turned up by the Atlanta press concerning irregularities in the decisive 58 write-in votes. Of these voters, 34 lined up in alphabetical order. Of the final 34 voters, 32 displayed identical handwriting when signing in. A pair of votes came from dead men, and individuals who had long since moved out of the county cast another five. Five of the write-in voters swore that they had not voted. A dozen voters were never located, and yet another of the voters was listed as the wife of a bachelor.

The Talmadge forces suffered only a temporary setback when the courts made Thompson acting governor. Herman Talmadge won the special election held in 1948 and defeated Thompson for a second time in 1950. In 1954, Marvin Griffin, who had been Herman Talmadge's lieutenant governor, succeeded to the governorship, and in 1958, Griffin's lieutenant governor succeeded him.

In 1956, Herman Talmadge flexed such intimidating political muscles that Walter George, who had served in the U.S. Senate for 34 years, opted to retire rather than face the head of the Talmadge faction in the Democratic primary. Once the younger Talmadge reached the Senate, his interest in maintaining the family machine waned. After 1958, even the rudiments of factional politics in Georgia had vanished to be replaced by an emerging bipartisan competition within less than a decade.

CONCLUSION

Politics in Georgia in the first half of the twentieth century illuminates the tensions that shaped subsequent political events in the state: rural versus urban, populist versus progressive, white versus black, and tradition versus change. As we will see in subsequent chapters, these tensions permeated nearly every aspect of Georgia politics, including the constitutional institutions, the allocation of power, and the allocation of benefits from government. Change came not from within government but from below, in the form of grassroots efforts of blacks, urbanites, and Republicans; and above, in the form of the United States Department of Justice, the federal courts, and the United States Congress.

CHAPTER 2

Georgia Geography and Politics

The allocation of political power and national and state gubernatorial administration are based on geography. Senators and representatives are apportioned to states. Representatives are elected from a geographically designated district. In the states, power in the legislature is apportioned into districts to ensure that all geographic areas receive representation subject to requirements that districts have equal population. States divide into counties or parishes or townships, which exist to implement the law as creatures of the state.

In Georgia, as much as in any state of the Union, geography matters. Georgia has distinct geographic regions, long identified in the politics and culture of the state. Those regions have historic political and economic relevance, though the influence of some regions on the politics of the state has waned. Georgia has a strong tradition of county government, and counties continue as a prominent source of local identity for Georgians. For generations, strong county government and the apportionment of political power into counties guaranteed a dominant voice for rural Georgia.

The rise of the one-person, one-vote standard in representative politics and Atlanta's growth accelerated political change. Metropolitan Atlanta has come to dominate the politics and economics of Georgia. And with Atlanta's dramatic growth has come a shift in the relative power and influence of different historic regions and a redefinition of *region* as sprawling suburbs obliterate old regional lines.

THE FALL LINE AND GEORGIA REGIONS

The geography of Georgia creates distinct divisions that have structured political competition, both within the Democratic Party during the long epoch of one-party rule and later in the era of two-party competition. The Fall Line

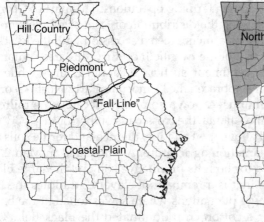

A. The Piedmont, the Coastal Plain,
and the Fall Line

B. Regions of Georgia: North Georgia,
South Georgia, and the Black Belt

MAP 2.1   Regions in Georgia

Source: Bartley, *From Thurmond to Wallace: Political Tendencies in Georgia, 1948–1968*, 21.

where the foothills meet the fertile, rolling lowlands bisect Georgia (See Map 2.1A). The Fall Line arcs across the state from Columbus through Macon to Augusta, an extension of a topical feature that extends between the American Lowland and the American Piedmont. Political scientist V. O. Key notes a politically distinct Fall Line division in South Carolina and North Carolina, as well as in Georgia. Georgia historian Numan Bartley divides the state into three geographic regions:[1]

1. The broad Black Belt or "Middle Georgia," a 100-mile wide arc of rich soil straddling an arc from Augusta to Macon to Columbus to Albany;
2. North Georgia, roughly north of a line running from Elberton and Athens in the east to LaGrange in the west;
3. and South Georgia, south of Dublin and east of Albany and Thomasville.

The area above the Fall Line encompasses four distinct topographic regions. Most of North Georgia is in the Piedmont, a rolling, hilly stretch ranging from 200 to 800 feet above sea level. The Piedmont stretches from New Jersey to central Alabama and constitutes about 80% of Georgia above the Fall Line. The balance of Georgia above the Fall Line, to the northwest, is part of three other geomorphic features: the Blue Ridge; the Valley and Ridge; and the Appalachian Plateau. This mountainous country was unsuited to anything other than small-scale farming, mining, lumbering, and eventually the development of small industry including textiles and the world's largest concentration of carpet manufacturing in the Dalton area. Unsuited to plantation farming, the

[1]Numan V. Bartley. *From Thurmond to Wallace: Political Tendencies in Georgia, 1948–1968*. Baltimore: Johns Hopkins Press, 1970.

hill country supported small yeoman farming operations. This part of Georgia was settled relatively late, following the distribution of farm-sized plots in the Land Lottery of 1832. Hill country farmers greeted secession with the least enthusiasm and during the first half of the twentieth century, this area contained the rare nuggets of Republican sentiment, such as in Fannin County, while the rest of the state overwhelmingly embraced the Democratic Party. North Georgia developed industry, and Terminus—a town so named because the railroad ended here—eventually became Atlanta, the crossroads of the South.

Immediately below and above the Fall Line, the rich and fertile soils are well suited for large-scale plantation agriculture. As indicated in Map 2.1B, the historic Black Belt, named for both its productive soil and the large black population of those counties that is a remnant of slavery, straddles the Fall Line. Before the Civil War, large plantations where slaves toiled at the back-breaking work of producing a cotton crop dominated the Black Belt. This swath of Georgia continues to be heavily African American.

Below the Fall Line is the southeastern coastal plain that stretches from Tidewater Virginia to Texas. East of I-75 and south of I-16 lies the sawgrass country, a less-developed part of the coastal plain. Areas of richer soil, and therefore greater agricultural potential, sometimes featured sizeable black populations although not at the levels in the Black Belt. Generally speaking, this part of the coastal plain had small towns and smaller scale agriculture than the large operations of the Black Belt.

ECONOMIC IMPLICATIONS OF THE FALL LINE

The physical distinction of land above and below the Fall Line, together with the falls that disrupted water transport, contributed to the long-term development of alternative agricultural and economic models for north Georgia, the Black Belt, and south Georgia.[2] Bartley and V. O. Key illustrated economic consequences of the geography of Georgia. North Georgia was more industrial; the Black Belt and south Georgia were more agricultural. Politics followed, in part, these economic models, making geography politically relevant through the local economic models and the political cultures that grew up based on the variable dependency on slave (and later black sharecrop) labor.

Numerous rivers flow across Georgia toward the Atlantic or the Gulf, including the Chattahoochee, the Savannah, the Ocmulgee, the Oconee (which joins with the Ocmulgee to form the Altamaha), the Flint, and the Saint Marys. Many of these rivers cross the Fall Line. Towns and cities such as Augusta, Columbus, Macon, and Milledgeville grew up along the Fall Line because of transportation economics. Early nineteenth-century transit of goods by boat required off-loading and reloading at the falls, although a canal was dug in Augusta to get around the rapids on the Savannah River. These hubs became centers of commerce and settlement because of their critical location in the transportation infrastructure. Eventually, railroads supplanted water as a

[2]*Ibid.;* and Key, *Southern Politics.*

means of transportation. However, the rail heads went to existing population centers, producing a second boom of development related to the transportation infrastructure.

South of the Fall Line, agriculture continues to dominate the economy. Above the Fall Line, especially outside of the rural Black Belt counties, industry arrived before the Civil War in the form of textiles. Georgia experimented with textiles early in the mountainous western part of the state and the name "Empire State of the South" was hung on Georgia because of its extensive industrialization. Cotton mills and wool processing initially boomed, until rail transport allowed northern mills to compete directly. Georgia's antebellum industrialization then turned to paper milling and metal foundries. Industry in the antebellum period ran counter-cyclical to agriculture: when cotton boomed, industry suffered, and when cotton busted industry grew. This cycle exacerbated a growing political division in the state between the agricultural barons of the Black Belt and the mechanics and yeomen of the Piedmont. The ensuing economic division would infuse the politics of Georgia and would help establish politics that resonate into the twenty-first century.

Map 2.2 illustrates this geographic difference in economic emphasis. Map 2.2A indicates the distribution of slave population at the county level in 1850. The highest concentrations of slaves were in the rice-growing counties along the coast and in cotton-growing counties in the Savannah River basin and on either side of the Fall Line. In north Georgia, slaves rarely made up as much as a quarter of the population, while south of the Fall Line slaves no longer constituted a majority but still made up between a quarter and half of the population.

Map 2.2B shows that farm values tracked with the slave population. Much of the most valuable land lay along the Fall Line, or in the Savannah or

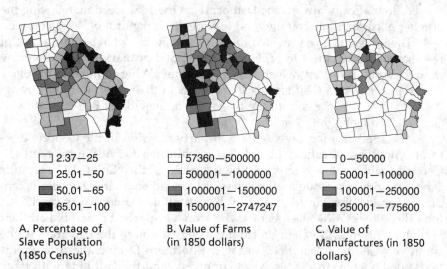

	A	B	C
□	2.37−25	57360−500000	0−50000
▨	25.01−50	500001−1000000	50001−100000
▨	50.01−65	1000001−1500000	100001−250000
■	65.01−100	1500001−2747247	250001−775600

A. Percentage of Slave Population (1850 Census)

B. Value of Farms (in 1850 dollars)

C. Value of Manufactures (in 1850 dollars)

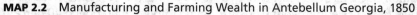

MAP 2.2 Manufacturing and Farming Wealth in Antebellum Georgia, 1850

Source: Data compiled from 1850 U.S. Census.

Chattahoochee River basins. Values fell off moving further north into the Piedmont or toward the sawgrass country. Georgia lands that opened up by the 1820, 1821, and 1827 land lotteries (which distributed former Native American lands) had farm values comparable to the Black Belt. After the Civil War, these counties, along with those in the Black Belt, would see black tenant farmers working the land.

Map 2.2C shows the value of manufacturing by county in 1850. Other than along the coast, most manufacturing was located on or above the Fall Line, and a cluster of industrial towns emerged in the counties surrounding Fulton and DeKalb. Little industrial wealth existed south of Fall Line. Even before the Civil War, the predominantly agricultural character of south Georgia and the industrial and commercial character of north Georgia had begun to take shape.

GEOGRAPHY OF ANTEBELLUM POLITICS

Georgia experienced remarkably stable bipartisan politics throughout the 1840s. As indicated on Map 2.3A, the Whigs' greatest support came along the Savannah River, in the eastern part of the Black Belt, and southern counties formed from the 1820 Land Lottery. Democratic strength was concentrated in counties with few large slaveholders—above the Fall Line, in the hillier parts of the Piedmont, and in an arc just below the Black Belt. The Black Belt had some of the most competitive counties, and these are not shaded. Political competition was well developed in both the manufacturing and the prosperous farming counties.

By the 1850s, the destabilization of the national party system that undid the Whig Party had started to realign Georgia politics. The Whigs' unsuccessful effort to deal with the slavery issue caused its demise. Georgia voters moved dramatically toward the Democrats in the 1852 election, reducing the number of competitive counties and leaving just a handful of Whig counties.

The Whig collapse provided the initial chapter in what became a time of Democratic dominance. In 1856, the Democrats' primary opposition came from the American Party, which won a few former Whig counties in the Black Belt. Democrats had their strongest showings in their north Georgia strongholds of the 1840s, the counties of the emerging new Black Belt in southwest Georgia, and along the coast.

The 1860 election revealed a two-party division in the Georgia electorate. Because Abraham Lincoln's Republicans did not appear on the Georgia ballot, voters had the following options: the National Democratic candidate, Stephen Douglas; the secession-minded Southern Democratic candidate, John C. Breckinridge; and the Constitutional Union Party candidate, John Bell. Breckinridge Democrats who won a 49 percent plurality had their best showing in south Georgia from the coast through the Sawgrass to the southwest Georgia Black Belt, and in the northern Democratic strongholds that dated back to the 1840s. Most counties along the Fall Line with large numbers of slaves either went Constitutional Union, which polled 40 percent of the Georgia vote, or were closely contested. Industrial counties split, some

A. Democrat–Whig Strength, 1840s

B. Democrat–Whig Strength, 1852

C. Democrat–American Party
Strength, 1852

D. Breckinridge Democrats–Bell
Constitutional Union Party, 1860

MAP 2.3   The Evolution of Two-Party Competition in Antebellum Georgia

Source: Data compiled by authors.

going Constitutional Union, others going Breckinridge Democratic. Stephen Douglas ran generally poorly throughout the state.

GEOGRAPHY OF RECONSTRUCTION GEORGIA

The Civil War devastated rural Georgia and as anyone who has watched "Gone with the Wind" knows, burned Atlanta to the ground. Where the great plantations had been, much of the wealth disappeared, having been tied up in slaves or invested in Confederate bonds and bills. Reconstruction witnessed the onset of patterns that shaped Georgia politics for decades. The three elements discussed here are the redistribution of the black population, the richest agriculture counties, and the nascent manufacturing counties.

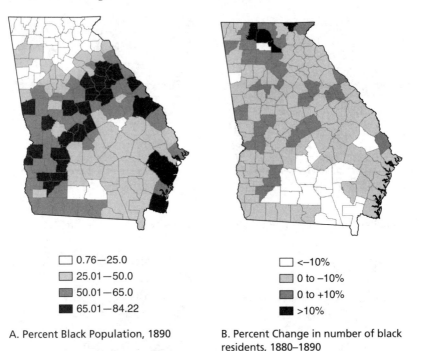

□ 0.76—25.0
▨ 25.01—50.0
▨ 50.01—65.0
■ 65.01—84.22

□ <–10%
▨ 0 to –10%
▨ 0 to +10%
■ >10%

A. Percent Black Population, 1890

B. Percent Change in number of black residents, 1880–1890

MAP 2.4   The Black Belt and the Pattern of the Black Exodus in Georgia, 1890

Source: Data compiled from 1890 U.S. Census.

Map 2.4A displays the distribution of African Americans in 1890. A comparison with Map 2.2A shows that the number of heavily black counties along the Fall Line and in the southwestern part of the state had increased substantially. The Piedmont continued to have only a handful of majority-black counties. Many counties south of the Fall Line had a net loss in black residents from 1880 to 1890, except in those Black Belt counties.

A comparison of the counties with the heaviest black concentrations in 1890 (Map 2.4A) with the wealthiest agricultural counties (Map 2.5A) shows an extensive overlap. Tenant farming had replaced slave labor in these counties, but the economic situation remained the same—a wealthy planter class that was a racial minority in its own county. A notable change is the increase in the value of agricultural products in the Piedmont counties just north of the Fall Line.

Manufacturing spread slightly from 1850 to 1889 (Map 2.5B), although the most profitable manufacturing centers were in four old water transportation hubs—Savannah (Chatham County) and the Fall Line cities of Columbus (Muscogee County), Macon (Bibb County), and Augusta (Richmond County)—and the new transportation hub, the rail center of Atlanta (Fulton County). Ten of the sixteen remaining counties with over a half-million dollars in manufacturing in 1889 are north of the Fall Line, largely along rail lines connecting to Atlanta.

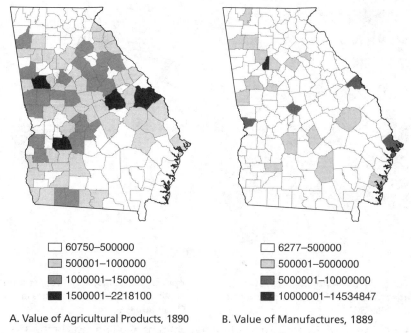

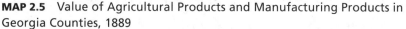

A. Value of Agricultural Products, 1890   B. Value of Manufactures, 1889

MAP 2.5   Value of Agricultural Products and Manufacturing Products in Georgia Counties, 1889

Source: Data compiled from 1890 U.S. Census.

Immediately after the 1890 census, the 1892 Democratic ticket fared relatively poorly in Georgia. Former president Grover Cleveland challenged Republican President Benjamin Harrison with James Weaver, running on the People's Party line. Cleveland won Georgia's electoral votes taking 58 percent of the vote. Harrison received 21.7 percent of the vote to edge out Weaver who took 18.8 percent of the vote.

Map 2.6 shows the counties of greatest strength for each party. Democrats won most counties and did best in Savannah, Augusta, Columbus, and in majority-white rural counties near to majority-black counties. Republican votes, as shown in Map 2.6, were concentrated in the heavily black coastal counties, in the western Black Belt, and in mountain counties on the North Carolina border. Populists ran strongest in some of the oldest settled regions, taking black and white ballots across the eastern part of the Black Belt and in the eastern Piedmont.

The purging of black voters and the cooption of the Populists secured the dominance of the Democratic Party in Georgia and in the process eliminated any semblance of a party political geography. With the exception of Herbert Hoover who took 43 percent of the Georgia vote in 1928, another three generations would pass before Republicans would seriously contest Georgia elections. However, the factors that emerged as important components of the politics of the late nineteenth century—agriculture versus

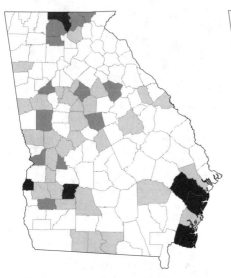

A. Republican Strength: Majority-GOP
counties shaded in black; dark-gray counties
are 35–50% GOP.

B. Populist Power: Majority-Populist counties
shaded in black, dark gray counties are
35–50% Populist.

MAP 2.6   Areas of Greatest Strength of Republicans and Populists in the 1892
Election

Source: Data compiled by authors.

industrial development, Populism, and the status of Georgia blacks—would
influence the state's political geography once Democratic hegemony began
to erode.

REGIONALISM IN THE ONE-PARTY SYSTEM AT MID-CENTURY

Writing in the middle of the twentieth century after decades of Democratic
dominance, Key characterized Georgia politics as the "Rule of the Rustics" because of the power of rural voters and rural demagogues such as Gene
Talmadge.[3] A more recent assessment in *The New Politics of the Old South*
observes that:

> While farmers and small-town residents had disproportionate in-
> fluence in every state prior to the one-person, one-vote revolution
> of the 1960s, rural counties had greater influence in Georgia poli-
> tics than elsewhere. Not only did rural voters have more than their
> fair share of legislative seats, but also their influence in elections
> was magnified at city dwellers' expense.[4]

[3]Key, *Southern Politics*.
[4]Charles S. Bullock, III, "Georgia Election Rules and Partisan Conflict." In Charles S. Bullock, III,
and Mark J. Rozell, eds., *The New Politics of the Old South* (Lanham, MD: Rowman and Littlefield,
1999), 49.

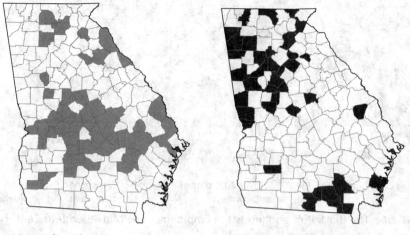

A. Strong for Talmadges   B. Weak for Talmadges

MAP 2.7   Patterns of Persistent Strength, Weakness for the Talmadges

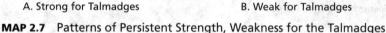

Source: Key, *Southern Politics,* 112.

The county unit system severely skewed power to the countryside. A politician active during that period observed that, "give me five good men in 100
rural counties and I could run the state under the county unit system."[5]
      The demise of the two-party system after Reconstruction left formless,
candidate-centered politics. As an interlude on the way to partisan competition
that took its first tentative steps in the 1960s, Georgia experienced a generation
of bifactional politics that structured choices in many top-of-the-ticket contests.
The successes of the Talmadge machine prompted the opposition to coalesce,
and this brought much of the structure often associated with party politics to
the Democratic Party primary. The Talmadges combined race-baiting with
Populist appeals. Electoral support for the Talmadges generally followed the
wealth, development, and ideological patterns of old. Map 2.7 shows the
counties that consistently gave strong support to Talmadge candidates or
their opponents. Map 2.8 shows the location of African-American concentrations in 1940 and the distribution of high and low manufacturing employment
in 1940. According to Key and Bartley, the Talmadges ran better in rural counties with less industrial development, and with small populations and in and
on the edge of the Black Belt.[6] Gene Talmadge had strong appeal in places
where the Populists had run well in the late nineteenth century.
      The first hint of the potential for two-party politics emerged in 1928 when
Catholic, anti-prohibition New York Democrat Al Smith ran for President
against "dry" Protestant Republican Herbert Hoover. Smith attracted 55 percent

[5]J. Phil Campbell, personal interview with Bullock, March 1, 1983.
[6]Key, *Southern Politics;* and Bartley, *From Thurmond to Wallace: Political Tendencies in Georgia,*
1948–1968.

A. Majority-black as of 1940   B. Over 20% manufacturing   C. Less than 5%
                                   employment   manufacturing employment

MAP 2.8   The Black Belt and Industrial Employment at Mid-Twentieth Century

Source: Key, *Southern Politics,* 6, 114

of Georgia's vote—18 points off the Democratic performance in 1924 and 1920. Hoover performed best outside the Black Belt, mainly in the hill country and the urban centers (see Map 2.9). This pattern would generally prevail among rural whites in Georgia until after World War II, when national Democratic presidential candidates (other than Jimmy Carter in 1976) became increasingly unacceptable to most rural white voters, setting up revolts supporting independents Strom Thurmond (1948) and George Wallace (1968) and bolts to Republicans Barry Goldwater (1964) and Richard Nixon (1972).

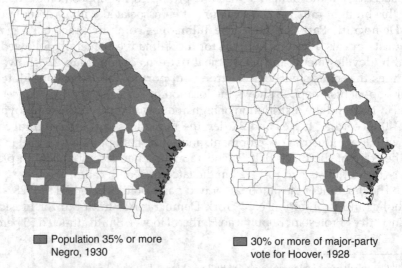

■ Population 35% or more   ■ 30% or more of major-party
  Negro, 1930   vote for Hoover, 1928

MAP 2.9   The Black Belt and the 1928 Election for President

Source: Key, *Southern Politics,* 327.

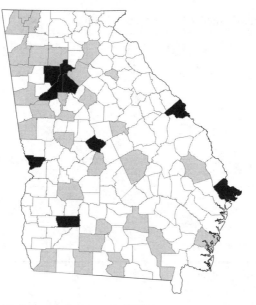

MAP 2.10   County Unit Apportionment, 1958

Source: William G. Cornelius. "The County Unit System of Georgia: Facts and Prospects" *The Western Political Quarterly*, 14 (1961): 943.

The malapportionment of state electoral power for major offices and in the legislature empowered rural, interests of south Georgia over the growing urban centers and north Georgia. Map 2.10 shows the distribution of seats and influence of counties during the last days of the county unit system. The counties that cast six unit votes in statewide primaries and had three members of the state House included the cities that grew up along the Fall Line (Augusta, Columbus, and Macon). Savannah, Georgia's primary port city, also had six unit votes. In southwest Georgia, Dougherty County (Albany) was the most populous in that corner of the state. The other three counties with six unit votes provided the core for Atlanta (Fulton, DeKalb, and Cobb Counties). Twelve of the 30 four-vote counties lay south of Fall Line and another two were just north of it. Thus, barely half of the four-vote counties were in north Georgia.

Table 2.1 shows the inequity between the population distribution in the middle of the twentieth century and the distribution of seats in the state senate. The apportionment plan in place from 1949 until 1962 divided seats evenly between north and south Georgia. The five core Atlanta counties filled less than five percent of the Senate seats and accounted for just over six percent of the House seats, despite having about a quarter of Georgia's population. Following the first redistricting in 1963, the Atlanta core's share of seats rose dramatically to more than a fifth of the chamber, which better reflected the area's share of the state's population, although this remained four percentage points below the area's share of the population. Representation from south Georgia plummeted to barely a third of the membership which closely approximated that region's

TABLE 2.1:   The Changing Geography of Political Power

	Percent of State Votes Cast in General Election			
	1960	*1980*	*2000*	*% CUV, 1958*
Atlanta Core	26.83	34.16	37.31	6.30
Suburban Donut	9.64	10.18	16.21	11.30
North Georgia	25.15	22.28	20.27	30.20
South Georgia	38.38	33.37	26.20	52.20

	Percent of State Senate Seats				
	1949	*1963*	*1982*	*1992*	*2004*
Atlanta Core	4.30	22.80	30.40	34.80	33.90
Suburban Donut	7.40	7.40	12.50	14.30	17.00
North Georgia	38.70	35.50	27.60	24.10	27.70
South Georgia	49.40	34.30	29.50	26.80	21.40

Source: Data compiled by authors.

population share. The 1963 apportionment plan left north Georgia outside metro Atlanta substantially underrepresented.

Since 1983, the Atlanta core has elected approximately a third of the Senate while south Georgia's representation has continued to decline and now constitutes barely a fifth of the seats. The plan drawn by a federal court in 2004 underrepresented south Georgia as well as the part of north Georgia not in metro Atlanta core.

After the Supreme Court dismantled the county apportionment system in 1962 (see Chapter 10), Republicans began winning elections in Atlanta and other urban areas and their suburbs, but not until the 1990s would they secure one-quarter of the seats in either chamber of the General Assembly or in the congressional delegation.[7] Still, it is these geographic entities—north versus south, Atlanta versus the country, industry versus agriculture—that define Georgia politics. The reapportionment revolution unleashed growing Republican support, but it would take decades for the GOP to come to power.

POPULATION TRENDS

Population trends in Georgia demonstrate dramatic changes over a century and a half. Map 2.11 shows the populations for Georgia counties in 1850, 1890, 1950, and 2007.

In 1850, the population center of Georgia was near the Fall Line, in the middle of the Black Belt. The state's counties divided roughly into three categories based on their population. About a sixth, located mainly in the saw-grass country, had fewer than 5,000 residents. Half the counties had between

---

[7]*Ibid.*, 51.

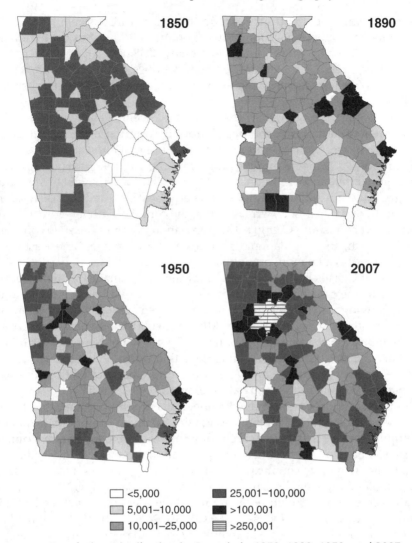

MAP 2.11   Population Distribution in Georgia in 1850, 1890, 1950, and 2007

Source: Various U.S. censuses.

5,000 and 10,000 residents, and the remainder had populations between 10,000 and 25,000. Georgia had a few small towns, but most residents lived on farms and in villages. With few exceptions, most of the populous counties lay along the Fall Line and largely in the Black Belt. Of the fifteen least-populous counties, only two were in north Georgia.

By 1890, the arc of post–Civil War population development in Georgia was established. Of the nine most populous counties, five would rank among the most populous in the state in 1950: Fulton, Richmond, Muscogee, Chatham, and Bibb. The fastest-growing urban centers were at transportation nodes of the nineteenth century in terms of water in 1850 or rail in 1860. Four of the nine most populous counties were on the Fall Line, but the population center moved north toward Atlanta, and many Black Belt counties lost ground in population relative to whiter Piedmont counties. Only eight counties had fewer than 5,000 residents, but the modal category of county had between 10,000 and 25,000 residents.

By 1950, in the twilight of the Talmadge Machine and when V. O. Key wrote of Georgia politics, the population distribution of modern Georgia started to emerge. Of the six most populous counties, Fulton and DeKalb were in metropolitan Atlanta, another three were the Fall Line urban counties of Muscogee, Bibb, and Richmond, with only Chatham (Savannah) in south Georgia. Two-thirds of the counties with between 25,000 and 100,000 residents were north of the Fall Line, while most of the counties with fewer than 25,000 residents were in south Georgia. The population center of the state continued to move north, and population disparities between the most and least populous counties became more pronounced.

Recent Census Bureau estimates indicate the dramatic transformation of the state in the past half-century. Since 1990, Georgia has been among the fastest growing states in the nation and surpassed New Jersey to become the nation's ninth most populous state. Atlanta is still the population center and the 28-county metropolitan area contained 5.4 million of Georgia's 9.7 million residents in 2008. That made Atlanta the nation's eighth largest metropolitan area as it passed Washington. Five metro counties had populations in excess of a quarter million, four over a half million. In 2009, Fulton County exceeded one million and projections have Gwinnett eventually reaching that threshold. The counties on the Fall Line along with Chatham County that were major population centers in 1850 are today the state's most populous outside metro Atlanta. However, tremendous population growth has followed the interstate highways into counties adjacent to the core counties of metro Atlanta, and a similar pattern emerges near the other, old population centers. New population centers have grown up along four-lane highways, such as Lowndes County (Valdosta) and Athens-Clarke County. Metro Atlanta has spread out even as portions have become incredibly dense with population.

While Georgia's urban sprawl cannot match that which spreads from Boston south to Richmond, Virginia, metropolitan areas in the southeast are beginning to run together. Just to the north and west of the Atlanta metropolitan area lies the four-county Athens metropolitan area, and it is just one county away from the Augusta metropolitan area. Going to the northwest, only one county separates the Atlanta and Chattanooga metropolitan areas. Towards the south, Atlanta's metropolitan area abuts the Macon and Columbus metropolitan areas. The latter comes within one county of the Albany metro area.

Contemporary Atlanta sits in the center of a booming metropolitan area.[8] While the city's boundaries have not changed in almost 60 years, so that the

---

[8]See, for example, Frederick Allen, *Atlanta Rising* (Atlanta: Peachtree Press, 1996).

city did not experience the explosive population growth, surrounding counties have undergone dramatic suburbanization. From 2000 to 2008, only the Dallas metropolitan added more people than the 1.13 million new Atlantans. The growth pattern is often described as a "donut" with heavily white Republican suburbs surrounding the urban core in Fulton and DeKalb Counties, with their diverse populations. As the demand for housing grew, Atlantans trailed out I-85, I-75, I-575, I-20, and Georgia 400, building farther and farther from the city, turning quiet corners like Woodstock, Covington, Cumming and Dacula into sprawling, gridlocked suburban bedroom communities. Whites have moved mainly to the north and northeast, blacks mainly to the south and southeast from the city proper. Clayton County, home to Atlanta's airport, has become the second most heavily black county in the state. More recently an increasingly diverse population that includes many recent immigrants has moved into the older suburbs.

Meanwhile, below the Fall Line, growth is slower in most counties and almost non-existent in others. Not even a third of counties below the Fall Line have 25,000 residents, and of nine counties with fewer than 5,000 residents, eight are on or below the Fall Line. South Georgia and the southwestern Black Belt grew along the major transportation corridors, but even the growth along I-75 and I-16 pales compared to booming north Georgia. In the rest of Georgia below the Fall Line, few people move in and many young people leave in search of better jobs.

CONCLUSION

The economic and political history is driven by regional forces. Industry is located in the north and where transportation hubs stimulated the creation of population centers. Prosperous agriculture and rural black populations grew up together, with all of the social, economic, and cultural complications associated with slavery and later the sharecrop model of agriculture. Before the Civil War and on through Reconstruction, two-party politics paralleled these differences. Into the middle of the twentieth century, the bifactionalism of the Democratic Party structured itself on these factors.

It is out of this legacy of bifactionalism - of agriculture versus industry, north versus south Georgia, urban versus rural, and especially racial conservatism that Georgia politics began its march toward realignment to a two-party system, which was finally achieved at the close of the twentieth century. In the midst of population growth, black suffrage, and an evolving economic model and growing urban populations, the opportunity for two-party growth emerged. The process shaped Georgia politics as issues in the state became defined more by ideology and race, and the geography of the politics changed to one of urban centers versus growing unincorporated suburban communities versus declining rural counties.

CHAPTER 3

Republican Rebirth, Democratic Delaying Actions

In 1960, Georgia once again proved to be among the most fervent supporters of the Democratic Party. Only Rhode Island gave John Kennedy more than the 62.5 percent of the vote he won in Georgia, a percentage that eclipsed the 60.2 percent from Massachusetts, his home state. Even after mid-century, overwhelmingly conservative, white Georgia voters still flocked to a liberal, integrationist candidate from New England.

Four years later, however, the presidential environment had been rearranged as if tilted by an earthquake scoring 9.0 on the Richter scale. For the first time in its history, Georgia gave its Electoral College votes to a Republican. Barry Goldwater carried the state by a margin of 94,000 votes, winning with 54 percent of the total.[1] Significantly, this breakthrough victory came not against a northerner but against the first southerner to be nominated for president since before the Civil War.[2] Most Georgians found the Arizona Republican preferable to Texan Lyndon Johnson who had succeeded to the presidency following Kennedy's assassination. Johnson, a one-time protégé of Georgia Senator Richard Russell, alienated conservative whites by supporting the 1964 Civil Rights Act. The new president had urged Congress to enact the sweeping legislation designed to eliminate racial discrimination in education, employment, public accommodations, and voting as a lasting memorial to the slain John

---

[1]Bernard Cosman, *Six States for Goldwater* (University, AL: University of Alabama Press, 1966); Numan V. Bartley, *From Thurmond to Wallace* (Baltimore: Johns Hopkins Press, 1970).

[2]Some would argue that Woodrow Wilson was a southerner since he was born in Virginia and spent much of his youth in Georgia and South Carolina. However, Wilson's political career played out in New Jersey, where he served as governor.

Kennedy. Goldwater, a member of the National Association for the Advancement of Colored People, voted against the Act because he considered it an unconstitutional infringement on states' rights. Georgia, which along with its southern neighbors, continued to fight a rearguard action against the Civil Rights movement, eagerly embraced the opponent of the new legislation.

RACE, REPUBLICANS, AND GEORGIA

Goldwater's philosophical objection to the Civil Rights Act activated segregationist whites. By invoking concepts such as states' rights, Goldwater communicated in a code that promoted white supremacy and segregation without ever explicitly mentioning race. In the 1964 general election, he won his home state of Arizona and also the Deep South, dominating the white vote as the first Republican to carry the Black Belt states since Reconstruction. He took 54.1 percent of the vote and carried 112 of Georgia's 159 counties, including almost all of the Black Belt counties.[3]

Goldwater had coattails. Bo Callaway, who campaigned openly against integration policies, won an open seat in Middle Georgia to become the first Republican sent to Congress from Georgia in almost a century. Callaway was one of seven additional Republican congressmen elected from the South in 1964, even as Republicans lost a net of 42 seats nationwide. Republicans also registered dramatic gains in the state legislature. The state House, which had just been redistricted to meet the one-person, one-vote standard recently enunciated by the U.S. Supreme Court, saw its Republican ranks expanded from two who represented mountain counties to 21, most of whom came from urban and suburban communities. In the Senate, Republicans tripled their numbers to nine.

The Goldwater phenomenon continued to reverberate after 1964. Republicans made significant headway in municipal elections in Macon and Savannah. Their most tantalizing prospect came in the gubernatorial election of 1966. After decades of dormancy, the GOP offered a viable gubernatorial candidate. The party still had not developed to the point of conducting a primary and instead chose its standard bearer at a convention. They picked for the honor Representative Callaway who, in addition to having a successful campaign under his belt, offered the advantage of being from a wealthy family of textile mill owners and so could contribute to the cost of the campaign.

Since Republicans did not stage a primary, their supporters could participate in the Democratic selection process.[4] The 1966 Democratic gubernatorial choices spanned a wide ideological range. On the left stood Ellis Arnall, the reformist chief executive from 1943 to 1947. On the far right was Atlanta restaurateur and outspoken opponent of black civil rights, Lester Maddox, who attracted national media attention when he defied the 1964

---

[3]Earl Black and Merle Black, *The Vital South* (Cambridge, Harvard University Press, 1992).

[4]Georgia has an open primary system rather than requiring voters to express a party preference when registering.

Civil Rights Act by threatening potential black diners at his restaurant with an axe handle. Other candidates included young state Senator Jimmy Carter, who finished a surprisingly strong third in a six-candidate field. Arnall led with 29.4 percent, followed by Maddox with 23.5 percent, and then Carter with 20.9 percent.

Following the demise of the county unit system, invalidated by the courts for violating the one-person, one-vote standard, Georgia adopted a majority vote requirement. Arnall and Maddox faced off in a runoff. Maddox mobilized rural, conservative voters who had been the mainstay of the Talmadge dynasty and handily defeated Arnall.[5] The nascent Republican Party urged its supporters to vote for Maddox, believing him to be the weaker Democrat. With support from Republicans and the last of the Talmadge machine, Maddox won 54.3 percent of the runoff vote.

Callaway's fatal miscalculation was not to take Maddox seriously. It was easy to understand why that might happen, since Maddox had no money and was opposed by all of the state's leading political forces.[6] The state's newspapers rejected the Democratic nominee, and the financial interests of the state found Maddox and his racist rhetoric to be an embarrassment and worried that should he win the governorship, it might scare off northern investors. The Maddox campaign consisted of little more than the candidate driving around the state in his aging station wagon, stopping periodically to tack up crude signs to telephone poles, proclaiming simply, "MADDOX COUNTRY."

Despite having won a term in Congress, Callaway showed himself to still be a political neophyte. At the same time that Republican gubernatorial nominees in Florida and Arkansas were exploiting the opportunity to appeal to black voters when opposing racist Democrats, Callaway failed to take a similar approach. Maddox's frequent diatribes in the Atlanta papers condemning the Civil Rights movement made him unacceptable to African American voters. But when an advisor suggested that Callaway campaign for that vote, he rejected the idea: "No. The Negroes would just say I was playing politics." To this the frustrated advisor asked, "Well, for God's sake, Bo, what do you *think* you're playing?"[7]

Callaway alienated Democrats who opposed Maddox. Several members of outgoing Governor Carl Sanders' inner circle were working covertly for Callaway. Their enthusiasm waned, however, when Callaway needlessly attacked their mentor.

Even with these blunders, in any state other than Georgia, Callaway would have won the governorship because he outpolled Maddox by 3,000 votes. The Callaway margin would also have been sufficient in Georgia but for the presence of a write-in candidacy. Moderate-to-liberal Democrats found neither partisan choice acceptable. As loyal Democrats, they refused to vote

---

[5]Bartley, *From Thurmond to Wallace.*

[6]Marshall Frady, *Southerners* (New York: New American Library, 1980), 46.

[7]Robert Sherrill, *Gothic Politics in the Deep South* (New York: Ballantine Books, 1968), 292.

for a Republican, especially a Republican who seemed to be about as conservative as the Democratic nominee. On the other hand, Maddox's repeated displays of racism made him unacceptable. Facing this Hobson's choice, liberal Democrats mounted a write-in campaign for Ellis Arnall. The logistics of a write-in campaign are always difficult, and this effort came up far short, because it managed to attract less than 5 percent of the total vote. That 5 percent, however, proved critical since Georgia law required that a governor win a majority of the popular vote. Callaway barely missed achieving 48 percent, so the decision went to the overwhelmingly Democratic state legislature, where Maddox prevailed by a 182–66 margin; in all 38 Democrats crossed party lines to vote for Callaway, and 11 other Democratic legislators—all of the African American legislators in the General Assembly—did not cast ballots.

Georgia partisan history might have been radically different had it joined Florida and Arkansas in becoming the first southern states to elect a Republican chief executive in modern times. A Republican governor in Georgia might have given the party the same kind of legitimacy that Senator Strom Thurmond conferred on the Republican Party in South Carolina with his conversion in 1964. But when Democrats in the legislature lined up behind their party's standard-bearer and made Maddox governor, it set back GOP hopes by more than a generation. Rather than being one of the first southern states with a Republican governor, Georgia became the last state to achieve that feat.

Although Callaway's ineptitude allowed the governorship to slip through GOP fingers, the party scored successes down ticket. Republicans won both of the Atlanta-area congressional districts, more than offsetting their inability to retain the seat Callaway vacated. Unfortunately for Republicans, these two seats would be their high-water mark in the Georgia congressional delegation for the next quarter century.

Despite Callaway's loss at the hands of the state legislature, the GOP seemed poised to make a giant leap forward in 1968 when five statewide Democratic officials changed parties. At a dramatic news conference, these officials renounced their commitment to the party of their ancestors, turning away from the liberal Democratic presidential nominee Hubert Humphrey. The disaffected included individuals just one step below the very top Democratic leaders. The headliners in the set of converts were Jimmy Bentley and Phil Campbell. Bentley, closely aligned with the Talmadge faction, had demonstrated his political skills in 1962 when he defeated longtime Controller General (Insurance Commissioner) Zack Cravey. Observers anticipated that if Bentley ran for governor, he could count on Talmadge supporters in rural Georgia. Should he run for governor, he might find himself opposing Agriculture Commissioner Phil Campbell.

Joining these two, who would be on most observers' short lists of likely gubernatorial candidates, were the state treasurer and two members of the Public Service Commission. These five broke with the Democratic Party because they found it to be too liberal. In changing parties, these early converts offered an explanation repeated innumerable times since: "I didn't leave the

Democratic Party, it left me." As Hubert Humphrey swung to the left in an effort to mobilize greater support in the North and to placate the supporters of Eugene McCarthy and the late Bobby Kennedy, who had been sorely disappointed with Humphrey's nomination, the Minnesota Democrat alienated southern conservatives.

The movement of these Democratic leaders to the GOP was carefully scrutinized with the expectation that it might be a harbinger of further defections. Would Senator Herman Talmadge follow the lead of family protégé Jimmy Bentley? No other major Georgia political figure followed the risk-taking five. Democrats who withstood the temptation to switch parties proved wise. None of the five switchers ever held elective office again. Campbell arguably fared best. He became the undersecretary of agriculture in the Nixon administration. Bentley ran for governor in the 1970 Republican primary. Rather than flocking to the Bentley banner as someone whose strong credentials might attract Democrats in November, most Republicans rejected the convert for insufficient longevity in the party. Hal Suit, the news anchor on Atlanta's most watched station, won the nomination easily, taking 59 percent of the vote. After losing the nomination, Bentley dropped out of politics. Suit's television persona proved insufficient, and he lost his gubernatorial bid with 40.6 percent of the votes.

The 1968 presidential election dealt Democrats another blow as Georgia joined the rest of the Deep South, except for South Carolina, in voting for third-party candidate George Wallace who, like Maddox, exploited racial tensions. Liberal Democrat Hubert Humphrey placed third in Georgia with only 26.7 percent of the vote, relying heavily on recently franchised black voters.

Georgia Republicans suffered major setbacks in the mid-1970s. The fallout from Watergate and the resignation of President Richard Nixon caused some voters to question their support for the GOP. The selection of native son Jimmy Carter as the Democratic presidential nominee in 1976 compounded the GOP's problems in Georgia. This one-two punch staggered Georgia Republicans, who saw their ranks in the state Senate fall from a high of nine to only four in 1977. In the Georgia House, Republican ranks thinned from 29 to 21 between 1973 and 1979. The lean years of the mid-1970s wiped out much of the GOP gains registered in the post-Goldwater era.

REBUILDING THE GOP

Georgia Republicans who had carried the state in the presidential election of 1964 and had then seen Richard Nixon take three-fourths of the state's popular vote in 1972—a margin that has yet to be surpassed by a Republican nominee—were confronted with the task of rebuilding in the 1980s. The leadership of these efforts to resurrect the GOP came from transplants who had come to Georgia as young adults. Paul Coverdell came from the Kansas City area. His parents opened an insurance agency in Atlanta just after their son won election as student body president of Lee's Summit High School outside Kansas City, Missouri. Young Paul remained in Missouri to complete his leadership responsibilities and then attended the University of Missouri. After a tour in the Army, he joined his parents in the insurance agency. In 1970, he won a state Senate seat in a suburban Atlanta district.

At about the same time that Coverdell was selling insurance and thinking about politics, Minnesotan John Linder, just out of the Air Force, opened a dental practice. Like Coverdell, the young dentist made his first bid for public office less than a decade after moving to Georgia, and in 1974, he won a seat in the state House from the Atlanta suburbs.

Another recent arrival set his sights even higher. Newt Gingrich, a "military brat" born in Pennsylvania, had earned his undergraduate degree from Emory. In 1970, he returned to Georgia to teach History and Geography at West Georgia College after doing graduate work at Tulane University. Gingrich bucked the Watergate tide and challenged 20-year veteran Jack Flynt in Georgia's Sixth congressional district. Flynt, a traditional southern Democrat, had a record of opposing civil rights legislation. Gingrich, as something of a Rockefeller Republican, was to the left of Flynt on a number of issues.[8]

As detailed by Richard Fenno, when the two candidates appeared at a forum, Gingrich displayed far better debating skills than the incumbent. Gingrich's youth and command of the issues appealed to Republicans who were pouring into the Atlanta suburbs at the northern end of the district. Even in the bleak Republican year of 1974, Gingrich did well taking 48.5% of the vote. Two years later, he challenged Flynt a second time. With Jimmy Carter's lead over Gerald Ford rapidly evaporating, the Democratic presidential nominee had very short coattails. Indeed, it may be that Flynt was the only Democrat who owed his election to the Democratic standard bearer. The irony here was that Flynt was not a supporter of his state's former governor, who he thought to be too liberal. But the conservative Flynt did adapt to the changing times, and for the first time sought black support—a component of the electorate becoming increasingly critical for the electoral survival of southern Democrats. By mobilizing black support and holding on to Carter's coattails, Flynt eked out a victory of 5,000 votes. With Gingrich riding a rising tide of Republican support in the Atlanta suburbs, Flynt bowed out in 1978, and the young professor went to Congress as his party's only representative from the Peach State.

A fourth architect of the Republican renaissance came to Georgia from Indiana to work for IBM. Like Gingrich, Mack Mattingly made his first bid for public office by running for Congress in 1966, when he polled an unimpressive 23 percent of the vote against Bill Stuckey, the heir to the green-roofed filling stations specializing in pecan logs that dotted the South. Mattingly next suited up for political battle in what seemed to be a hopeless challenge to four-term Senator Herman Talmadge. But Talmadge had recently encountered a tsunami of negative publicity as a result of his alcoholism, divorce, and charges of financial improprieties in his office.

In retrospect, the election of Mack Mattingly proved to be one of those instances in which it was not so much that the challenger won, but rather that

---

[8]Richard F. Fenno Jr., *Congress at the Grassroots: Representational Change in the South, 1970–1998* (Chapel Hill: University of North Carolina, 2000).

the incumbent lost. The vote for Mattingly, which included a surprisingly high level of support from African Americans eager to punish Talmadge for decades of racist rhetoric uttered by him and his father, did not constitute a major improvement in GOP prospects. Not only did Mattingly's election not spawn other Republican success, but Mattingly also failed in his own reelection bid in 1986.

Perhaps due to his political inexperience, Mattingly chartered a disastrous course in his bid for reelection. He chose to forego campaigning in Georgia in order to cast often meaningless votes on the Senate floor. In contrast, his opponent, Representative Wyche Fowler, all but abandoned Washington to campaign full-time in Georgia. Fowler, recognizing the need to develop name recognition outside of his Atlanta congressional district, spent months criss-crossing the state. Since he had compiled the state's most liberal record when representing his predominately black district, Fowler needed to convince voters in other parts of the state that he was not a liberal, but rather that he had simply been a delegate representing his constituency's policy preferences. He promised that if elected by the statewide constituency he would effectively represent the state's more conservative preferences. To make that claim credible, Fowler had to make repeated presentations throughout the width and breadth of the state.

Mattingly tried to defend his decision to stay in Washington while denigrating Fowler's by repeatedly running a television ad critical of Fowler with the catch line, "Fowler, missing for Georgia." One flaw in this ad was that it ran far too often, thereby blunting any impact it might have had. Second, for voters who were paying only minimal attention to the content of the ad, it could have been interpreted as advocating the election of the challenger, if all the voter remembered was "Fowler . . . for Georgia." A third problem was that once Mattingly committed himself to staying in Washington rather than campaigning in Georgia, he could not leave the Capitol even to attend a fundraiser on his behalf that featured President Ronald Reagan. Mattingly found himself missing from Georgia far too often.

One of the early native-born Georgians in the Republican movement was Johnny Isakson, who followed in his father's footsteps as an executive at Atlanta's ultra-successful Northside Realty. Isakson caught the rising tide of Republicanism created by executive transfers moving into suburban Cobb County and, in his early 30s, he won a seat in the Georgia House in 1976. Perhaps it was because of his Georgia background that Isakson was less of an ideologue than some of the other young Republicans. His moderation and understanding of Georgia politics enabled him to establish closer ties with the Democratic House leadership and made him a more effective voice for his constituents than many of his fellow partisans.[9]

---

[9]Bo Callaway, who had the potential to be a leader among the emerging Republicans, forfeited that role when he decamped to Colorado. There he helped develop the popular Breckenridge ski resort area and became involved in Republican politics in the Centennial State. His active political involvement in the West proved no more successful than in Georgia, as he lost Colorado's GOP Senate nomination by 1,600 votes in 1980.

GOP BREAKTHROUGH

A review of the Georgia political scene in 1991 reveals a political topography lit-tle changed over the previous 25 years. Indeed, the strength of the two parties in 1991 bore much more similarity to that of two, three, or even four generations earlier than with what would be visible a mere decade later. In 1991, Democrats held every statewide office just as they had, with the brief Mattingly interlude, for more than 100 years. Gingrich gave Republicans a toehold in the congres-sional delegation, but it appeared to be precarious. In 1990, young attorney David Worley came within 1,000 votes of defeating Gingrich, even though the challenger received little encouragement from the Democratic Party. In retro-spect, had Democrats helped Worley with fund-raising and get-out-the-vote activities, Gingrich might have been sent back to the college classroom. In the General Assembly, Republicans had finally rebounded to the level attained before Watergate, but held only a fifth of the seats.

Republican fortunes began to turn around in 1992. An important factor in changing party fortunes was Georgia's prolonged struggle to adopt a redis-tricting plan. Georgia, like other states, must equalize the population among its legislative and congressional districts following each census. Because of its historic repression of black participation, the 1965 Voting Rights Act requires that before it can implement a redistricting plan, Georgia must secure ap-proval either from the U.S. attorney general or from the federal district court sitting in the District of Columbia.

Georgia had frequently had problems getting preclearance for districting plans in the past. But after the 1990 census, its problems magnified. The greater difficulty in getting approval stemmed from changes in federal law. In 1982, Congress renewed the Voting Rights Act for another 25 years, and in doing so it beefed up the part of the law known as "Section 2." Prior to 1982, Section 2 had been seen as simply a restatement of the Fifteenth Amendment guarantee of black suffrage, allowing plaintiffs to challenge election laws as racially discrimi-natory. A 1980 Supreme Court decision, *Mobile* v. *Bolden*, ruled that a plaintiff must prove that there had been an intention to discriminate when putting the election law in place. In 1982, Congress rewrote this provision to "correct" the Supreme Court decision. After 1982, a plaintiff needed only demonstrate that mi-norities had less opportunity to elect their preferred candidates than did white voters. The intent standard had been replaced with an "effects," or results test.

To comply with Section 2, the Department of Justice (DOJ) demanded that Georgia maximize the number of majority black congressional districts. This ne-cessitated splitting an extraordinary number of counties to separate African Americans from whites. Sorting blacks and whites into different districts re-sulted in three majority-black districts where previously there had been one.

It took the legislature three attempts to draw districts that satisfied DOJ. This extended legislative debate kept the focus on racial issues. Prior to this, the General Assembly's Democratic leadership had managed to unite Democrats by avoiding racially divisive issues. Black and white Democratic legislators who had worked in reasonable harmony for years now distrusted one another.

In the general public, the more politically attentive voters increasingly came to believe that the Democratic Party had become the pawn of black interests. This resulted in a growing number of white voters forsaking the Democratic Party.

The redistricting plans produced unprecedented rewards for the Republicans as they increased from one to four congressional seats. In the General Assembly, Republicans picked up 17 House seats and four Senate seats in 1992. GOP gains continued on into 1994, a year that was particularly good for Republicans across the country as they gained control of the U.S. House for the first time in 40 years. In Georgia, Republicans added four more congressional seats, giving them an 8-to-3 advantage. Republicans also added 14 more House and six more Senate seats. The 1994 election also marked the first time that Republicans won any of the state's constitutional offices as they elected the superintendent of education and the insurance commissioner. In addition, they picked up two more seats on the Public Service Commission, giving them a 3-to-2 advantage on that regulatory body.

By demanding that majority-black districts be created whenever possible, the DOJ forced Georgia to adopt a plan that paid far greater dividends to Republicans than African Americans. To create majority-black districts, neighboring ones had to be "bleached," and because most whites vote Republican, the whiter the district, the more likely it would elect a Republican. While it is true that two more African Americans went to Congress from Georgia, after 1994, the rest of the delegation was all Republican, and these new Republican legislators gave little support to the policy concerns of African Americans. Instead, the state's congressional delegation had become polarized along racial, partisan, and ideological lines, with all of the Democrats being moderate-to-liberal while all of the Republicans were quite conservative.

While Republicans did not win the governorship in 1994, they clearly announced their arrival as self-made millionaire Guy Millner took 48.9 percent of the vote against Zell Miller, who was seeking his second term. By coming within 32,600 votes of victory, Millner set a new high-water mark for Republican gubernatorial performance, exceeding the 47.8 percent won by Bo Callaway 28 years earlier. The GOP had become fully competitive in Georgia.

CONCLUSION

The GOP had now become the party of choice among white voters. The departure of much of the white electorate to the GOP left the Democratic Party increasingly reliant on black support. Ironically, the party of Jim Crow that had disfranchised African Americans after Reconstruction and fought to maintain segregation was now dependent upon unified black support for its survival. By the mid-1990s, a white, conservative Republican Party faced off against a biracial, moderate-to-liberal Democratic Party. Without 80, 90, and sometimes even 95 percent of the black vote, Democrats had poor prospects for winning statewide in Georgia. Even with 90 percent of the black vote, Democrats needed 40 percent of the white vote, and by 2000 that proved increasingly difficult.

PART TWO

Constitutions and Institutions

CHAPTER 4

The Georgia Constitution

Laws can be passed, amended, or even repealed by the vote of a majority of the General Assembly. Governors can veto laws, or even parts of laws, in Georgia so long as they can statutes the veto against further legislative action. The courts can strike down statues using the power of judicial review (an ancient practice from England that allows the court to interpret statute in the context of higher law, to judge it unconstitutional). However, provisions of the state constitution escape attacks by courts. The constitution takes precedence over statute and is more difficult to change—though change is not impossible, as the case of Georgia demonstrates. The constitution sets out the basic rules under which the government will operate. For this reason, those who draft constitutions try to thwart hasty or insufficiently thought-out changes.

CONTRASTING THE GEORGIA AND U.S. CONSTITUTIONS

Georgia's constitution serves much the same function as the U.S. Constitution, but the format of the two documents differs markedly. The national Constitution, ratified at the end of the eighteenth century, remains in place. It has seven articles, has been amended twenty-seven times, and is only about 30 pages long. Georgia, on the other hand, operates under its tenth constitution. The current constitution has 11 articles. The most recent version of the state constitution took effect in 1983, but it already has 67 amendments—more than twice as many as the U.S. Constitution, which was drafted 196 years before Georgia's latest effort.

Both the national and Georgia constitutions have articles devoted to the legislative, executive, and judicial branches. In contrast to the U.S. Constitution, which largely describes the design of institutions and the general grants of authority to same, Georgia's constitution provides specific details absent from some legislation. For example, in Article VI, dealing with the judiciary, the state constitution specifies in which county a divorce action will be filed and in which county a challenge to a land title will be filed. Article III of the Georgia Constitution deals with the General Assembly and, among other topics, specifies how to handle disorderly conduct among members and has lengthy sections dealing with the appropriations process and management of the state's employee retirement system.

Some topics that are not found at all in the national Constitution get extensive coverage in the Georgia document, such as Article VIII, which deals with education. One of the reasons that the federal document has remained more concise, less frequently amended, and never replaced is because of its elastic clause (Article I, Section 8), which authorizes Congress "to make all laws which will be necessary and proper for carrying into execution the foregoing powers . . ." Once the U.S. Supreme Court gave broad interpretation to that provision of Article I in *McCulloch* v. *Maryland*, it became possible to broaden the range of concerns addressed by federal statutes as the country matured, as technology developed, and as the economy became more complex (subject, of course to continued agreement from the Supreme Court). Georgia, rather than leaving it to the legislature interacting with the courts to address new problems as they arise, opted for precision in the grants of power included in the constitution. Efforts at precision explain why Georgia has rewritten its constitution more frequently than any state other than Louisiana and why it continues to add amendments every two years. (Lest one thinks that Georgia's 10 constitutions are an extraordinary number, France, which overthrew the Bourbons at about the same time that Georgia became a state, has lived under 16 constitutions.)

GEORGIA AND THE BILL OF RIGHTS

The 10 amendments attached to the Federal Constitution in 1791 are popularly termed the Bill of Rights; designed to protect the rights of citizens against the national government. The common conception is that the first 10 amendments are the Bill of Rights, in that they were all proposed and adopted at the same time. However, the Ninth and Tenth Amendments acknowledge the existence of rights beyond those explicitly enumerated, though they rarely find their way into debates over individual rights and liberties. The Tenth Amendment affirms that powers not explicitly granted to the national government are retained by the states or the people therein. This last provision has been historically advanced as a vehicle for states' rights and is usually in conflict with guarantees of individual liberties.

The first article of the current Georgia Constitution is also a Bill of Rights. Originally termed a Declaration of Fundamental Principles, these guarantees have grown from five to over 30 in various iterations of the constitution. Section 1 details the rights of persons and contains many of the same protections found in the federal Bill of Rights. The Georgia Bill of Rights guarantees freedom of speech and press, a right to bear arms, the right to assemble and petition the government, a right to trial by jury, and a right to counsel. Citizens are protected against unreasonable searches and seizures and self-incrimination. In the following sections, we detail the evolution of these rights as well as other institutional features and grants of power through the 10 Georgia constitutions, with a historic overview from the original trust colony charter.

FROM TRUSTEE CHARTER TO CONSTITUTIONAL COLONY

From 1732 to 1752, Georgia was governed by a Board of Trustees operating under a charter from the government of Great Britain. The charter provided for a corporate body (the Trust) and an unspecified number of trustees in England who would govern the colony through an elected executive committee of 15. This charter guaranteed religious freedom except for Roman Catholics and Jews. The initial trust did not provide for slavery until 1750 and for the sale of rum until 1742. Trustees had to go to Parliament for most substantive policy changes, such as licensing trade with Indians. In 1750, the Trustees asked Georgians to elect delegates to a council that would advise the Trustees. Savannah was apportioned four delegates; Augusta, two; Ebenezer, two; and every other town received one delegate each. The 16 delegates then met in Savannah, constituting the first representative assembly in Georgia. They immediately sought authority to enact local legislation. The next year, the Trust started to negotiate to turn Georgia over to the government.

From 1752 to 1776, Georgia was administered by the British Crown through the secretary of state. A royal governor was selected by the Crown, and a royal charter was crafted that was intended to be a model of colonial administration. The governor could call an assembly to pass laws, create courts, and engage in other administration. Each county had two representatives, and a council was created to serve as an "upper house," infusing bicameralism into the colony. When colonial loyalties to Great Britain eroded to the point of revolution in July 1775, the delegates of the assembly called a provincial Congress, which assembled at Tondee's Tavern in Savannah and agreed to join the revolution. This provincial Congress, in turn, authorized a Council of Safety, which usurped the authority of the royal governor. The colony then set about organizing a constitutional convention. By February 1777, the first constitution was completed and ratified.

THE CONSTITUTION OF 1777

The preamble to the initial Georgia Constitution draws inspiration in part from Jefferson's Declaration, declaring that "Whereas the conduct of the Legislature of Great Britain for many years past has been so oppressive on the people of America . . . conduct being repugnant to the common rights of mankind, hath obliged the Americans, as freemen, to oppose such oppressive measures, and to assert the rights and privileges they are entitled to by the laws of nature and reason." Voiding the authority of the Crown and seeing no government otherwise constituted, the people of Georgia moved "to adopt such government as may . . . best conduce to the happiness and safety of their constituents in particular and America in general." The Georgia framers claimed their authority as "representatives of the people, from whom all power originates" to constitute the new government.

The initial constitution consisted of 63 articles. It established separate legislative, executive, and judicial functions, with most of the power in the legislature, terming the branches' powers "separate and distinct" in Article I and noting that "neither exercise the powers properly belonging to the other." The balance of the constitution dealt with those issues typical of American constitutions—creating institutions, making grants of authority, indicating suffrage, and delineating some rights and liberties:

> Articles II through XV dealt with aspects of legislative powers, the apportionment of representatives, grants of authority, and procedures for the conduct of legislative business.
>
> Articles XVI through XVIII dealt with matters of eligibility for office, Continental office, and forbade holding more than one "post of profit" under the state.
>
> Articles XX through XXXIII dealt with the office of the governor and his executive council, interactions between the executive and the legislature, and grants of executive authority. The governor was elected for a term of one year.
>
> Articles XXXIV and XXXV authorized and organized a militia.
>
> Articles XXXVI through XLIX authorized the judiciary, designated courts and their jurisdictions, and provided for grand and petit juries, and also their selection and eligibility.
>
> Articles L through LVI authorized and detailed the obligations of county government, including record keeping and the construction of jails.
>
> Article LVII authorized the great seal of the state of Georgia.
>
> Article LVIII through LXII set forth rights and liberties of freepersons. Among these were protection from excessive fines or bails (Article LIX); a guarantee that "the principles of the habeas corpus act shall be a part of this constitution" (Article LX); freedom of the press and the guarantee of jury trial "to remain inviolate forever" (Article LXI); and the exclusion of "clergyman of any denomination" from the legislature (Article LXII).

Georgia's initial constitution created a strong legislature, a weak governor, a judiciary, local governments, and various protections that would later be included in the U.S. Constitution.

THE CONSTITUTION OF 1789

Georgia ratified the U.S. Constitution in January of 1788 and then went to convention in Augusta to revise its constitution. Georgia's new document, just 2,700 words long, was modeled on Madison's document. It created a bicameral legislature that had the authority to select the executive. Article II of the 1789 constitution provided that the "house of representatives shall . . . vote by ballot for three persons [for governor]; and shall make a list containing the names of the persons voted for, and of the number of votes for each person" and then deliver that list to the Senate, which "shall, on the same day, proceed, by ballot, to elect one of the three persons [governor by] a majority of the votes of the senators." The governor was given broad veto power to revise "bills passed by both houses, before the same shall become laws" though his revisions could be overturned by a two-thirds vote within five days, presaging the strong line-item budget veto of current Georgia governors. There is little detail on the judiciary, but the document included a state bill of rights, as Article IV contained a variety of guarantees to citizens and inhabitants of the state, specifying suffrage, guaranteeing freedom of the press, trial by jury, habeas corpus, and free exercise of religion.

THE CONSTITUTION OF 1798

The 1798 constitutional revision arose directly out of an episode of Georgia history known as the Yazoo Land Fraud. This event entailed the corrupt sale of most of present-day Alabama and Mississippi by the state of Georgia to four land speculation firms. The state, which held land claims over this territory, acted because of the efforts of U.S. Senator James Gunn (Federalist-Ga.) to coordinate bribery of state officials. Reaction from his Senate colleague James Jackson, a Jeffersonian Republican, led to the ouster of the Federalists from control of state government and the rescinding of the sale by the next legislature (the Rescinding Act of 1796). The subsequent constitutional convention was called to rein in the power of the legislature and also codify in a new constitution the Rescinding Act. As a result, the new constitution was twice as long as its predecessor, due largely to the detail related to the rescinding of the Yazoo land swindle.

Among the substantive revisions in the new constitution was the provision for the popular election of the governor, thereby removing the governor's dependency on the legislature. The constitution authorized a state supreme court, but it would be 40 years before the legislature would create the Supreme Court and another decade after that before it was seated. The constitution continued the institution of slavery but prohibited importation of slaves after 1798. The 1798 constitution remained in force for 63 years, making it the second longest-lived constitution in state history.

THE CONSTITUTION OF 1861

As much as the 1789 constitution was crafted to conform to and reflect the 1787 Philadelphia document, the 1861 Georgia Constitution was patterned after the Confederate Constitution. It was the first of *four* constitutions adopted by the state in less than two decades. It was also the first constitution to be submitted to a vote of the people. The major enhancement of this constitution is a detailed Bill of Rights, titled the "Declaration of Fundamental Principles," presented prominently at the front of the document as Article 1 with the introduction

> The fundamental principles of Free Government cannot be too well understood, nor too often recurred to. God has ordained that men shall live under government; but as the forms and administration of civil government are in human, and therefore, fallible hands, they may be altered, or modified whenever the safety or happiness of the governed requires it. No government should be changed for light or transient causes; nor unless upon reasonable assurance that a better will be established.

These principles continue into the current state constitution. Beyond previous guarantees such as jury trial and adherence to habeas corpus, among the numerous explicit guarantees appearing in the 1861 constitution are:

> Protection to person and property
>
> An explicit guarantee of numerous due process rights, including a right to counsel for the accused, access to the accusation, ability to confront witnesses, protection from double jeopardy
>
> The right to keep and bear arms
>
> An enhanced freedom of speech and press, which cautions "while every citizen may freely speak, write and print, on any subject, he shall be responsible for the abuse of the liberty"
>
> Petition and peaceable assembly guarantees

Also, the state constitution for the first time explicitly incorporated the concept of judicial review of legislative acts by the judiciary and granted the ability to nullify acts "in violation of the fundamental law."

The Georgia Constitution of 1861 reflects a literal thinking on rights and liberties: that these are conferred explicitly in the constitution, rather than being part of a larger body of rights that existed under the Fundamental Law even though they are not enumerated. This nod to literalism is also evident in the explicit incorporation of judicial review into the constitution. The concept existed at the Federal level without explicit constitutional guarantee and had been previously practiced in the English system without benefit of a written constitution, indicating its origins as part of the function of courts in enforcing the fundamental law.

THE CONSTITUTION OF 1865

In order to regain admission to the Union and secure removal of federal troops, Georgia had to adopt a new state constitution which included three important elements: a repeal of the 1861 secession ordinance, abolition of slavery, and repudiation of its war debt from the Civil War. The constitution left the Declaration of Fundamental Principles largely unchanged. The only enhancement was the following, designed to win readmission:

> The Government of the United States having, as a war measure, proclaimed all slaves held or owned in this State, emancipated from slavery, and having carried that proclamation into full practical effect, there shall henceforth be, within the State of Georgia, neither slavery nor involuntary servitude, save as a punishment for crime, after legal conviction thereof; provided, this acquiescence in the action of the Government of the United States is not intended to operate as a relinquishment, waiver, or estoppel of such claim for compensation of loss sustained by reason of the emancipation of his slaves, as any citizen of Georgia may hereafter make upon the justice and magnanimity of that Government.

The new document also incorporated a preamble largely modeled on that of the U.S. Constitution, declaring:

> We, the people of the State of Georgia, in order to form a permanent Government, establish justice, insure domestic tranquility, and secure the blessings of liberty to ourselves and our posterity, acknowledging and invoking the guidance of Almighty God, the author of all good government, do ordain and establish this Constitution for the State of Georgia.

Other notable changes include the following: The governor was placed under a two-term limit, judges would be elected instead of appointed, and home rule for municipalities was expanded by granting localities the power to tax. When Georgia failed to ratify the Fourteenth Amendment to the U.S. Constitution, the national government unseated its congressional delegation and rejected the new constitution. Military forces returned to Georgia and did not leave until 1871.

THE CONSTITUTION OF 1868

Once again under military occupation, Georgians met in convention for four months in the winter of 1867 to 1868 to craft a new constitution that might end Reconstruction. The Declaration of Fundamental Principles expanded from 21 sections in the rejected 1865 constitution to 33.

Much of this language captured the substance of the Fourteenth Amendment to the U.S. Constitution. Section 2 of the Declaration declared

> All persons born or naturalized in the United States, and resident in this State, are hereby declared citizens of this State, and no laws shall be made or enforced which shall abridge the privileges or immunities of citizens of the United States, or of this State, or deny to any person within its jurisdiction the equal protection of its laws.

Such amending of the state constitution made sense, because the Fourteenth Amendment empowered Congress to regulate the states, so that they might not violate the rights and liberties of individuals. In other words, the guarantees and protections from governmental violation of liberties and rights under the Bill of Rights were also applied to the state, and Congress had the authority to enforce them through legislation.

Changes directed at the previous slave culture included the provision, required for readmission to the Union, that "[t]here shall be within the State of Georgia neither slavery nor involuntary servitude" (Section 4). Other changes directed at elements of the former slave culture included a declaration that "[t]he social status of the citizen shall never be the subject of legislation" (Section 11), and that "whipping, as a punishment for crime, is prohibited" (Section 22).

The Declaration also prohibited a state lottery; authorized a poll tax, though only for educational purposes; and permitted laborers to place liens on the property of employers to guarantee payment for labor or "material furnished." This last provision protected in particular the ability of Freedmen to obtain pay for their skilled or unskilled labor, though Jim Crow would make it ineffective.

The new constitution established universal male suffrage and called on the state to provide free general education to all children. The suffrage provisions provided for an oath taken by the voter, registration requirements, and both felon and "idiot" disfranchisement. All male citizens over 21 who had resided in the state for a year and had met all their tax obligations could vote.

In order to provide that secession would never happen again, the 1868 constitution affirmed the perpetual state of union between Georgia and the other United States, declaring that "Georgia shall ever remain a member of the American Union" whose people are part of the American nation, and who owe "paramount allegiance to the Constitution and Government of the United States."

THE CONSTITUTION OF 1877

Six years after exiting Reconstruction and four months after the bargain that made Rutherford Hayes the president, which also ended national government intervention in the South, 193 Georgians convened to replace the Reconstruction constitution of 1868, producing a document of 13 articles and 16,000 words. The document was much more explicit—and restrictive—with regard to the treatment of both individual rights and the grants of authority to the government.

The new constitution renamed the Declaration of Fundamental Principles as the Bill of Rights. The Bill of Rights was divided into five sections, largely incorporating the previous Declaration but including three important changes. First, in Section 2, Paragraph 5, the practice of lobbying the legislature was declared to be a crime enforceable by penalties prescribed by the legislature. In Section 5, the framers reasserted aspects of states' rights, declaring that the "people of [Georgia] have the inherent, sole and exclusive right of regulating their internal government, and the police thereof, and of altering and abolishing their Constitution whenever it may be necessary to their safety and happiness." The second paragraph affirmed a less fundamental interpretation of the constitution than implied by the extensive Bill of Rights, declaring that "The enumeration of rights herein contained as a part of this Constitution, shall not be construed to deny to the people any inherent rights which they may have hitherto enjoyed."

This constitution, the longest lived in the history of Georgia at 68 years, began the tradition of excessive amending. The constraints on the legislature imposed by the constitution required extensive changes. The voters successfully altered the document over 300 times. Amending activity included a variety of changes to enforce the reestablishment of white supremacy, leading to an era of Jim Crow rule.

THE CONSTITUTION OF 1945

Prompted by a decade of debate regarding the need for constitutional reform, in 1943 progressive Governor Ellis Arnall appointed a constitutional commission to follow up on the 1931 recommendations of the University of Georgia's Institute for Public Affairs. The product, presented in January 1945 and ratified by the electorate in August, streamlined the 1877 constitution. Among the most notable changes were the creation of an elected lieutenant governor (which would lead to controversy within two years during the Three Governors' Controversy), extending eligibility for jury duty to women and enlarging the state supreme court. For the first time, it also provided for a state merit system and public employee retirement system.

The new constitution continued the amended suffrage requirements of 1877. Voters had to be persons "who are of good character" and literate. The literacy requirement read:

> All persons who can correctly read in the English language any paragraph of the Constitution of the United States or of this State and correctly write the same in the English language when read to them by any one of the registrars, and all persons who solely because of physical disability are unable to comply with the above requirements but who can understand and give a reasonable interpretation of any paragraph of the Constitution of the United States or of this State that may be read to them by any one of the registrars.

These provisions continued until suspended by the Voting Rights Act of 1965, and they were permanently abolished by Congress in 1970.

The 1945 constitution continued until 1976, when voters ratified a new constitution promoted by incumbent Governor George Busbee. Busbee had run for office on the promise of an "article-by-article" reorganization of the document. The Constitution of 1976 was just that—a reorganization of the existing articles of the 1945 constitution and its amendments, rather than a document that contained any substantively new content.

THE CONSTITUTION OF 1983

Immediately after the ratification of the Constitution of 1976, the General Assembly created a Select Committee on Constitutional Revision chaired by former Governor Busbee that included major constitutional officers, lawmakers, and members of the judiciary. This committee fully revised the state constitution, which was initially approved by the legislature in special session in September 1981, was amended in the 1982 regular legislative session and sent to the voters at the 1982 general election. The new constitution went into effect July 1, 1983.

The new constitution was less than half the length of its predecessor. It authorized the legislature to deal directly with matters previously requiring a vote of the people. The new constitution explicitly incorporated the federal equal protection clause, which finally brought Georgia into constitutional alignment with the national Constitution's Fourteenth Amendment and made judicial elections nonpartisan. Amendment became less common since that path was no longer required when the legislature regulated local governmental units. This eliminated the need to keep the state constitution in a loose-leaf notebook, although Georgia ratifies new amendments in each general election.

The new constitution contains a preamble (carried over from previous versions) and 11 articles.

Article I: Bill of Rights, which derives from the Declaration of Fundamental Principles in Constitution of 1861, and is largely unchanged except for provisions added by the Reconstruction-era constitutions.

Article II: Voting and Elections, which describes qualifications for suffrage; procedures for registering to vote; and mechanisms for suspending public officials.

Article III: Legislative Branch, which established qualifications for office; legislative powers and grants of authority; impeachment authority; session length and timing; and apportionment of legislative seats.

Article IV: Constitutional Boards and Commissions, deals with the creation of, and grants of authority to, the Public Service Commission, State Board of Pardons and Paroles, State Personnel Board, State Transportation Board, Veterans Services Board, and a Board of Natural Resources.

Article V: Executive Branch, which deals with the election of the Governor and Lieutenant Governor, grants of authority to the Governor, grants of authority to other elected executives, and handling of disability of executive officers.

Article VI: Judicial Branch, which details the role of the seven different types of courts, including their jurisdictions and grants of power, as well as the powers and authority of district attorneys.

Article VII: Taxation and Finance, which describes both the taxation powers of the legislature and limits thereon, exemptions to ad valorem and property taxes, grants from the state to local governments, and the management of the state debt.

Article VIII: Education, which discusses public school systems, school boards, and taxation related to education.

Article IX: Counties and Municipal Corporations, which discusses the creation and role of counties; home rule; the creation of special districts; and the tax powers, debt, and bonding authority of municipalities.

Article X: Amendments to the Constitution, which describes the process of amending the constitution.

Article XI: Miscellaneous Provisions, which addresses a potpourri of issues arising from the transition from the old constitution to the new, including judicial review and the continuation of existing law under the new constitution.

AMENDING: U.S. CONSTITUTION VERSUS GEORGIA CONSTITUTION

Several amendments to the national Constitution expanded suffrage, with the Fifteenth Amendment guaranteeing the right to vote to African Americans who previously had been held as slaves. The Nineteenth Amendment extended the suffrage to women. The Twenty-Fourth Amendment banned the poll tax as a prerequisite to voting, while the Twenty-Sixth Amendment lowered the age for voting to 18. Other amendments to the federal Constitution freed the slaves, extended most of the protections of the Bill of Rights to individuals in their dealings with their states through the due process clause of the Fourteenth Amendment. The Sixteenth Amendment authorized the income tax, while the Seventeenth Amendment provided for the popular election of senators. To the extent that the federal Constitution contains matters that might be thought of as trivial, the primary candidates would be the Eighteenth Amendment, which prohibited the manufacturing and consumption of alcoholic beverages and the Twentieth Amendment, which repealed the Eighteenth Amendment after 14 years.

In contrast, the Georgia Constitution has been amended to provide for a variety of activities so unusual or mundane as to defy imagination. For instance, since 1950 the voters of Georgia have been asked to approve the following proposals via constitutional amendment:

To limit the ability of the city of Waycross to levy city taxes on property owned by persons over age 65 (1954)

To allow credit for work at a state prison to count against medical school loan debt (1964)

To "preserve the right to not associate" in order to preserve segregation through school choice (1962)

To allow cities and counties to clear slums (1962)

To approve an ad valorum tax exemption for fraternities and sororities (1958)

To allow recorder's courts and police courts to dispose of cases of marijuana possession involving less than one once of pot (1980)

In addition, when the state constitution of 1982 was placed on the ballot, it was accompanied by four proposed amendments before it ever took force.

Note that these seemingly trivial amendments were to versions of the constitution prior to the current one. As noted above, the present constitution sought to avoid the necessity of amendments to address local concerns.

AMENDMENT PROCESS

To amend the Georgia Constitution, the proposal must be approved by two-thirds of the members of both chambers of the General Assembly. Then the proposal must be approved by a majority of the voters at the next general election. The brief explanations that accompany the amendments on the ballot, limited to a sentence or two, often leave voters uncertain as to what they have been asked to vote on. Having these items on the ballot can also slow down the process of voting, because many voters arrive at the polls unaware of the amendments. In one instance, the wording of an amendment was so confusing that it was later challenged in court. Opponents unsuccessfully sought to invalidate the ratification, claiming that the wording of the amendment relating to sovereign immunity made it appear that it would become easier to sue the state, when in fact, the amendment made it more difficult to bring suit.

MAKING CHANGE MORE DIFFICULT

One motivation for amending the constitution is to make policy changes more difficult. Thus, some amendments take provisions that are currently in statutes and convert them into provisions of the constitution. Two examples are worth mentioning. The first is the program that created the HOPE scholarships, which pay for college or vocational education for any Georgia high school graduate with a "B" average, now has constitutional protection. Governor Zell Miller, who created this program by getting the legislature to authorize a lottery to pay for it, worried that his successors might not be as committed to limiting the use of the lottery money for HOPE scholarships and the pre-kindergarten program for four-year-olds. Therefore, coincident with the election of his successor in 1998, he persuaded the legislature to place on the ballot an amendment restricting lottery proceeds to these two programs.

The second was the 2004 Georgia constitutional amendment prohibiting gay marriage. While Georgia law already defined marriage as between a man and a woman, the Massachusetts Supreme Court decision that struck down a similar statute in the Bay State led legislators in Georgia and some other states to believe that if this were not written into their constitutions, courts might undo the legislative bans.

The amendment banning gay marriage passed with more than 70 percent of the vote. It also had the advantage, from the perspective of its supporters, of encouraging religious conservatives to turn out and vote. While there may have also been some counter-mobilization in the gay and lesbian community, there are far more religious conservatives than gays or lesbians in Georgia. Therefore, the inclusion of this provision helped Republicans not only carry the state for George Bush, but also to win majorities in both chambers of the state legislature.

CONCLUSION

Georgia has used 10 constitutions. There are, generally speaking, three eras of constitution writing in the state. The first is at the time of the establishment of the colony as a state, as Georgia experimented, often unsuccessfully, with institutions and grants of power and authority to those institutions. The second era, surrounding the Civil War, arose out of efforts to enumerate individual rights and liberties while also dealing with the changing status of black Georgians, initially as slaves, later as freedmen, and then again as a political force to be contained by ascendant white Georgians after Reconstruction. This same era of constitution-writing entailed further experimentation with institutional power that made it very difficult for any state branch to exercise substantial authority. The last era, since World War II, has dealt with attempting to rein in the amending activity and reorganizing an arcane and cumbersome document into a modern functioning constitution for a modern, urbanizing state.

The product is a document that is still subject to frequent amending. Amendments increasingly deal with altering the constitution to accommodate policy initiatives or to attempt to enact as higher constitutional law policy priorities of the legislative and political electoral majority in order to constrain the policy alternatives of a future, different majority. Constitutional revision has eliminated many of the most arcane aspects of Georgia's governing document, but much of the constitutional structure of Georgia, including its institutions, guarantees of rights and liberties, and grants of institutional power, trace back at least 150 years.

votefordanae.com

Danae Roberts grew up in politics. Her father, U. D. Roberts, was once Republican Party chair. Danae began working in campaigns when she was 14, stumping for U.S. Representatives Mac Collins and Linda Schrenko. She observed, "Working these campaigns gave me a tremendous opportunity to work with people who have represented us at the state and even national level . . . so even before I could vote, I was involved and just had a passion to lead in government." In 2000, Danae, a political science major and Alpha Omicron Pi (AOII) sister, quickly went from vice president of the Georgia College Republicans to alternate delegate to the Republican National Convention in Philadelphia to be a candidate for the state legislature in her hometown of Columbus.

The district she filed for was held by GOP incumbent Tommy Davis. Georgia Republicans typically adhere to Ronald Reagan's "Eleventh Commandment" when it comes to incumbents, but Davis was not a typical incumbent. Tim Bentley of the *Georgia's Capitol Report* described Davis's ascent to the legislature in 1998 thus: "Ronnie Culbreth qualified for the GOP primary, but withdrew his candidacy within hours of the qualifying deadline. Davis immediately filed to run for the post. No other Republican or Democrat has time to qualify."[1] Davis was a backdoor incumbent, unproven against other politicians in the district, and he fully expected a challenge, but not a 21-year-old recent UGA graduate.

Roberts sought to differentiate herself from the incumbent and to tie him to Democratic Governor Roy Barnes. Her attacks of Barnes's education reform bill, and Davis's support for it, won her support from various Republican politicians and conservative groups. She mounted a classic, grassroots effort that cost just under $11,000. Roberts received tremendous support from fellow church members and members of the University of Georgia's College Republican chapter, who campaigned for her on the weekends. The result was a surprising upset that made headlines in the national political press, which

[1]Tim Bentley, *Georgia's Capitol Report*, Monday, July 17, 2000 v2(9)

immediately seized on the uniqueness of her youth.[2] Her father's evaluation spoke of the strong bond between father and daughter. "I am extremely proud of my daughter . . . when she graduated college she just went for it."[3]

Roberts evoked both the potential impact of her election on her friends, and her belief in God's will as a guiding force in her life. "My campaign piqued some of my friends' interest in possibly running for an elected office in the future . . . if the Lord wants me to go to another office, I'm sure that will become available in the future."[4]

LAWMAKING 101

The Georgia House of Representatives was among the last cigar-chomping, back-slapping, good-old-boy political institutions in the modern world. Long a bastion of rural white men, it gradually admitted women and minorities into the inner sanctum. In 2001, though, the reins of power were in the hands of rural white Democrats who remembered a legislature without blacks, without women, and without Republicans. The election of a youthful, exuberant, smart Republican woman from the suburbs caused notice.

> It was one of those unremarkable, yet poignant moments last Wednesday morning in the House Chamber . . . Danae Roberts strode toward the Speaker's dais past a phalanx of mostly male, dark-suited colleagues. She reached Tom Murphy, the venerable crusty, 76-year-old House Speaker with wood gavel in hand, an unlit cigar in mouth . . . Murphy smiled. Roberts—with "Meg Ryan hair," shiny teeth and perfect posture—did likewise. Flash. The Speaker rediscovered his cigar.[5]

Her good looks attracted attention from the press and her colleagues. Octogenarian Speaker pro tempore Jack Connell observed happily "'Isn't she attractive?" The "little lady" comments didn't seem to phase the freshman, who told the Atlanta press, "I feel like I've been accepted.'"[6]

Her first session in the legislature did not continue as smoothly as the photo op with the Speaker. Roberts and fellow Columbus freshman Seth Harper (R) voted against a variety of budget measures including a $20-million-dollar appropriation for Muscogee County-area projects. The *Columbus Ledger* reported that

> [Harper and Roberts] ruffled a few feathers during their first session in the Georgia General Assembly. But that is what their constituents

---

[2]*CNN.Com/allpolitics:* "Veteran Lawmakers Fall or Face Runoffs in Georgia Primary," archives.cnn.com/2000/ALLPOLITICS/stories/07/19/gaprimary.ap/index.html (July 19, 2000).
[3]Ibid.
[4]"GOP House Nominee, 22, May Have Made History," Associated Press, July 20, 2000.
[5]"New House No Sorority," **Atlanta Constitution**, February 11, 2001, 3C.
[6]Ibid.

elected them to do, say the Columbus delegation's newest members . . . Their opposition was tolerated by some Democrats in the local delegation as part of the political process and rejected by others.[7]

The Columbus delegation was known for its cohesiveness. That cohesiveness was highly prized by the Democratic floor leadership. Speaker Murphy was "shocked" that Roberts would vote against so much money for the Columbus area, saying, "It was a little outrageous, to tell you the truth."[8] Some legislative colleagues complained that the votes would make it more difficult for the delegation to negotiate in the legislature, because they were not lock-step for the budget.

Danae Roberts steeled herself in her faith. "I went in there praying that I would not be disfavored by people . . . but when people got to know me, they found out I didn't think I knew it all—I am one that wants to listen, observe, and then take part."

She stood on principle and made difficult votes on controversial measures, especially when confronted with the backroom approach to legislating that sometimes raises its head in the General Assembly. When Governor Barnes shotgunned his controversial state flag through the House, Roberts voted "nay." She voted against the new flag because Democrats pushed for a quick vote with no time for representatives to get constituent input, and observed afterwards, "It was shoved in our faces . . . I wasn't opposed to change. I was opposed to the process."

Reflecting on her first term, Roberts described it as her "learning term" spent "listening and learning." When asked about her agenda and goals, she emphasized education and her strong commitment to developing business opportunities in metro Columbus. She did not shrink away from her vote against the fiscal year 2002 budget, but she did vote for the next budget because "this time, the bond debt was reduced, and I felt better voting for it." Roberts criticized the "opaque nature" of the Georgia budgeting process; she argued that the whole budget process should be more open, so that the entire lawmaking body and the people would be able to see what goes into the "multi-billion dollar spending plan."

During her second legislative session, Roberts scored a legislative success, notable not only because she was a junior member of the minority party, but also because she was a junior minority party member marked for extermination by the majority-party leadership. Together with another Columbus representative, Democrat Carolyn Hugley, she coauthored the Sex Offender Notification Act (HB 1054). The act created a mechanism to ensure that public and private schools would have up-to-date knowledge about the presence of convicted sexual predators in their community. The previous state law

---

[7]*Columbus Ledger-Enquirer,* "Freshmen Georgia Lawmakers Say They Have No Regrets" [URL no longer available] (April 12, 2001).

[8]Ibid.

required that schools be updated on an annual basis, but the Roberts-Hugley bill created a secure, electronic notification system that would allow schools and day-care facilities to access the daily-updated databases of the Georgia Bureau of Investigation. The bill passed through the House on a voice vote on March 25, 2002, and the Senate by an electronic vote of 43-to-0. Governor Barnes signed the bill on May 3, 2002.[9]

Roberts did not buck the system at every turn, but rather sat back and learned, thereby earning support from veteran lawmakers. She did her homework, attended to her duties, and had a stellar attendance record, missing just five votes. And, despite the assumptions of folks on the left, her strong Christian faith did not translate into an arch-right voting record. Act-Up's legislative scorecard for Georgia in 2002 revealed that, among all legislators for the past four years, Roberts had an average "C" score for supporting homosexual issues in the General Assembly, placing her ahead of many Democrats.

"TARGET ON THE BACK"

Redistricting is the most critical, contentious act a legislature undertakes. In order to meet the mandates of equal population required by federal courts, legislatures must redistrict after every census to reflect population shifts. In fact, redistricting represents much more than that; it is the opportunity for incumbents to choose their constituents or for the dominant party to enhance its majority. Legislators take care of themselves, their partisans, and their friends. Redistricting usually increases the electoral security of incumbents. The 2001 Georgia remap eschewed the historic incumbent-protection gerrymander for the blood sport of the partisan remap. Among the Republican scalps hung on the redistricting wall was that of Danae Roberts.

Columbus had not grown as fast as the rest of the state and had to give up a seat. To meet the equal population mandate, Democrats sacrificed Robert's old district. Jim Houston of the *Columbus Ledger* observed, "When the ink dried on Georgia's reapportioned House districts . . . Roberts' House District 132 was dismantled."[10] Political observer and longtime *Atlanta Journal* editorial page associate editor Jim Wooten was indignant over the partisan fingerprints on the new legislative maps.[11] The new map placed Roberts's home in the same district as fellow Republican Representative Vance Smith. In order to continue her political career, she would have to compete in another district, one that was close by and with enough Republicans that she would have some prospects for success. She opted to contest District 109, an open seat with four precincts from her old district. However, 109 contained substantial new inhospitable territory for a Republican: Black Belt Talbot County. She moved into an apartment in the

[9]Andy Peters, "Legislative Notebook," *Macon Telegraph,* March 26, 2002.
[10]Jim Houston, "Roberts Refuses to Let Redistricting Stop Her." *Columbus Ledger-Enquirer,* October 31, 2002.
[11]Jim Wooten, "Democrats Put On Squeeze: Redistricting Process Takes Toll on Conservative Women," *Atlanta Journal-Constitution,* August 17, 2001, A20.

BOX I.1

Election Results, Danae Roberts

	2000	2002
Primary Election		
Danae Roberts (R)	2,210 (56.8%)	2,944 (100.0%)
Tommy Davis (R-Inc.)	1,681 (43.2%)	No opponent
General Election		
Danae Roberts (R-Inc.)	12,152 (100.0%)	5,543 (48.5%)
Debbie Buckner (D)	No opponent	5,589 (51.5%)

Source: Data compiled by authors.

Windsor Village complex a year before the election in order to comply with the state's one-year residency requirement. As Roberts stumped her new, sprawling districts, she emphasized education, focusing on classroom size, infrastructure, and the return of local control to school systems since "each school system finds itself facing different situations that have different requirements."[12]

The fall election wrote a premature end to the electoral career of Danae Roberts. Meg Pirtne, writing for the Columbus paper, observed that

> Strong home-county support in Talbot County led political newcomer Debbie Buckner to victory in the Georgia House District 109 race . . . although Roberts led by 710 votes in Muscogee County, Buckner secured victory by dominating Talbot County with 1,532 votes to Roberts's 478 [a 1,044-vote margin]. Buckner campaigned door-to-door with family and friends, listening to constituents and learning along the way.[13]

So the unseating of Roberts was attributed to the same circumstances as her ascendancy—a hard-working newcomer took to the streets and beat her at the doors with the enthusiastic support of friends and family. The account, however, ignores an inconvenient reality: Danae Roberts encountered the adverse effects of redistricting on an incumbent, when the constituency base is disrupted and career decisions of the past impede the electoral future.

POST-ELECTIVE CAREER

After losing her legislative seat, Roberts did not slow down. She went to work for the state Department of Education, representing its policy and budget interests to her former colleagues. Holding the position of external

---

[12]Houston, "Roberts Refuses to Let Redistricting Stop Her."

[13]Meg Pirtne, "Buckner Unseats Roberts," *Columbus Ledger-Enquirer,* November 6, 2002.

BOX I.2

The Tale of the Tape

	Richard B. Russell, Jr.	C. Danae Roberts
Age at First Election	23 years, 1 month	22 years, 9 months
Education	A.B., Letters University of Georgia	A.B., Political Science University of Georgia
Greek House	Sigma Nu	Alpha Omicron Pi
Father's Politics	State Supreme Court	State GOP Chair
Hometown	Winder	Columbus
Subsequent Careers	House Speaker Governor U.S. Senator	State Legislator Lobbyist Government Affairs Specialist

Source: Data compiled by authors.

affairs specialist, she stayed at DOE for two years. She also got married (she's now Danae Roberts Gambill) and settled in Cartersville. In 2005, she joined the Georgia Chamber of Commerce as vice president for governmental affairs. This position again placed her in a lobbying role, representing the state chamber and its membership to the General Assembly. She left after a year to go to the Georgia Hospital Association as director of government relations. This last change placed her with a not-for-profit trade association representing 170 hospitals and numerous health-providing and health-maintenance systems in the state. It also placed her in contact with both the state legislature and the U.S. Congress, lobbying on issues of health and clinical care provisions and health care management.

CHAPTER 5

The Georgia General Assembly

The General Assembly, composed of the House of Representatives and the Senate, has primary responsibility for enacting legislation for the state. It can also monitor implementation of legislation, which includes oversight of the executive branch (the governor and state agencies). For most of its history, the General Assembly has been very deferential to the governor, far less likely to challenge actions of the governor and to grant his or her policy requests than Congress is when dealing with the president. One-party Democratic control of both branches of government from the early 1870s until 2003 contributed to this deference.

A second reason for the deference shown by the legislature to the governor has been the part-time nature of legislative service. For many years, the General Assembly met only every other year, in a 70-day session. Currently the legislature meets annually but only for 40 legislative days. Legislators are paid $17,000 a year, receive $173 per diem when on official legislative business, and have a $7,000 expense account. The Speaker received almost $100,000 in 2008. Because they earn so little, legislators must be concerned about practicing their vocations and therefore, they are not regularly in the Capitol except during sessions. A consequence of what political scientists would term part-time, amateur legislators is that they frequently rely on the greater expertise of the governor and his or her staff, who are involved full-time in the state's policy arenas.

Georgia has one of the nation's largest legislatures, with 56 senators and 180 representatives. All lawmakers currently represent single-member districts, although historically some House members came from multi-member districts (the 2004 redistricting eliminated the last multi-member districts). Members of both chambers serve two-year terms. Unlike many other states, Georgia does not limit how long a legislator can serve. In 2009, five representatives had served more than 30 years, while the most senior senators' service began in 1991.

Enactment of legislation requires the approval of both chambers, in identical form, by a constitutional majority—more than half of each chamber's members. For most of the state's history the House was the dominant chamber, which is unlike Congress, where the Senate is generally seen as the more powerful chamber. Beginning in the 1960s, the Senate asserted its prerogatives so that now members of each chamber believe their body to be the more important one. Disagreements between the chambers over the terms of new public policy increased dramatically in 2003, when Republicans controlled the Senate but Democrats retained a majority in the House. Even after Republicans took control of both chambers in 2005, the House and Senate continued high profile disagreements over the budget and taxes.

Although Georgia is the nation's ninth most populous state, it has a short legislative session. The General Assembly meets for only 40 days with sessions beginning on the second Monday in January and usually ending around the first of April. In 2004, the 40 days extended over the longest period in more than a century when frequent recesses taken to work out compromises between the Democratic House and Republican Senate stretched the session almost into May. In a largely symbolic move in 2005, the first legislative session under complete Republican control wrapped up its work in 39 days. Despite the 40-day limit, the governor infrequently calls special sessions, except after the census, when the legislature meets at the end of the summer to redraw legislative and congressional districts.

PERSONNEL

Until the last four decades of the twentieth century, the General Assembly was an exclusive preserve of white, Democratic males, mostly from rural districts. U.S. Supreme Court decisions requiring equal population among legislative districts opened the door for greater diversity.

While rural communities enjoyed disproportionate influence in all state legislatures, Georgia went further than most in limiting urban and suburban areas. Until 1966, each county had at least one representative in the state House with only minimal deference given to differences in county populations. The eight most populous counties each had three representatives, while the next 30 in size each got two seats. The remaining 121 counties had a single legislator each. Obviously, if rural legislators united, they could defeat urban initiatives. The rural flavor of the past continues in events like the Wild Hog Supper held the night before the legislature convenes.

The Senate also gave small rural counties disproportionate influence. Prior to 1962, Senate districts, with two exceptions, consisted of three counties. The choice of a district's senator rotated among the three counties. In the year in which a county got to choose a senator, only its voters could participate. Only rarely did a county pass up its chance to name the senator and allow another county to take its place. The rotation system ensured that even the smallest counties got to choose the senator every third election. The constant rotation of senators among the counties in a district meant that only the senator from Fulton County, the state's most populous, which contains most of Atlanta, could gain seniority since the county did not share a district with two others. The lack of seniority in the Senate helps explain the greater influence traditionally exercised by House members who could seek reelection. Indeed, the Senate was so woefully prepared to legislate that House members would often cross over to the Senate to run committee meetings for procedure-deprived senators.

The rotation system ended when the courts required roughly equal population among Senate districts.[1] With multiple seats now allocated to Fulton County, the first African American to serve in the General Assembly in decades won election to the Senate. Leroy Johnson has the distinction of being the first African American southern legislator in modern times.

Following the Supreme Court decision that both legislative chambers must be based on population, Georgia redrew its House districts in the mid-1960s. With more seats allocated to urban areas, African Americans also won places in the House, where they joined growing numbers of Republicans. During the earlier period when representatives ran countywide, the few Republicans came from mountain counties since GOP strength in more urban areas got outvoted.

Since their initial entry into the General Assembly, the trajectory for black representation has been upward. As shown in Figures 5.1A and 5.1B, by the end of the 1960s, African Americans held 7 percent of the House seats. Within a decade the figure had reached 12 percent. In the early 1990s, in the face of demands from the U.S. Department of Justice to maximize the numbers of majority-black legislative seats, the ranks of African Americans serving in the House hit 17 percent. In 2009, the House had 43 African Americans (24 percent of the membership), including two Republicans.

In the Senate, black membership reached 10 (20 percent of the membership) in 1995 and has hovered around that number ever since. In 2009, the Senate had a dozen black members. African Americans make up just under a quarter of the membership of the General Assembly.

Until very recently, the presence of all African American legislators in the Democratic Party proved advantageous for the representation of black interests. In 2002, the last session in which Democrats dominated both chambers of the General Assembly, blacks chaired six Senate and six House committees including the powerful Rules Committees in each chamber. An African American served as Senate majority leader, while another chaired the Democratic House Caucus. But when Republicans took control of the General Assembly, black Democrats—like their white Democratic colleagues—lost

---

[1]Former President Jimmy Carter describes this special election necessitated by the end of the rotation system in his part of Georgia. The need to choose a senator in a newly configured district provided Carter with his first opportunity to run for elective office. As his account details, the election was initially stolen from him, although he did manage to have the initial vote thrown out and another election held, which he won. Thus, this proved to be the first step on a route that took him to the presidency. See Carter, *Turning Point*.

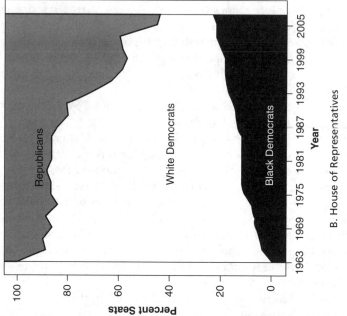

A. Senate

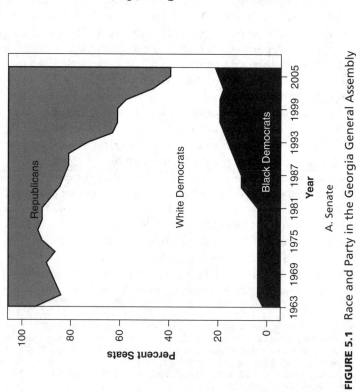

B. House of Representatives

FIGURE 5.1 Race and Party in the Georgia General Assembly

their committee chairs, with the exception of a black senator who chaired a minor committee in 2009.

The number of women in the General Assembly has also increased dramatically. The first women entered the legislature in 1923 with the election of Viola Ross Napier of Bibb County and Bessie Kempton of Fulton County. In 2009, women constituted just over one-fifth of the House membership. The Senate, however, had only seven women, down from the high point of 13 in 2003. The decline is in part attributable to women who gave up Senate seats to seek higher office and also to a shift of voter preferences toward Republicans.

Thus far, variation in the number of women legislators has been due to the share coming from the Democratic Party. The Republican Party has never elected more than two female senators, while the number of Democratic women senators has ranged from one to 11 over the last 20 years. In the House, the number of Republican women has fluctuated between 10 and 12 since 1993. During that period, the number of Democratic women in the House has gone from a low of 17 to a high of 30. Today's number of 37 female representatives is two short of the high-water mark for female presence in the lower chamber. In 2009, women chaired one Senate and four House committees.

The number of Republican legislators jumped in 1964, the first year in which a Republican candidate won Georgia's presidential electors. A number of the voters who supported Barry Goldwater for president voted for Republican legislators, whose numbers grew from two to 23 in the House and from three to nine in the Senate. After this initial burst, Republicans' ranks stalled, and even declined, as shown in Figures 5.1A and 5.1B. After having 29 Republican House members in 1973, the Watergate scandal that drove Richard Nixon from the White House reduced their ranks so that Republican numbers achieved in 1973 were not exceeded for more than a decade.

The election of the first Republican governor since Reconstruction provided the leverage for Republicans to win control of the Senate. Sonny Perdue's election as governor in 2002 coincided with 26 Republicans winning Senate seats. Within days, Perdue convinced four Democratic senators to change parties, giving the GOP a 30-to-26 advantage in the upper chamber. Each convert got a committee chair, with Jack Hill, Perdue's former roommate, becoming chair of the powerful Appropriations Committee.

The 2004 elections, which took place in districts redrawn under the watchful eye of a federal court in order to eliminate a Democratic gerrymander, netted Republicans 20 additional House seats. As had occurred in the Senate two years earlier, four Democrats switched parties to give Republicans a 99-to-80 advantage in the House. The Republican majority in the Senate increased from 30 to 34 seats with the new maps.

In addition to the changes chronicled above, the 2003 session welcomed the first Latino legislators in recent memory. Currently the House has three Latino members. Unlike in many jurisdictions where Latinos win heavily Hispanic districts, Georgia's Latino members come from districts that have few Hispanics, indicating that the legislators won with a diverse coalition that included Anglo voters.

Substantial increases in the numbers of African American, female, and Republican legislators have changed the stereotype of the Georgia legislator. In the 2005 session, only 21 white, rural, male Democrats remained in the House and just a pair were left in the Senate.

The trends that changed the personnel in the General Assembly also brought a more serious approach to the responsibilities of lawmaking. Legislators increasingly demand justifications for the votes they are asked to cast, rather than just helping their friends in the lobbying corps. The partying, drinking, and high jinks that used to be part of a legislative session have largely disappeared. Open bars paid for by lobbyists are less common, although receptions sponsored by organizations with concerns before the legislature are held almost every night of the session just down from the Capitol at the old Freight Depot.

CAMPAIGN FINANCE

Georgia law limits the individual contributions to a legislator to $2,000 each for the primary and general election, and if the campaign should involve a runoff, an additional $1,000 can be given. Since the vast majority of incumbents get reelected, political action committees (PACs) give disproportionately to incumbents and beggar challengers. Incumbents generally get others to pay for their campaigns, while challengers often must dig into their own pockets or take out a second mortgage to finance their runs.[2]

PACs give disproportionately to legislative leaders because they are better positioned to help the organization achieve its objectives. Even leaders who have weak or no opposition get showered with money. For example, over a seven-year period beginning in 1996, Democrat Terry Coleman, who chaired the House Appropriations Committee before becoming Speaker, raised more than $300,000 and never had a serious challenge. In his first year as president pro tempore of the Senate, Republican Eric Johnson raised $145,000, even though he had not been challenged since 1998.[3] In 2008, Speaker Glenn Richardson, who faced a potential challenge to his leadership, distributed $37,000 to 18 Republican candidates while giving $175,000 to the Republican Party.[4]

Table 5.1 shows how money has followed the change in partisan control of the legislature. Democratic fund raising increased every election year until the year after the party lost control of the Senate. GOP fundraising increased

---

[2]Robert E. Hogan, "Self-Financing of State Legislative Campaigns," *American Review of Politics* 20 (Fall 2000): 329–47.

[3]James Salzar, "Lawmakers Spread Campaign Wealth Around," *Atlanta Journal Constitution* (March 22, 2004): A1, A7.

[4]James Salzer, "GOP Leads in Georgia Fund-Raising Race," *Atlanta Journal Constitution* (November 3, 2008), B6.

TABLE 5.1	Partisan Fund Raising in Legislative Races, 1996–2004	
Year	Democrats	Republicans
1996	$5.77 million	$5.37 million
1998	$9.00 million	$7.42 million
2000	$9.59 million	$7.28 million
2002	$14.20 million	$10.00 million
2004	$12.12 million	$17.28 million

Source: James Salzer, "Georgia GOP Finds There's Money in Winning," *Atlanta Journal Constitution* (May 9, 2005), A1, A7.

by more than a third in 2002 when the party won the Senate and after they won the House, it had more than doubled in four years. Some of this largess came in *after* Republican victories to help pay off debts.

Incumbents with sizable war chests have several options. They may increase their campaign bank account, expecting that this alone will discourage potential challengers who will recognize that not only will they have to overcome the advantages of incumbency, but, should they mount a serious campaign, they also face the vast resources of the incumbent.[5] A second alternative is "regifting," which allows generously funded incumbents to share their wealth with their less-endowed fellow partisans. In 2003, the Senate Republican leadership gave as much as $30,000 to seven Republicans thought to have marginal districts.[6] In the House, Speaker Coleman distributed money to 70 Democratic candidates.

The third option allows incumbents to spend excess funds on "ordinary and necessary" expenses for gaining and retaining office. Among the kinds of expenses that have passed muster under this definition have been $330 for a tuxedo, fines paid the state Ethics Commission for a late campaign report, and $266 for a mattress given to an assistant, along with expenditures for tires, a vacuum cleaner, and a camcorder.[7]

The cost of running for the General Assembly has increased as candidates have begun hiring consultants, pollsters, direct-mail experts and advertising on radio and even occasionally on television. Campaigns costing more than $100,000 are common. In the most expensive contest, Senator Renee Untermann spent more than $650,000 to defeat Joyce Stephens in a 2002 runoff for which Stephens spent more than $360,000. In addition to these two heavy hitters, two other candidates competed in the primary, pushing the total cost well over $1 million.

---

[5]Robert E. Hogan, "Campaign War Chest and Challenger Emergence in State Legislative Elections," *Political Science Quarterly* 54 (December 2001): 815–30.

[6]James Salzer, "Law Makers Spread Campaign Wealth Around" *Atlanta Journal Constitution* (March 22, 2004), pp. A1, A7.

[7]Lucy Soto, "A Tuxedo, a Hog: Spending Rules Lax on Campaign Cash," *Atlanta Journal-Constitution* (February 21, 2000), B1, B4.

LEGISLATIVE ELECTIONS

Georgia legislators win reelection in overwhelming numbers. As one progresses through a decade, the likelihood of defeat decreases. Then, the redistricting that takes place after the census endangers some incumbents whose districts get reconfigured to adjust for population shifts. In many districts, only one party even offers candidates. In the past, Democrats often had no GOP challenger. Now that Republicans have become the majority, their nominees more often avoid a general election confrontation, as shown in Figure 5.2. With the demands on legislators increasing, it became progressively more difficult to recruit candidates, and the lack of competition has had obvious implications for legislator responsiveness to constituent preferences. One incumbent, when asked whether he might be defeated because of constituent unhappiness about a roll call vote, said, half in jest, "Let me go home and have a pay raise." Another legislator who recently left a leadership position in the House claims to have tripled his earnings.

Immediately after a new census and subsequent redistricting, some incumbents' districts get reconfigured to adjust for population shifts, and that

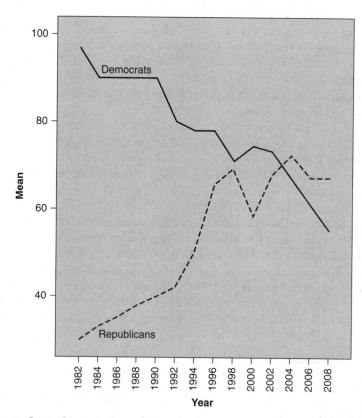

FIGURE 5.2   Party Contestation of Seats in the Georgia House of Representatives, 1982–2008

can inject uncertainty into the political system. In the worst-case scenario for incumbents, two or more get thrown together in a district. Georgia law requires a person to live in the district that he or she represents for at least a year before filing for election, so moving to another district is not an alternative. Democrats who controlled the 2001 redistricting process went out of their way to pair Republican incumbents as a means of reducing the talent pool in the opposition party and passed a final redistricting bill with less than a year until filing, forcing Republicans to run where they lived.[8] Half the Republicans in the General Assembly confronted the prospect of meeting another incumbent in the primary. Republicans have yet to control redistricting of the state legislature, but should they be in control in 2011, they might return the favor to Democrats.

PARTY LEADERSHIP

While the chairs of committees like Appropriations and Rules have great power within their chamber, the most important officers are those selected by the majority party to run the chamber. In the House, the leader of the majority party serves as Speaker. In 2005, for the first time in 130 years, the House chose a Republican Speaker, Glenn Richardson from the Atlanta suburbs. Richardson, a trial lawyer, had been the floor leader for Governor Sonny Perdue during the previous two years. As the Speaker, he is the person most likely to be seen on the dais, presiding over the legislative debate.

Prior to Richardson's election, the Speaker had total control over assigning members to committees. Unlike in Congress where each party assigns its members to committees, the minority party in Georgia has no input into the selection process. Richardson democratized the process somewhat by creating a committee on committees. However, he retained the authority to reject recommendations from the committee. The Speaker assigns legislation to committees, decides which bills to call up off the Rules Calendar for floor debate, and recognizes those wishing to speak.

The Speaker's chief lieutenant is the Speaker pro tempore. The current occupant of that post, Mark Burkhalter, a potential candidate for the speakership, was selected as part of a pact to avoid conflict within the new GOP majority. The third person in the GOP hierarchy, Majority Leader Jerry Keen, has close ties to religious conservatives, having once headed up the Georgia chapter of the Christian Coalition. The fourth position in the hierarchy, the whip, is assisted by a number of deputies who disseminate information to the rank-and-members of the party and alert the leadership to membership concerns. In 2009, Jan Jones became the first woman to occupy the post for Republicans.

The opposition party is led by the minority leader who would likely become Speaker should partisan fortunes reverse. The minority party also

---

[8]Ronald Keith Gaddie and Charles S. Bullock III, "From Ashcroft to Larios: Recent Redistricting Lessons from Georgia," *Fordham Urban Law Review*, 34 (April 2007): 997–1048.

has a whip and several assistant whips. Democrats in the 2009 General Assembly selected DuBose Porter as floor leader and Carolyn Hugley as minority whip.

The lieutenant governor presides over the Senate. From the creation of that office in the 1945 until 2003, the lieutenant governor, although not a member of the Senate, had more power than any senator. He assigned members of *both* parties to committees, named committee chairs, decided which committee would review legislation, and determined what legislation would be called up off of the Rules Calendar for floor debate. This all changed when Lieutenant Governor Mark Taylor, a Democrat, confronted a Republican majority. Republicans cut the lieutenant governor's budget and staff and set the agenda for the Senate. Republicans created a Committee on Assignments made up of the lieutenant governor, president pro tempore and majority leader to assign members and bills to committees. Following Casey Cagle's installation as the first Republican lieutenant governor in 2007, the Senate restored the authority traditionally exercised by the lieutenant governor.

The highest-ranking senator, the president pro tempore, leads the majority party. In promoting the party agenda, the president pro tempore is assisted by the majority leader, the majority whip, and the whip organization, which carry out much the same functions as their counterparts in the House. The minority party has a leader, a whip, and deputy whips.

Unlike other American legislative chambers, Georgia has not just a majority and minority leader, but also an administration floor leader. The governor names his own floor leaders, who typically have two lieutenants, and charges them with shepherding his agenda through to enactment. At times the responsibility for passing the governor's program puts his team members at odds with their party leaders in the chamber. Governor Roy Barnes (D) broke with tradition in 1999 and crossed party lines to include one of his former law partners, Charlie Tanksley, a Republican, to be part of his Senate leadership team. Tanksley's selection did not promote bipartisan support for Barnes' initiatives, and some Republicans fretted about Tanksley's loyalty when he attended GOP caucus meetings.

The selection of an administration floor leadership team goes back to the mid-1960s when the General Assembly began to assert its independence from the governor. Prior to 1967, the governor handpicked the Speaker of the House and named committee chairs in both chambers. This practice ended when the 1966 election failed to choose a governor and, as explained in Chapter 3, the legislature had to choose the governor. Before it could vote for governor, the House had to get organized. With no governor in place to name the Speaker, the body acted on its own and selected as its new Speaker a former occupant of that position, George L. Smith. A strong leader who knew how to use power, Smith retained his new authority and that of his chamber after it chose Lester Maddox as chief executive. Since then, the House has enjoyed substantial freedom from executive control, which makes the Speaker one of the most powerful figures in Georgia politics.

THE LEGISLATIVE PROCESS

With only a 40-day session, legislation must move quickly to secure enactment. To speed the process, legislators can prefile bills before a session begins. Legislation can begin in either chamber, with the exception that money bills must originate in the House. The Office of Legislative Counsel reviews bills to ensure that they not violate the state or federal constitution. With rare exception, all legislation gets assigned to a committee. Senators usually have four assignments, while representatives serve on at least two committees. The Senate had 26 committees while the House had 36 in 2009, and it is these subunits that hold hearings and modify legislative proposals. It is also in committee that many legislative proposals die. Unlike in Congress, where committee hearings may drag on for weeks, in Georgia it is rare for them to extend more than a day or two. Floor debate is also brief in Georgia, with multiple bills being considered every day.

Each chamber's Rules Committee controls the flow of legislation. Bills approved by substantive committees must be put on the Rules Calendar to become eligible for debate on the floor. Supporters of legislation appear at the daily meetings of the Rules Committees to urge inclusion of their proposal on the calendar. In 2005, the House Rules Committee adopted some of the procedures that made it more like its counterpart in the U.S. House when it set time for debate and issued closed rules for some legislation to preclude consideration of amendments on the floor. Prior to the adoption of the closed-rule option, the only way to bar amendments was by engrossing a bill. Engrossing a bill happens when the chamber, rather than the subset of members who serve on the Rules Committee, makes decisions to prohibit all amendments, similar to a closed rule in the U.S. House. Engrossing legislation is still the method for barring amendments in the Senate.

A chamber's presiding officer calls up bills from the Rules Calendar. Should a bill not be called up for debate, its sponsor must appear before the Rules Committee again, because a bill is on the Rules Calendar for only a single day. The control of the flow of legislation, first by the Rules Committee and then by presiding officers of the chambers is absolute, so that a frustrated legislator has no appeal should a piece of legislation be blocked at either of these stages.

Figure 5.3 shows the legislative process in Georgia. Passage of a statute requires support from a constitutional majority, which is one more than half of the membership. A failure to achieve 91 positive votes in the House or 29 votes in the Senate defeats a bill. Approval of constitutional amendments, which are placed on the next general election ballot, requires the support of two-thirds of the membership in each chamber.

As in Congress, when the two chambers pass different versions of a bill, it goes to a conference committee to iron out the differences. The Speaker of the House and the lieutenant governor each appoint three conferees, all of whom invariably come from the majority party. The report explaining the compromises agreed on by the conferees must be supported by at least two of the three conferees from each chamber. Once a conference report has been prepared, it must be passed by both chambers, or the legislation dies.

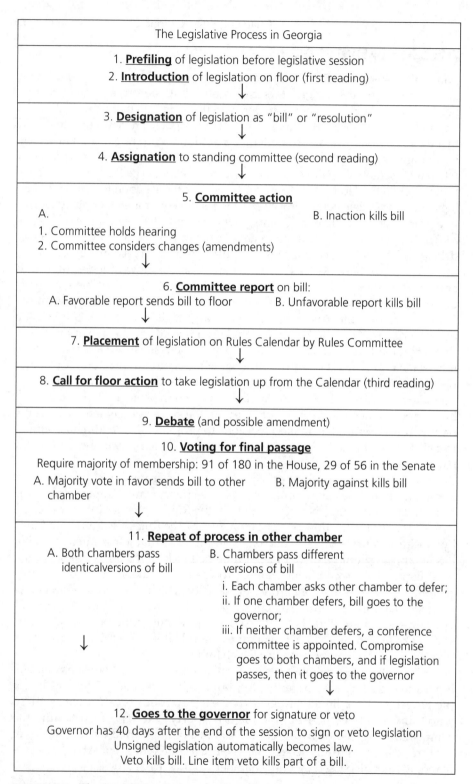

The Legislative Process in Georgia

1. **Prefiling** of legislation before legislative session
2. **Introduction** of legislation on floor (first reading)
↓

3. **Designation** of legislation as "bill" or "resolution"
↓

4. **Assignation** to standing committee (second reading)
↓

5. **Committee action**

A.   B. Inaction kills bill
1. Committee holds hearing
2. Committee considers changes (amendments)
↓

6. **Committee report** on bill:
A. Favorable report sends bill to floor   B. Unfavorable report kills bill
↓

7. **Placement** of legislation on Rules Calendar by Rules Committee
↓

8. **Call for floor action** to take legislation up from the Calendar (third reading)
↓

9. **Debate** (and possible amendment)

10. **Voting for final passage**
Require majority of membership: 91 of 180 in the House, 29 of 56 in the Senate
A. Majority vote in favor sends bill to other   B. Majority against kills bill
   chamber
↓

11. **Repeat of process in other chamber**

A. Both chambers pass   B. Chambers pass different
   identicalversions of bill   versions of bill
                                      i. Each chamber asks other chamber to defer;
                                     ii. If one chamber defers, bill goes to the
                                         governor;
                                    iii. If neither chamber defers, a conference
↓   committee is appointed. Compromise
                                         goes to both chambers, and if legislation
                                         passes, then it goes to the governor
                                                                        ↓

12. **Goes to the governor** for signature or veto
Governor has 40 days after the end of the session to sign or veto legislation
Unsigned legislation automatically becomes law.
Veto kills bill. Line item veto kills part of a bill.

FIGURE 5.3 The Legislative Process in Georgia

The governor has 40 days from the end of the session during which to sign or veto legislation. New laws typically take effect either immediately upon being signed by the governor or on July 1, the beginning of the next fiscal year. Georgia's governor, like most chief executives, can exercise a line-item veto to exclude specific items from appropriations bills while signing the rest of it into law.[9] In 2005, Governor Perdue used the line-item veto to remove several projects that legislators had added to help schools in their districts.

Tension between the legislative and executive branches is to be expected, but it reached unprecedented levels in the few years since the GOP takeover. Just before the close of the 2007 session, Governor Perdue vetoed a property tax rebate bill favored by Speaker Richardson. The House responded by rejecting the governor's proposal to remove the state income tax from some wealthy retirees. The House voted to override the governor's veto, but that effort failed when the Senate declined to follow suit. An angry Speaker Richardson accused the governor of being childish and showing his "backside" to the House, a comment for which he later apologized.[10] Relations remained testy in 2008 as the House began the session by voting to override a series of vetoes that Perdue had used to block legislation passed in 2007. Georgia found itself in a financially challenging situation in 2009 and needed to trim almost 10 percent from the budget, and relations between Governor Perdue and the legislature involved far fewer spats.

INNOVATION AND CHANGE

During the era when the Senate seats rotated among counties, the post of state senator was largely honorific, since senators could not run for reelection.[11] Once reelection became an option for senators, they wanted more influence over legislation. The House could thwart senators' involvement by not sending legislation to the upper chamber until the closing days of the session. To allow time to review the handiwork of the House and to make changes, the Senate stipulated that it would consider only legislation passed by the House by no later than the thirty-third of the 40 legislative days. This thirty-third day became known as "crossover day," and on it, and the day before, the Senate confronted a logjam of legislation passed by the House. In time the House also adopted the thirty-third day as crossover day for Senate bills. In 2005, Republicans moved the crossover day forward to the thirtieth day.

---

[9]The line-item veto is an executive power to nullify or cancel portions of legislation, typically in budget bills. Governors in 43 states, including all southern states except for North Carolina, have this power. The Confederate Constitution included the line-item veto in the powers of the president. A 1996 effort to give the president a line-item veto by statute was ruled unconstitutional by the U.S. Supreme Court.

[10]James Salzer, "Budget Brawl of '07 Ends," *Atlanta Journal-Constitution* (May 9, 2007), A1, A8.

[11]The exceptions were Fulton County, which had a non-rotating senator from 1931 until 1963, and the experience of eventual governor Carl Sanders, who went from his home county of Richmond into Columbia County and convinced voters there to send him back to the Senate.

Unlike in Congress and in some state legislatures such as South Carolina or Florida, where senators have longer terms than representatives, members of both Georgia chambers run every two years. The Senate has greater prestige because each senator has more influence than a representative since a senator represents more than three times as many constituents as does a representative. Following the 2000 census, the average population in a Senate district stood at 146,187 compared with 45,480 in the average House district.

Speaker Richardson instituted a unique innovation in 2005 when he named three Republicans as "hawks" who could swoop down into any committee or subcommittee meeting and vote. Holding these "wild cards" strengthened the hand of the Speaker, because this raised the ante in terms of what would be needed for Democrats and a rump group of Republicans to succeed at the committee level. Democrats criticized the hawks as undemocratic and blamed them for undermining the committee structure. Republicans believed that this reform promoted party government. The potential impact of the hawks proved to be greater than their actual usage. Usually hawks intervened to create a quorum so that a committee or subcommittee could conduct business. Less often, a hawk's vote altered the decision the committee would have taken.

The hawk system helped the new Republican leadership exercise a degree of influence that his longtime predecessor had achieved through sheer force of personality. Tom Murphy, who served 28 years as Speaker prior to losing reelection in 2002, could secure his policy objectives by simply appearing at the back of a committee hearing room and glowering at the membership. While there were a few instances towards the end of his career when Speaker Murphy experienced policy disappointments, more frequently his preferences prevailed.

In the U.S. Congress, membership on virtually all committees approximates the partisan ratio of the chamber. In contrast, Georgia's General Assembly rewards the majority party with a disproportionate share of the seats, especially on the most important committees. For example, in the Senate, only three Democrats serve on the 17-member Rules Committee and the Appropriations has seven Democrats among its 32 members. Had the Democrats received a share of seats proportional to their percentage in the chamber, they would have held seven Rules and 12 Appropriations seats. Minority party members are disproportionately relegated to committees that have little influence and often sit on committees that meet infrequently. In the Senate a member of the minority party usually chairs at least one committee. In 2005, the Interstate Cooperation Committee had an exclusively Democratic membership. The five Democrats on the committee, however, were given few responsibilities. All House committees have Republican chairs. The disadvantages Democrats face today mirror the conditions imposed on Republicans when Democrats ruled the legislature.

CLEAVAGES

As in most states, Republicans are generally more conservative than Democrats. The Democratic Caucus has at times experienced division along racial lines. The Legislative Black Caucus tends to have the legislature's most liberal members. Historically rural, white Democrats were quite conservative and would have been Republicans in many other states. In Georgia, the allure of being part of the majority party with the potential of chairing a committee and the opportunity to obtain funding for pork barrel projects back in their districts kept conservatives in the Democratic fold. Thus, the Democratic Party frequently had not only the most liberal but also some of the most conservative members.

At times, Republicans exploited the racial division within the Democratic Party as they did on redistricting in the early 1980s and 1990s. Conservative Republicans and moderate and liberal black Democrats both wanted to win more seats.[12] With white Democrats holding the vast majority of seats, any expansion by the Legislative Black Caucus or Republicans would come at the expense of white Democrats. In 1991, Republicans shared their mapping resources with the Black Caucus. White Democrats proposed creating a second majority-black congressional district, but Republicans developed a map with three black districts. Ultimately the U.S. Department of Justice forced the state to adopt a plan very much like that devised by the GOP and supported by the coalition. The new map rewarded both partners as two more African Americans went to Congress along with seven additional Republicans. After 1995, Georgia's congressional delegation had no white Democrats.

A second example illustrates how Republicans used an ideological division within the Democratic Party to their advantage. In 2004, all Republican senators and all but one of their representatives voted for a constitutional amendment banning gay marriage. On the Democratic side, all ethnic minority Democratic senators but only three white Democratic senators opposed the proposal. A similar but less stark division separated the Democrats in the House on this issue, with rural white Democrats voting with Republicans.

With the emergence of a viable Republican Party, some conservative Democrats switched to the GOP, while others either lost to Republicans or, upon their retirement, a Republican took their place. As a consequence, the median position of the Democratic Party has shifted leftward and is now much more liberal than the median position for the Republicans in the General Assembly.

It would be a mistake, however, to think that the Republican delegations in the House and Senate are homogenous. While virtually all Republican legislators are economic conservatives, not all suburban members are social conservatives. Thus within the Republican ranks, there are disagreements over the conditions under which an abortion should be available. The conservative stand permits an abortion only to save the life of a mother, while a more moderate position also permits abortions to terminate pregnancies resulting from rape or incest.

---

[12]Robert A. Holmes, "Reapportionment Strategies in the 1990s: The Case of Georgia," in Bernard Grofman, ed., *Race and Redistricting in the 1990s* (New York: Agathon, 1998): 193–6; Charles S. Bullock III, *The Georgia Political Almanac: The General Assembly, 1995–1996* (Atlanta: Cornerstone, 1995), 25.

STAFF SUPPORT AND RESOURCES

The General Assembly has relatively little staff support. Members can use part of their personal allowance to hire an aide, but otherwise none is provided to rank-and-file members. The only staff provided to all legislators is access to a secretary/receptionist.

Even committees are sparsely staffed, with most operating with the assistance of a secretary, usually shared by two committees, and an intern who, again, may be responsible to two committees. The legislature hires approximately 30 interns selected by the state's colleges and universities. The most important committees also have a full-time aide assigned to them. Some aides are recent college graduates and may have previously served an internship in the body. Only the most important committee, the Appropriations Committee in each chamber, has a more extensive staff component. As a consequence of the scarce staffing, interns have far more responsibility and access to insider information than they get if they go to Washington and work in a congressional office. The downside is that the legislators depend much more on lobbyists and representatives of the executive branch for information. The General Assembly has no entity comparable to the Library of Congress to research questions, although each chamber has a research office, many of whose staffers have advanced degrees.

The most significant staff support for the General Assembly comes from the Legislative Budget Office (LBO), created in 1969. This body is analogous to the Congressional Budget Office but predates the congressional entity by half a decade. Today the LBO helps House members conduct the annual hearings where representatives of the executive branch justify their budget requests and then digest the information from the hearings. With the onset of divided government in 2003, the Senate created its own budget office. Senate Republicans saw the LBO as a tool of the Democratically controlled House.

Each chamber also operates an information office that helps legislators with their press relations. These offices provide weekly summaries of the activities of the individual chamber that legislators often take with them when they return home over the weekend to meet with constituents.

Most legislators have offices in the Coverdell Legislative Office Building (CLOB), located across the street from the Capitol. This structure also contains hearing rooms for many of the committees. While the CLOB houses most legislative functions, a few coveted offices remain in the Capitol itself. The Speaker's office is just a few steps away from the House floor. Senior committee chairs also enjoy the convenience of being able to move from office to chamber floor without having to cross a street.

NORMS GOVERNING BEHAVIOR

Every organization has unwritten rules that regulate behavior. Those who want to get ahead in the organization pick up on the cues and react accordingly, and those thought to be a bit strange often are too obtuse to discern the

TABLE 5.2 Common Legislative Norms	
General Benefit Norms:	*Expertise*
	Specialization
	Hard work
	Respect and Reciprocity
	Trust
	Institutional Loyalty
Limited Benefit Norms:	*Seniority*
	Freshman Apprenticeship

"dos and don'ts." Legislatures have two types of norms (see Table 5.2). The first, general-benefit norms, benefit all legislators. Limited-benefit norms provide advantages for a subgroup of legislators, most often either senior members or members of the dominant "club" that enforces the norms of the institution. Norms persist as long as members find them helpful.

Many General Assembly norms exist to some degree in Congress. For example, members are encouraged to specialize and become experts in some facet of legislative activity.[13] The reward for this is that experts get to play a predominant role when legislation in their area of expertise comes up for debate. Other legislators turn to the experts for guidance as to how the proposals might affect their districts and what would be the appropriate vote.

The reciprocity norm often goes hand-in-hand with specialization and encourages legislators to help one another. For example, a legislator who votes for a pet proposal of a colleague expects the colleague to reciprocate. While this mutual logrolling is usually very informal, one long-time senator maintained lists of the colleagues for whom he had done favors so that when he needed help from one of them, he could remind the target of what he had done for him or her in the past.

Institutional loyalty is another norm much in evidence in the General Assembly. Members of each chamber feel that theirs is far superior to the other. These feelings are so strong that interns quickly become co-opted and become convinced that they work in the "better chamber." Loyalty also applies to relations with the media and outside political actors. At one time, lawmakers avoided public criticism of their chamber, but this norm suffered damage with the rise of partisan competition.

Seniority is practiced to a degree in the General Assembly. During Tom Murphy's speakership, a legislator needed roughly 10 years of service to become eligible to chair a committee. Once on a committee, the seniority norm usually allows a legislator to retain that assignment. However, unlike in

---

[13]Donald Matthews does an excellent job of describing old legislative "folkways" of the U.S. Senate in his 1960 book, *U.S. Senators and Their World*; Samuel Patterson explained the presence of norms similar to congressional norms in state legislatures back in the 1950s.

Congress, where the most senior member of the majority party frequently chairs a committee, the leadership in each chamber can name any legislator as chair. Some first-termers get tapped to chair minor Senate committees. The Senate seemingly gives some credit for House service: new senators who have previously served in the lower chamber tend to get better assignments and are more likely than those without legislative experience to be tapped to chair or serve as vice chair on a committee early in their careers. Nor does seniority guarantee a legislator's continuation as chair. Occasionally, legislators who have voted against their chamber's leader have been removed from leadership positions in mid-session, as happened in 2008 to legislators who voted against Speaker Richardson's preference for a seat on the Department of Transportation board.

The apprenticeship norm has largely disappeared from Congress but continues to operate in the General Assembly. Freshman often get poor committee assignments, and their desks on the floor tend to be further from the dais. They are also discouraged from making speeches, especially in the House. There, freshmen can get their points across with a parliamentary inquiry asking, "Mr. Speaker, isn't it true that . . ." and then stating an opinion. When freshmen first present a bill on the floor, they can expect to be hazed. As they try to explain their legislation to the membership, they will be peppered with difficult questions, often from the procedural experts in the body. When it comes time to vote on the proposal, all of the legislators will vote against it and then at the last moment change their votes, allowing the bill to pass.

In debate, members are expected to the courteous, to respect others' viewpoints, avoid personal attacks and not lose their tempers. In the conduct of legislative business, members should be cooperative. Members are expected to keep commitments, to engender trust, and to not break confidences.

The local legislation norm facilitates enactment of bills that affect a single county or city. The general rule is that if all the legislators representing the jurisdiction affected by the bill favor it, the legislature will pass the proposal. Larger delegations can adopt a less demanding rule than unanimity.[14]

Demands for extraordinary support from legislators from the affected area can be a stumbling block. For decades, failure to achieve sufficient support within the Fulton County delegation thwarted efforts of residents of Sandy Springs to incorporate their community. (This saga will be explored in the chapter on local government.) The community finally incorporated in December 2005 amid controversy over the effort to overturn the preferences of the majority-Democratic Fulton County delegation. When they became the majority, Republicans made the incorporation of Sandy Springs a piece of state rather than local legislation, thereby nullifying the veto of the Fulton delegation.

---

[14]Clayton T. Moore, "The Local Legislation Process in Georgia Comes Under Fire" (honors thesis, University of Georgia, 2002).

BOX 5.1
First Time Out—A Freshman Introduces a Piece of Legislation

By mid-March 1999, when she got up to speak on behalf of her first pieces of legislation, the old boys of the legislature welcomed her to the club in a fashion that is typical of the General Assembly:

Speaker Tom Murphy likes to call the Georgia House "one of the world's greatest fraternities." If so, that might make freshman Stephanie Stuckey (D-Decatur) a little sister. And when new legislators make an initial visit to the podium—or "well" in Capitol parlance—they're often barraged with inane, obscure, and irrelevant questions. It's sort of like hazing frat pledges. This week, Stuckey, a lawyer, expected the worst as she explained three bills she sponsored. The first two bills passed without a ripple. On the third, the vote tally board lit up with red lights symbolizing "no" votes next to nearly all the reps' names. She shrank a bit, until the lights turned green and it was clear the class was up to tomfoolery . . . [A member] asked for reconsideration, meaning the bill would be held for a day. A few minutes later he undid his motion. Just joking.

So, from inside Stephanie's head, what was it like going into the well for the first time? "It is intimidating. You can really get picked apart." Most freshmen go to the well with a noncontroversial bill that has high prospects for success, such as a piece of local legislation. "The bill will probably be noncontroversial, if only because the Rules Committee won't let a freshman go to the well with a hard bill . . . Details? Well, that's the problem. You could go to the well and go into every detail of the legislation, and the leadership is standing there saying, 'Hurry up and pass it,' or you could just go down and say, 'Pass this, it is a good bill.' . . . There is a strategy to going to the well; you don't want to talk it to death, but I always want to explain everything. I passed a complex, 48-page statutory revision of the child custody law with two sentences . . . Most members trust the leadership and the committees to get a bill right before the bill comes to the floor."

Source: Ronald Keith Gaddie, *Born to Run: The Origins of the Political Career* (Boulder: Rowman and Littlefield Press, 2004), 106–7.

CONCLUSION

The last two generations have witnessed dramatic changes in Georgia's General Assembly. The changes begin with the membership, which prior to 1960 was white, male, Democratic, and rural. Today both chambers have

Republican majorities, are more than one-fifth African American and consist primarily of members from the sprawling Atlanta metropolitan area. Women remain underrepresented but now constitute almost 20 percent of the legislature.

The legislature has become less a tool of the governor, and the two chambers now exercise equal authority. Since Republicans consolidated control of the legislative and executive branches, conflict between the House and the governor has reached unprecedented intensity, with the governor freely wielding his veto pen and the House voting to override those vetoes. The Senate has generally sided with the governor.

The majority party dominates legislative activities more completely than in Congress. Today, Republicans, like the Democrats who ruled Georgia for generations, make all committee assignments, fill all the slots on conference committees, and control the flow of legislation.

CHAPTER 6

The Executive Branch

A diagram of Georgia state government would show the governor at the top of the organizational pyramid. The governor is the most powerful and most visible office in the executive branch. It is also the only position in state government that is term limited, indicating an unwillingness to allow an individual to hold the position indefinitely. As we shall see in this chapter, while the position of governor is more powerful than any others, it has its limitations.

THE GOVERNOR

Two individuals won the office four times: Joseph Brown accomplished the feat during the nineteenth century, and Eugene Talmadge won the governorship in 1932, 1934, 1940 and a four-year term in 1946, after losing in 1942. These governors were also the only ones whose sons served as the state's chief executives.

Until 1942, governors could serve a maximum of two consecutive two-year terms. From then until 1976, the constitution limited a governor to a single four-year term. Since 1976, the governor is permitted to serve two consecutive four-year terms. All but one of the governors able to serve eight years have done so. Allowing governors a second term strengthens their hand, especially vis-à-vis a number of appointed boards, since in the course of eight years, the governor can appoint all of the members of the board, even when terms are staggered.

With the governorship being the highest position in the state, it is not surprising that the incumbents have worked their way up. Table 6.1 shows that most governors since 1930 previously served in the General Assembly. Richard Russell and E. D. Rivers advanced to the governorship after being Speaker of the House, while Carl Sanders did a term as Senate president pro tempore. While no other governor led a legislative chamber, some served in powerful support positions. Joe Frank Harris chaired the House Appropriations Committee, while George Busbee was Governor Sanders' assistant floor leader.

TABLE 6.1   Governors of Georgia 1931–2005

Governor (Party)	Term	Political Experience	Home County
Richard Russell (D)	1931–33	State House, 1921–31	Barrow
Eugene Talmadge (D)	1933–37	Agriculture Commissioner, 1927–33	Telfair
Euith D. Rivers (D)	1937–41	State House, 1925–27, 1933–37; State Senate, 1927–29	Lanier
Eugene Talmadge (D)	1941–43	Agriculture Commissioner and Governor	Telfair
Ellis Arnall (D)	1943–47	State House, 1933–35; Attorney General, 1938–43	Coweta
Herman Talmadge (D)	1947*	None	Telfair
Melvin Thompson (D)	1947–48**	County School Superintendant 1927–33	Jenkins
Herman Talmadge (D)	1948–55	Governor, 1947	Telfair
Marvin Griffin (D)	1955–59	State House, 1935–36; Lieutenant Governor, 1948–55	Decatur
Ernest Vandiver (D)	1959–63	Lieutenant Governor, 1955–59	Franklin
Carl Sanders (D)	1963–67	State House, 1955–57; State Senate, 1957–63	Richmond
Lester Maddox (D)	1967–71	None	Fulton
Jimmy Carter (D)	1971–75	State Senate, 1963–67	Sumter
George Busbee (D)	1975–83	State House, 1957–75	Dougherty
Joe Frank Harris (D)	1983–91	State House, 1965–83	Bartow
Zell Miller (D)	1991–99	State Senate, 1961–65; Lieutenant Governor, 1975–91	Towns
Roy Barnes (D)	1999–2003	State Senate, 1975–91; State House, 1993–99	Cobb
Sonny Perdue (R)	2003–	State Senate, 1991–2001	Houston

*Chosen by the General Assembly when his father died after being elected but before taking office. Removed by decision of the state supreme court after serving for 67 days.

**Elected as lieutenant governor in 1946 and served as acting governor after Herman Talmadge's removal pursuant to a court order until a special election could be held.

Roy Barnes had been a respected member of both chambers and was often referred to as the "smartest man in the legislature." Ellis Arnall held the number two position in the House, Speaker pro tempore. Three governors advanced from the understudy position of lieutenant governor; one governor, Lester Maddox, became lieutenant governor after serving as governor. Only Maddox and Herman Talmadge became governors without previous office-holding experience, although Talmadge had managed his father's last campaign, while Maddox had run unsuccessfully for mayor of Atlanta.

Prior to Carl Sanders, Georgia governors came from rural areas.[1] Sanders came from Augusta, and his successor, Lester Maddox, is the only governor in modern times to come from the city of Atlanta. Roy Barnes, the last Democrat elected governor, comes from one of the state's most populous counties (Cobb), which contains suburbs of Atlanta, while Joe Frank Harris's home has become one of Atlanta's outer suburbs.

Until the 1980s, south Georgia often provided governors. The Talmadges, Rivers, Griffin, Carter, and Busbee all came from the southern half of the state. More recently, with south Georgia providing only about a fifth of the electorate, governors from that part of the state have become less frequent, although Sonny Perdue's home in Houston County is just below the Fall Line that bisects the state. As noted above, Harris and Barnes come from Atlanta's suburbs and, while Zell Miller is a proud son of Georgia's mountains, for many years before his governorship, he lived in Atlanta's suburbs.

The future of Georgia politics likely lies in the Atlanta suburbs, if only because most of the population and a proportionate share of the General Assembly come from the suburbs, which increases the likelihood that these communities will spawn gubernatorial candidates.

GOVERNOR'S RESPONSIBILITIES

The governor has a wide range of responsibilities in dealing with the legislature and other components of the executive branch. During the state's long period of one-party government, the governor was titular head of the Democratic Party, which provided another tool that could be used to dominate Georgia's politics.

While the legislature need not defer to the governor to set its agenda, it does. The governor's State of the State Address early in the session provides most of the proposals that the legislature focuses on during the session. Prior to 1966, governors named the Speaker of the House and chairs of important committees. Even after the legislature shook off the governor's dominance, it often enacted virtually all of the legislation he proposed. In each chamber, a three-person team of gubernatorial floor leaders shepherds the governor's program through the legislative process. As explained in the previous chapter, part-time legislators often defer to the full-time executive.

During his first term, Eugene Talmadge was one of the few governors to have problems getting the legislature to enact the proposals. Conservative legislators thought that Talmadge, like fellow Populist Huey Long of Louisiana, was too radical. After a frustrating initial session, Talmadge took

---

[1]It is worth noting that Sanders was also the southpaw backup quarterback on Wally Butts' great University of Georgia football teams of the 1940s. UGA running back and Maxwell Award winner Charley Trippi said of Sanders, "Carl, you were a lot smarter than we were. We were on the football field beating our brains out, and you were on the sideline politicking with everybody." See Daniel Brush, David Horne, Marc C. B. Maxwell, and Keith Gaddie, *University of Georgia Football* (New York: Savas-Beatie, 2008), 166–7.

matters into his own hands and delivered on one of his key campaign pledges, which had been to reduce the price of vehicle tags to $3. But even these attempts at legislative independence failed when Talmadge simply removed all of the state tax on car tags that exceeded $3, a proposal that the legislature had rejected.[2]

A second example of a balky legislature involved changing the state flag, which had been adopted in 1956. Most of this banner displayed the Saint Andrew's cross, which had dominated the Confederate battle flag. As African Americans became an important component of the Democratic Party, they sought to change the flag, which they saw as celebrating slavery. Even though Governor Miller failed in his effort at a new flag, his effort endangered his reelection.

Eight years later, Governor Barnes, dealing with a more progressive legislature, engaged in extensive arm-twisting and secured just enough support for a new banner that drastically reduced the size of the Saint Andrew's cross. Adoption of this new flag necessitated threatening committee chairs with loss of their positions, threatening Democrats who did not chair committees with an unfavorable district in the upcoming redistricting, and inducing some Republican support by offering their districts funding under a new education program.[3] Outraged conservative voters, who tacked up signs showing the 1956 flag along with the simple message, "Boot Barnes," got their revenge and contributed to Barnes' defeat in 2002.[4]

The governor can call special sessions of the legislature. Although done infrequently, the governor has tremendous control since he alone sets the agenda for a special session. He cannot guarantee that the legislature will adopt his proposals, but it forces the General Assembly to take a look at what he wants and prevents them from spending time on other issues that they might prefer to address. In recent years, special sessions have been called to redraw legislative districts and to deal with budgetary crises. In 2004, Governor Perdue called the legislature back into session after it failed to enact a balanced budget.

Governor Perdue became the first Georgia chief executive to experience divided government when Democrats retained control of the House following his election in 2002. Democrats showed that they could thwart the aspirations of a governor of the opposite party, just as both parties in Congress have frustrated presidents in previous decades. Perdue succeeded in getting his programs through the Senate only to see them die in the lower chamber. The Republican Senate approved the governor's efforts at ethics reform, tort reform, and limiting access to abortion. None of these bills even came to a vote in the House, where Democrats refused to report them out of committee.

---

[2]William Anderson, *Wild Man from Sugar Creek* (Baton Rouge: Louisiana State University Press, 1975).

[3]Charles S. Bullock III, and M. V. Hood III, "When Southern Symbolism Meets the Pork Barrel," *Social Science Quarterly* 86 (March 2005): 69–86.

[4]In referendum, voters adopted a variant of the pre-1956 state flag, which lacks the cross of St. Andrew but does bear a striking resemblance to the Confederate national flag.

BOX 6.1

Sonny's Improbable Win

In the first election of the twenty-first century, it looked like Democrats would extend their 130-year control of the governor's office. While Roy Barnes had alienated traditionalists by forcing through a new state flag that minimized the size of the Confederate symbol, antagonized teachers with his education reforms, and lost rural support by dividing counties with his redistricting plan, he remained the overwhelming favorite. The smart money poured into his campaign, while challenger Sonny Perdue struggled to pay for television ads. Ultimately Barnes raised $20 million to less than $4 million for Perdue.

But even before Barnes overwhelmed Perdue in the advertising wars, the challenger had a plan. Four years earlier at the same time that Barnes won the governorship with 52 percent of the vote, U.S. Senator Paul Coverdell (R) had won a second term, also with 52 percent of the vote. Perdue assumed that he could probably retain support in the counties that had voted against Barnes. To oust the incumbent, Perdue set his sights on the 70 counties that had split their votes in 1998, giving majorities to both Barnes and Coverdell. If Perdue could win the bulk of these counties, he believed he could score the upset.

The Perdue strategy succeeded. By concentrating on these counties, his underfunded effort managed to win all but five. Although no preelection poll ever showed Perdue with a majority, or even leading his Democratic opponent, he scored a 104,000-vote victory.

Should the General Assembly pass legislation of which the governor disapproves, the chief executive can prevent the law from taking effect. Georgia's governor, like that of the other 49 states, can veto legislation. The Georgia executive's veto is especially powerful; a governor can veto legislation at any point up to 40 days after the legislature adjourns. In 1865, Georgia's chief executive became the first governor authorized to exercise a line-item veto, which allows the governor to remove specific lines in the budget.[5] From 1929 until the governorship of Jimmy Carter, no governor exercised a line-item veto.[6] That the authority fell into disuse simply underscores the control that Georgia's governors had over the legislature. When the legislature rarely ignored the governor's wishes, the chief executive had no need of a line-item veto. With most of Carter's predecessors naming committee chairs in both chambers, legislators recognized that should they buck the governor, they would lose not only their authority within the chamber, but also access to funding for pork barrel projects back in their districts. Even after the governor

---

[5]This paragraph draws on Thomas P. Lauth, "The Line-Item Veto in Georgia State Government, Revisited," ms.

[6]Thomas P. Lauth and Catherine C. Reese. 1993. "The Line-Item Veto in Georgia: Fiscal Restraint or Inter-Branch Politics?" *Public Budgeting and Finance* 26 (Summer 2006): 1–19.

lost his authority to name committee chairs, he continued using the carrot to bring along legislators. The governor's emergency fund became but another source of local funding. Legislators favored by the governor hoped to receive extra monies that might go for such "emergencies" as installing new lights at a ball field or buying new high school band uniforms.

Governor Perdue has used the line-item veto more than his predecessors. In 2005, he eliminated $233,000 from the $16.4-billion budget. Two years later, the governor vetoed the supplemental appropriations bill because it included $142 million in property tax relief. After the House voted to override, Perdue used the veto pen to remove projects in the districts of several House leaders.

Because of the short length of Georgia's legislative sessions and with the governor having 40 days after adjournment to decide on legislation, gubernatorial vetoes rarely get overridden because by then the legislature has usually adjourned. Should the governor veto a bill following the second session, no opportunity exists to override because the legislature will not meet again. Thus, while a governor may not have total ability to secure what he wants, he can almost always block proposals he opposes. In 2008, for the first time in 34 years, the legislature overrode a veto, but 39 other local projects Perdue had vetoed in 2007 remained unfunded when the Senate refused to join the House, which had voted to override the vetoes. The one veto that got overridden resurrected the plan to create a separate Senate Budget Office leaving what had been the Legislative Budget Office to work exclusively for the House.

The governor has relatively limited appointment powers because six departments have their own elected heads. The governor can, however, appoint the state school board, which is responsible for setting policy for public schools from pre-kindergarten through the twelfth grade, and the board of regents, which sets policy for the state's system of higher education. Members of these boards serve staggered terms so that when a governor could serve only four years, it would be impossible to gain control of the board in the absence of member deaths or resignations. However, now that the governor can serve a maximum of eight consecutive years, a governor will have named the bulk of the board's membership well before the end of a second term. The governor also names a number of department heads for entities such as the Department of Human Resources and the Department of Natural Resources.

Georgia governors have been the titular heads of their parties. The executive director of the party as well as its chair is invariably someone whom the governor approves and typically recommends for the position. The people tapped by the governor to lead the party have frequently worked on the governor's election campaign. Combining leadership of the state government and the party enhances the governor's leverage on fellow partisans.

Georgia's governor lost the power to pardon convicts or to commute sentences to the three-person Pardons and Parole Board in the 1940s, so he does not deal with last-minute appeals from death-row prisoners. This shift of authority to a board appointed by the governor came after the governors

TABLE 6.2 Major Categories of Expenditures in Georgia's Fiscal 2009 Budget as Initially Approved

Category	Share of the Budget
Public Education	38.70%
Community Health	11.90%
Board of Regents (Higher Education)	10.90%
Human Resources	7.90%
Corrections	5.50%
Debt Service	4.80%
Transportation	4.00%
Other	16.40%

Source: Thomas P. Lauth, "Budget Deficits in the States: Georgia," presented at the annual meeting of the Western Social Science Association, Albuquerque, NM, April 17, 2009.

in the 1930s commuted large numbers of sentences during the closing days of their terms. Although never proven, there was widespread suspicion that some of the forgiveness demonstrated by the chief executive came at a price: after his first two terms, Talmadge gave 660 pardons, and four years later his successor, E. D. Rivers, freed some 1,600 prisoners.[7]

Governor's Budgetary Powers

Georgia's governor has great influence over the budget since his revenue estimate sets the budget's maximum size. In consultation with the state economist in the Office of Planning and Budget, the chief executive estimates the expected revenues for the upcoming fiscal year. The state economist offers several estimates based on alternative scenarios for the economic health of Georgia during the next fiscal year. Most Georgia governors have chosen a conservative figure since Georgia's constitution prohibits running a deficit or, unlike in some states like California, borrowing for operating funds. The legislature is constrained to pass a budget no larger than the governor's revenue estimate. The legislature can shift the money around among programs but cannot set overall spending levels above the governor's estimate.

The lion's share of the budget goes to support education. As shown in Table 6.2, public education (grades K–12) receives almost two-fifths of the budget, with just over 10 percent more designated for higher education. In fiscal 2009, health care constituted another major component, as it takes about one in every eight dollars spent by the state. Georgia has a large prison population, and just over 5 percent of the budget goes to the Department of Corrections. Almost a nickel of every dollar spent goes for the debt service to pay the interest on bonds that have been sold to finance a variety of projects.

---

[7]Harold Paulk Henderson, *The Politics of Change in Georgia* (Athens: University of Georgia Press, 1992), 39.

TABLE 6.3   Major Sources of Revenue for Fiscal 2009

Source	Share of the Revenue
Personal Income Taxes	51%
Sales Taxes	35%
Motor Fuel	6%
Corporate Income Taxes	3%
Motor Vehicle	2%
Tobacco	1%
Alcohol Beverages	1%
Property	1%

Source: Thomas P. Lauth, "Budget Deficits in the States: Georgia," presented at the annual meeting of the Western Social Science Association, Albuquerque, NM, April 17, 2009.

Just over half of the state revenue comes from the slightly progressive personal income tax that reaches a maximum of 6 percent. A third of the revenue comes from the statewide 4 percent sales tax. Since 1989, medical prescriptions and groceries have been exempted from the sales tax, although the budget crisis prompted calls to eliminate these exemptions. In fiscal 2009, as reported in Table 6.3, a variety of other sources contribute small slivers to the state treasury. Although not adopted, proposals have surfaced in the legislature to eliminate the state property tax and to replace the annual ad valorem tax that owners must pay when renewing their car tags (the so-called birthday tax since owners must renew tags by their birthdays) with a one-time registration fee.

The legislature enacts the state's budget in March or April, months before the fiscal year begins on July 1. The governor's estimates for revenue collections and likely expenditures are projected from 3 to 15 months into the future. Because governors historically relied on conservative revenue estimates, by the time that a new legislative session begins—halfway through the fiscal year—the state typically has a surplus. When the legislature convened in January 2000, Georgia boasted a surplus of almost $1 billion. Relatively early in each session, the legislature enacts what is known as the supplemental budget which distributes much of the surplus accumulated during the first six months of the fiscal year. This money goes primarily for construction projects (often referred to as pork), which distribute state money to many legislators' districts. The legislature opts to devote the money to capital projects that are built and turned over to the authorities who will operate them so that the state has no lingering obligation. If the surplus went to hire new teachers, state highway patrol officers, or prison guards that would create a continuing obligation to pay their salaries and benefits. The distribution of funding in the supplemental budget heavily favors members of the majority party with members of the minority restricted to a few crumbs. Paraphrasing Orwell's *Animal Farm*, some legislators are more equal than others with the most equal legislators being those who hold leadership positions in the majority party.

BOX 6.2

Governor Perdue and the Budget Crisis*

During the last quarter of the twentieth century, each year Georgia took in more money in taxes than in the previous year. After two lean years at the beginning of Governor Sonny Perdue's term, the state's economy recovered, but in 2008, Georgia, like most of the rest of the nation and the world, went into recession. The state had experienced rapid population growth for more than a decade and extensive residential construction, especially in the Atlanta suburbs, made the state a prime candidate for the sub-prime loans that began to unravel the economy.

Governor Perdue had budgeted $21.2 billion for fiscal 2009. But from early in the fiscal year that began on July 1, 2008, the state's revenues failed to meet expectations. In August, most state agencies including the Board of Regents, which oversees Georgia's public colleges and universities, received an order to cut their planned spending by six percent. The budget for the Department of Education, which funds the basic needs of public schools, fared better than most agencies and had to reduce its budget by only two percent.

Revenue collections continued to lag and in January, the governor cut the budget from the $21.2 billion that the legislation had approved to $19.2 billion. In March, the fiscal 2009 budget was reduced again, this time down to $18.9 billion.

With numbers of students increasing even as it lost about a tenth of its state funding, the Board of Regents approved a temporary fee for students that ranged from $50 at junior colleges to $100 at universities. These additional fees continued into the 2009–10 school year.

With the recession deepening, the state budget approved for fiscal 2010 totaled only $18.6 billion. The governor and legislature, which avoided any tax increases as some other states had adopted, managed to balance this budget by incorporating $1.4 billion in stimulus funds from the federal government.

---

*Much of this draws on Thomas P. Lauth, "Budget Deficits in the States: Georgia," presented at the Annual Meeting of the Western Social Science Association, Albuquerque, NM, April 17, 2009.

For example, the 2005 budget had $3.5 million in projects much of which went to the districts of House leaders.[8]

GOVERNOR'S PERSONAL STAFF

To the delight of the Atlanta business community, Governor Perdue announced at the outset of his term that he planned to use a corporate model when organizing his office. He created the new positions of chief operating officer and chief financial officer.

---

[8]Brian Basinger, "Lawmakers Fight through Budget Battle," *Athens Banner Herald* (March 25, 2005), B1–2.

Governor Perdue has expanded the share of the Capitol Building devoted to housing the governor's staff, which includes individuals responsible for press relations, a speechwriter, a scheduler, legal advisors, and a number of policy experts. As explained earlier, the Office of Planning and Budget assists the governor in putting together budget proposals and in keeping track of revenues and expenditures. These all serve at the pleasure of the governor.

LIEUTENANT GOVERNOR

The lieutenant governor is the number two person in the executive branch. Georgia created this office in the 1945 constitution. The first individual to be elected to the post, Melvin E. Thompson, served only two months in that capacity before becoming acting governor after the state supreme court ruled he should succeed the late Eugene Talmadge. After Marvin Griffin held the office from 1948 until 1955, other early lieutenant governors each served a single term until Zell Miller won the office four times (1975 to 1991). Both of his successors—Democrats Pierre Howard and Mark Taylor—won second terms. In 2007, Casey Cagle became the first Republican incumbent in the office.

Unlike in states such as Florida, the governor and lieutenant governor do not run as a team. Instead, the lieutenant governor is elected separately. Griffin was very much Governor Herman Talmadge's understudy and successor, as both belonged to the Talmadge faction that dominated Georgia politics from 1933 until approximately 1960. In a few other instances, the governor and the lieutenant governor feuded. Carter's lieutenant governor, Lester Maddox, had preceded Carter as governor and hoped to succeed him. Especially during Carter's last two years, Maddox laid the groundwork for his next gubernatorial bid and provided little support for the increasingly unpopular Carter's initiatives.[9]

The period from 2003 to 2007 marked the first time that the individuals at the top of Georgia's executive branch represented different parties. Democrat Taylor, who had been lieutenant governor under Roy Barnes, won reelection in 2002, even as Barnes fell to Republican challenger Sonny Perdue. With a Republican in the Governor's Mansion, Taylor became the leading spokesperson for the Democratic Party and frequently criticized Perdue's policy initiatives. Taylor used this position to become the Democratic gubernatorial nominee in 2006 but lost the general election in a landslide.

Prior to Zell Miller's tenure, being lieutenant governor was seen as a part-time job, much like being a legislator. Since the mid-1970s, however, lieutenant governors have spent most of their time in the Capitol, although some, like Pierre Howard (1991–9), continued to practice law. Currently the lieutenant governor earns just over $80,000.

---

[9]Maddox lost a Democratic Party primary runoff to George Busbee, the candidate backed by House Speaker Tom Murphy.

The lieutenant governor's primary responsibility is to preside over the state Senate. As noted in the previous chapter, until 2003 when Republicans took control of the Senate, the lieutenant governor had a great deal of authority. But those lieutenant governors did not have to contend with an opposition-party majority. Republicans believed that in his first term, Taylor had been more of a partisan than his predecessor and unduly limited their influence. When they complained, Taylor responded, "Cry me a river." Once Republicans took control of the Senate, their theme might have been "Who's Crying Now?"[10] Republicans severely limited Taylor's powers by shifting his authority to make committee assignments and select chairs to a three-person Committee on Assignments, on which the lieutenant governor served but could be outvoted by the two Republicans. The Senate's highest ranking Republican, the president pro tempore, assigned legislation to committees and rulings by Taylor on points of order could be appealed to the president pro tempore. With a Republican as lieutenant governor, the Senate restored the powers Taylor lost to the office in 2007.

Many see the lieutenant governor's position as the premier stepping-stone to the governorship. The first three incumbents in the office each later served as governor, as did Zell Miller. While other lieutenant governors have not advanced, all but two ran for the top position.

OTHER CONSTITUTIONAL OFFICES

Georgians elect six department heads. While this is not the most—South Carolina elects seven and North Carolina elects eight—it is more than in many states. For example, Virginia elects only an attorney general, while in Tennessee no department heads are elected. By electing some department heads, Georgia differs from the national government, where department heads are part of the president's cabinet and are appointed by him and can be asked to resign by him. Since these Georgia department heads win office in their own right, they are not subject to demands made by the governor, as will be discussed shortly. Nor are the constitutional officers term limited, which enhances their power because they can continue in office while a governor must leave after two terms.

SECRETARY OF STATE

The secretary of state has many responsibilities, including running elections, handling the incorporation of businesses, overseeing 35 licensing boards of the state, and managing the regulation of securities exchanges within the state. The secretary of state also maintains the archives of the state of Georgia, is responsible for the maintenance of the grounds of the Capitol and the governor's mansion, and is the keeper of the Great Seal of the State of Georgia, which is

---

[10]The original "Who's Crying Now?" was recorded by Jo Dee Messina, though another song by the same title was recorded by the 1980s band Journey and was also covered by Randy Crawford.

used to authenticate state documents and is necessary to legitimize the actions of the state's chief executive.

Most of the incumbents have served multiple terms, with Ben Fortson holding the post from 1946 until 1979. Paralyzed and wheelchair bound, Fortson, an ally of outgoing Governor Arnall, hid the Great Seal of the State under the cushion of his wheelchair to secure it from being used by then-Governor Herman Talmadge during the Three Governors Controversy (described in Chapter 1). He later joked that sitting on the Great Seal for two months left a great impression on him.

In 1998, Cathy Cox became the first Democratic woman to win a constitutional office. Under her leadership, Georgia became the first state to adopt a system of touch-screen voting statewide. While computer wonks have criticized the system and claimed that it could easily be tampered with, Georgians who began using it in 2002 overwhelmingly approve of the ease and clarity that it provides. Karen Handel succeeded Cox in 2007 to become the first Republican to hold this office.

ATTORNEY GENERAL

The 1868 Georgia Constitution created the position of attorney general to represent the state in legal matters. Some attorneys general have clashed with other officials by speaking out on what they saw as improper behavior. Mike Bowers so frequently disagreed with Speaker Tom Murphy that when other state constitutional officers received pay raises, the legislature excluded the attorney general. Together with Governor Joe Frank Harris' chief deputy, Tom Perdue, Bowers had fired a ranking state patrol officer implicated in a ticket-fixing scandal. Murphy, a longtime supporter of the Georgia State Highway Patrol, turned his ire on Bowers. The attorney general's stature fell even further with the staunchly Democratic Murphy when Bowers switched parties and won reelection as a Republican in 1994.

Thurbert Baker became the first African American to hold the post when appointed by Governor Miller in 1997. Five years later, he won reelection even as Governor Roy Barnes lost. The Republican governor and Democratic attorney general had a major dust up. In his initial State of the State Address, Governor Perdue directed the attorney general to drop an appeal to the U.S. Supreme Court involving three state Senate districts. The district court had found Georgia noncompliant with the Voting Rights Act because it reduced the minority concentration in these districts, which might make it more difficult for an African American to win. Since blacks vote overwhelmingly for Democrats, having higher percentages of African Americans in some legislative districts results in whiter neighboring districts where Republicans have a better chance of winning. In the 2001 districting plan that was before the court, Democrats sought to distribute black voters so as to maximize the number of districts their party could win by reducing black concentration—the issue before the court. Should the attorney general succeed in the appeal, spreading blacks among a larger number of districts might endanger the GOP majority.

When Attorney General Baker ignored the governor's request, Perdue sought an injunction to stop Baker. The courts found in favor of the attorney general who, since he is elected and is not subject to removal by the governor, has his own popular mandate. The attorney general is charged with representing Georgia in court and that was what Baker was doing. By implication, other constitutional officers also can act independently of the governor.

The record length of tenure for an attorney general is held by Eugene Cook, who served for almost 20 years before resigning (1945–65). Cook's successors have now each served at least eight years. The phenomenon of attorneys general having tenures that cut across the terms of multiple governors makes it more difficult for the governor to control the state's chief lawyer.

INSURANCE COMMISSIONER

This position, which started out with auditor responsibilities, can trace its history back to 1782. In 1799, it changed from being called the auditor to being referred to as the comptroller general. Then in 1983, it was rechristened as the commissioner of insurance and was charged with regulating the insurance industry. The person in the position can set rates and determine what carriers will be licensed to operate in Georgia. Policyholders unable to resolve disagreements with their insurers can file complaints with the insurance commissioner, who periodically sends representatives across the state to meet with unhappy citizens. The insurance commissioner also serves as the state fire marshal. One recent commissioner got into trouble after having a siren and a flashing light mounted on his car and using them to speed through traffic.

When the GOP became truly competitive in Georgia in the mid-1990s, this was one of the first offices won by a Republican. In 2006, John Oxendine won reelection with two-thirds of the vote and became the first Republican to win four elections to a statewide office in Georgia.

Because of the responsibilities of regulating the insurance industry, that industry has been a major source of campaign contributions for insurance commissioners. Some question the wisdom of allowing the industry that is being regulated to play such an important role in selecting the individual responsible for its regulation.

STATE SCHOOL SUPERINTENDENT

Georgia established this office in the wake of the Civil War. For its first 40 years, the incumbent had the title of state school commissioner, but in 1910 it received its current title. Republican Linda Schrenko defeated the incumbent Democrat in 1994 and became the first woman to win a constitutional office in Georgia. After eight stormy years of frequent conflict with governors and members of the state school board, she lost a bid for governor in 2002.

The turmoil of the Schrenko years highlights the difficulties of the institutional arrangement surrounding this office. Schrenko sought to dominate education policy in the state. Georgia governors, however, like chief executives in many states, want to develop reputations for their support of education and three of the four most recent governors have instituted major education reforms. As Schrenko sought to put her mark on education policy, she came into conflict with the governor and was hamstrung by the state school board appointed by the governor. After frequent clashes early in Schrenko's tenure, Governor Zell Miller secured the resignation of most board members and replaced them with a group more willing to work with her. The role of peacemaker went to Johnny Isakson, the candidate defeated by Miller in 1990, who became chair of the board. Isakson, with years of experience working effectively in the overwhelmingly Democratic state House, managed to restore a degree of calm and cooperation between the board and the superintendent. Miller, who has a master's degree in history and taught the subject at Young Harris Junior College before entering politics, has always viewed himself as an educator. This may explain his desire to bring peace to the development of education policy.

Miller's successor, Roy Barnes, took an entirely different approach to dealing with Schrenko. Barnes pushed through a major education reform package developed by a commission he appointed that included little input from educators. Barnes's reforms called for smaller class sizes, a change that teachers favored, and proposed selective pay incentives including a permanent 10 percent salary increase for teachers who obtained National Board certification. However, he alienated teachers when he eliminated tenure, created massive new reporting responsibilities for faculty, and suggested that Georgia students fell at the bottom of the nation on average SAT scores and other examples of poor academic performance because of uncommitted instructors. Teachers, not surprisingly, did not appreciate being characterized as lazy and incompetent—or at least, that is how they interpreted the criticisms that accompanied the Barnes reforms.

Superintendent Schrenko, eager to become Georgia's next governor, sought to exploit the conflict and sided with the teachers, which put her in conflict with both the governor and the state board of education. As tensions mounted between the superintendent and the board, Schrenko devoted increasing amounts of her time to campaigning, only occasionally showed up in her Atlanta office, and avoided meeting with the board altogether. After her defeat by Sonny Perdue in the Republican gubernatorial primary, Schrenko was convicted of having misused federal funds. Some federal education money was allegedly funneled through a close Schrenko associate and made its way back into her underfunded campaign. A portion of the money allegedly went to pay for her face-lift.

Another Republican woman, Kathy Cox, succeeded the jail-bound Schrenko. Superintendent Cox had served in the state House after years as a high school history teacher. Contributing to her victory margin of a quarter-million votes was voter confusion, since she shared the same last name and, except for a different letter in the first name, the same first name as Georgia's popular secretary of state.

COMMISSIONER OF AGRICULTURE

Until well into the twentieth century, agriculture was Georgia's major industry. The commissioner of agriculture played an important role in providing information to farmers and in certifying the accuracy and quality of the fertilizer that they bought. Incumbents in this office often developed strong followings in rural communities across the state. The most successful in terms of career advancement, Eugene Talmadge, held this office for six years before winning the governorship in 1932. Several other agriculture commissioners were talked about as potential gubernatorial candidates, although none succeeded. The current incumbent, Tommy Irvin, holds a record for the longest tenure of any constitutional officer, having been appointed in 1969 and most recently reelected in 2006.

COMMISSIONER OF LABOR

This is the most recently created of the constitutional offices dating from 1911. The first incumbent, who served for a quarter century, carried the title of Commissioner of Commerce and Labor. All of his successors have had only the current title. The major function of the Georgia Department of Labor is occupational safety and the administration of labor laws, including child labor laws. Another major concern of the labor commissioner is addressing issues of unemployment in the state and seeing to the adequacy of training of the labor force, including vocational rehabilitation for reintegration of individuals into the workforce. Related to the occupational safety function of the commissioner, the Department of Labor also inspects boiler valves, pressure valves, and amusement park and carnival rides.

Michael Thurmond, a former state legislator and the father of a major welfare reform during the Miller administration, became the first African American labor commissioner in 1998. He and Attorney General Baker make Georgia the only state to have two African American constitutional officers. Thurmond had previously represented a majority-white legislative district in Athens.

PUBLIC SERVICE COMMISSION

Called the Railroad Commission from 1879 until 1922, the Public Service Commission (PSC) has had its mission dramatically expanded with the arrival of electricity and natural gas distribution. It regulates industries such as providers of telephones, electricity, and natural gas, whose rate increases must be approved by the PSC. The PSC also regulates the trucking industry and bus lines.

The PSC has five members elected statewide to staggered terms. In 1998, Democrats created five districts with one commissioner from each district, although they run statewide. Democrats hoped that the residency requirement would enable them to win most of the seats. This ploy collapsed in 2002 when Republicans defeated two Democratic incumbents. After 2007, Republicans held all the seats.

DEPARTMENT OF TRANSPORTATION

While the governor gets to name the members of many boards, the legislature has retained the authority to name members of the highly political Department of Transportation (DOT) Board, which sets priorities for road projects. In the past, when most of Georgia's budget went into roads, Governor Eugene Talmadge used highway contracts to reward his rural supporters eager for paved roads to get their goods to market and to make it easier to reach the county seats for their weekly shopping trips. One of Talmadge's largest battles came in his effort to gain control over the highway board. He summarily fired the head of the State Highway Department, which touched off a round of litigation in which the highway chair sued the governor in an unsuccessful attempt to regain his position. The Talmadge experience demonstrates that, at least in the past, a determined governor controlled highway funds. Today's governors still have some potential to influence highway policy, although it comes indirectly through influencing the selection of board members.

Caucuses representing each of the state's congressional districts elect one board member. A state legislator can vote on the selection of any highway board member who represents a part of the legislator's district. The frequent division of counties by both congressional and state legislative lines allows many legislators to participate in the selection of multiple highway board members since their districts may extend into more than one congressional district.

At times, the selection of a highway board member may be highly political. In 2005, the Republican Governor Perdue prevailed when his candidate defeated an incumbent Democrat who had previously served in the state legislature. Two years later, House Speaker Glenn Richardson lost a bitter fight to defeat two board members who had supported Perdue's choice for DOT commissioner over Richardson's candidate, a fellow legislator. The winner of the tug-of-war between the governor and Speaker, Gina Abraham, became the first woman to hold this office. She immediately set out to bring a degree of administrative order to this agency, which controls more than a tenth of the state budget. Shockingly, she found $360 million in contracts that had never been entered into the computer system.[11] Abraham's criticisms of her predecessor and challenges to the way things had been done created new enemies who became stronger upon the revelation of her affair with the chair of the DOT board. In early 2009, the board ousted her over the objections of Governor Perdue.

CAMPAIGN FINANCE

In 1998, Roy Barnes won the most expensive gubernatorial election in Georgia, up to that time, spending $11 million. Since he planned to seek a second term, he promoted legislation that would enable him to raise more campaign money and do it earlier. The laws regulating Barnes's 1998 campaign

---

[11]Ariel Hart, "Auditors Tell DOT Its Deficit Is Massive," *Atlanta Journal Constitution* (September 19, 2008), A1, A13.

limited individuals' contributions to statewide candidates to $1,000 in each of the first three years in office and then $5,000 during the election year. Under the new law, statewide candidates can raise twice as much as $8,000 from a single source during a four-year period; they also could get all of that money at any point during the four-year cycle rather than having it come in specified amounts in each year. An assessment made nine months before the 2002 election found that most of the contributors to Barnes's reelection in 1999 to 2001 gave more than the $1,000 maximum allowable under the old law.[12] Since incumbents often decide to seek reelection well before challengers choose to enter a contest, allowing candidates to raise the bulk of their money early in the four-year period benefits incumbents almost exclusively.

As with legislative contests, statewide incumbents in Georgia have generally won reelection and therefore receive far more funds than do the challengers. One of the most extraordinary imbalances saw Barnes raise more than $20 million for his reelection bid, an amount almost seven times that was raised by challenger Perdue. However, since Perdue upset the incumbent, raising the most money is no guarantee that the incumbent will always win.

CONCLUSION

Georgia has a historically strong executive. The governor has substantial powers to shape both the budget and legislation through the use of his line-item veto powers, as well as the array of informal powers available to (and used) by recent governors. Gubernatorial power is less than it once was, however. The General Assembly gained a great deal of independence in the 1960s when, for the first time, the House selected its Speaker and organized itself. The Senate has become more influential since service ceased to be term limited. Recent conflicts between Republican Governor Perdue and his fellow partisan Speaker of the House have been more visible than clashes in the past.

The governor's influence, while great, can be checked by the elected leaders of major state agencies. The opportunity to serve two consecutive terms has given governors greater influence over boards having staggered terms appointed by the governor.

Neither women nor African Americans have won Georgia's top elective positions. But a variety of secondary statewide offices have been held by African Americans or women, both Democrats and Republicans. The current electoral environment is leading to Republican domination of most down-ticket offices. The GOP will likely continue to dominate statewide elections barring scandal or a shift in white voter sentiment back toward Democrats.

---

[12]John McCosh, "Finance Law a Barnes Bonanza," *Atlanta Journal Constitution* (February 11, 2002), C1, C3.

CHAPTER 7

The Judicial System

A system of courts provides a way for society to resolve conflicts peacefully. Individuals who feel they have been wronged by fellow citizens need not exact retribution on their own; instead, they can sue their neighbor. If the wrongdoer has violated a law, then the government undertakes the prosecution. Moreover, the courts provide a check on the activities of the government. Laws or actions of public officials who are believed to exceed their authority can be challenged by any citizen in court. Courts also provide a venue in which to interpret the intentions of the legislature. Since legislative bodies usually write their statutes in broad language, many questions may arise. The legislature does not have the time, patience, and perhaps even the expertise to anticipate all of the situations that might arise. Therefore, the legislature indicates its general intentions in the text of the statute and leaves it up to the courts and the bureaucracy to fill in the details. Courts also frequently serve as the enforcers. Once the legislation has been passed, the General Assembly may largely wash its hands of the matter. Those who question the adequacy of enforcement can turn to the courts to nudge the bureaucrats responsible for implementing the legislation.

Courts hear both civil and criminal suits. Civil cases involve disagreements between private parties in which one person sues another for breach of contract or negligence. In criminal cases, the offense is against the public generally or the state, and the state, through a solicitor or district attorney, brings suit. Defendants charged with crimes get representation by an attorney of their choice if they can afford one, or a public defender if they cannot.

The U.S. court system is based on adversarial proceedings. Each party is expected to be represented and to put forward as strong a case as possible. It is believed that by having witnesses present testimony, which is then subject to cross-examination by the opposing counsel, the truth will emerge and justice will be done.

GEORGIA'S COURT SYSTEM

Georgia's early politicians regarded appellate courts with suspicion. Until 1801, Superior Court judges met in annual convention to make rules and occasionally to consider the constitutionality of recent legislative actions.

Currently, Georgia's judicial system consists of at least three levels of courts in every county. In some counties a fourth level exists, and there are specialized courts in some communities. Atop the pyramid is the state supreme court, authorized by the constitution of 1835 and created by the legislature a decade later. The court initially had three members, but since 1945 it has consisted of a chief justice and six associates. In 2008, the court had three African American members and two women. The chief justice is chosen by the other members of the court and is not a lifetime position but instead rotates. In 2005, Chief Justice Leah Sears became the first African American woman to hold that position. The supreme court has jurisdiction to hear appeals of all sorts. Since 1858, the state legislature has affirmed that state appellate court decisions have the force of law.

The state supreme court has exclusive appellate jurisdiction in the state court system over cases involving construction of treaties, the state and federal constitutions, and all cases where the constitutionality of a law, municipal ordinance, or other constitutional provision is in question, as well as all election disputes. The court has general appellate jurisdiction in a variety of other areas of civil and criminal law, cases certified to it by the court of appeals, and certain cases previously appealed to the state court of appeals that are of important public interest, an intentionally vague and flexible term.

Georgia's other appellate court is the court of appeals. Created by constitutional amendment in 1906, the court of appeals was designed to alleviate the heavy workload of the state supreme court. It has 12 members, and unlike the supreme court, where all of the justices participate in all cases, the court of appeals, like the Federal Circuit Courts of Appeals, reviews cases using panels made up of three judges. Currently the court of appeals has three African American members and three women. As in the federal system, a party disappointed in the decision of a three-judge panel can request an *en banc* review by the entire membership of the court of appeals. While a party can request the review, there is no guarantee that it will be granted. Until the enlargement of the court of appeals membership from 10 to 12, it had the heaviest workload of any appellate jurisdiction in the nation.

Not all cases are appealed to the court of appeals. The court of appeals reviews cases not explicitly reserved to the state supreme court or those cases where the superior courts have initial appellate jurisdiction. Some cases, such as capital felony appeals, go directly to the supreme court.

The superior court serves as each county's court of general jurisdiction. The state is divided into 49 superior court circuits that are organized into ten judicial districts. Each circuit consists of one or more whole counties. In urban areas, a single county will comprise a circuit. For example, Fulton County makes up the Atlanta circuit, while DeKalb County is the Stone Mountain circuit. In rural areas, a circuit consists of multiple counties. Every circuit has at least two judges and the largest, the Atlanta circuit, has 19 active judges, and these can be augmented by retired judges. The court must sit in each county in the circuit at least twice a year.

Approximately half of the counties have a state court that handles misdemeanors, while felonies are handled by the superior court. In counties with no state court, the superior court tries both felonies and misdemeanors. State court judges can also issue search warrants.

Each county has a probate court that deals with issues relating to wills and estates, appointment of guardians, and the involuntary hospitalization of individuals. Probate judges may hold habeas corpus hearings, preside over criminal preliminary hearings, and also hear some misdemeanor cases and other ordinance violations in the absence of a state court. In counties of more than 96,000 residents, a civil jury trial may be heard in probate court. In many smaller counties in Georgia, the probate judge also acts as the election administrator for the county, managing voter registration and supervising the conduct of elections. This latter function is subject to local statute. The probate court is presided over by the probate judge, who is elected to a four-year term. Unlike judges on other courts, probate judges need not be attorneys, except in counties with over 96,000 residents. There, probate judges must be at least 30 years old and have seven years of legal experience.

Twenty counties have a magistrate's court. These courts have limited jurisdiction, mainly confined to civil claims of less than $15,000 and procedural matters such as conducting preliminary hearings, issuing summonses, arrest warrants, search warrants, distress warrants, and dealing with county ordinance violations and check fraud claims. All trials in magistrate court are bench trials, that is, they have no jury. Magistrate courts have an elected chief magistrate, who can appoint other magistrates. Magistrates need not have a college degree or a law degree.

Each superior court circuit has a separate juvenile court that handles cases involving criminal activities by young people. Unlike actions in other courts, proceedings in juvenile court are less adversarial. The objective is to do what is best for the child in hopes that she or he can be rehabilitated and made a useful citizen. Juveniles convicted of crimes can be sentenced to separate juvenile facilities where they serve until they reach 18. The records of juvenile court are frequently sealed and may not be used in subsequent prosecution should the efforts to rehabilitate the juvenile fail and he or she be prosecuted as an adult. Most circuits have one or more appointed juvenile judges; however, in a few circuits, one or more of the superior court judges also functions as the judge of juvenile court. For particularly heinous offenses, juveniles as young as 13 can be tried as adults, and the case is handled in the superior courts. Municipalities have their own courts that deal with violations of city ordinances.

TRIAL COURT PROCEEDINGS

Trial courts allow witnesses to present testimony and juries to decide fact issues. A trial court is presided over by a single judge. If a jury trial is selected, the jury will consist of a dozen members. In complex cases that are expected to take several weeks, one or more alternate jurors may be selected in case a juror becomes ill or must be excused for some other reason.

When choosing a jury, until recently, the defense attorneys in criminal cases got more strikes than the prosecutor or district attorney. A strike is exercised when an attorney rejects a prospective juror. In 2005, the legislature leveled the playing field and gave prosecutors and defense attorneys the same number of strikes. Some see partisan politics influencing this change. Trial attorneys tend to be major supporters of the Democratic Party, and former House Speaker Murphy and Governor Roy Barnes are trial attorneys. With the changing of the guard, the new Republican rulers have little reason to please trial attorneys and can claim credit for promoting law and order by strengthening the hand of prosecutors.

Before a Georgian can be tried for a criminal offense, the defendant must be indicted by a grand jury. The district attorney presents evidence to the grand jury, which, if convinced that the evidence would be sufficient for a conviction, returns a true bill, also called an indictment. Grand jury proceedings take place in secret, and the defendant is not entitled to cross-exam prosecution witnesses, present witnesses on his or her behalf, or be represented by counsel. Those opportunities are reserved to the trial before the petit jury, also called a trial jury. Juries in criminal trials must agree unanimously to convict. A high standard of proof is set in criminal trials. To convict, the jury must be convinced of the defendant's guilt "beyond a reasonable doubt."

Civil suits where a plaintiff seeks damages require a lower standard of proof. To prevail in a civil trial, the plaintiff need only to prove a claim with a "preponderance of the evidence." The difference in the kinds of proof needed explains why a defendant who is acquitted on a criminal charge may lose on a related civil charge. In one high-profile example in California, O. J. Simpson won acquittal of charges that he murdered his wife and her friend. Later, the heirs of the two people that Simpson was accused of killing won damages in a civil suit for wrongful death.

Many cases are resolved before a trial. Both civil and criminal cases may be negotiated out. As any watcher of the television series *Law and Order* knows, prosecutors often allow a defendant to plead to a lesser charge in order to avoid the uncertainties and expense of a criminal trial. Increasingly, professional arbitrators resolve some civil disputes. This approach has the advantage of rendering a decision sooner and less expensively than awaiting a slot on the crowded court dockets. The arbiter need not be an attorney, although many are, and all are required to receive training. In a conflict dispute resolution, both sides present their side of the story and the arbiter renders a decision.

APPELLATE PROCEEDINGS

When decisions of trial courts are appealed, the process at the appellate level is very different. No witnesses are presented, no new testimony is given, and the parties frequently are not even in attendance. Appellate courts have multiple judges but no juries. With rare exceptions, the issues considered on appeal are questions of law and not of fact. Jury's findings of fact, if a jury trial has been conducted, are rarely reversed. The issues before an appellate court are those items to which an attorney has objected in the course of the trial. In an appeal, attorneys for each side present their contentions in the form of written briefs, which are reviewed by the appellate judges—or more likely their law clerks—before the hearing. At the hearing, the opposing attorneys are given limited time in which to argue the main points of their briefs. Attorneys may have little opportunity to present arguments before the judges interrupt to ask questions about assertions made in the brief. After the oral argument, judges consider the claims made in the briefs and oral arguments in light of statutes and prior court decisions.

AMICUS CURIAE

Sometimes, individuals who are not parties to the litigation—they are not the defendant or the plaintiff—participate in a case. The basis for participation is the third party's claim that it has an interest in the outcome of the case and is concerned that neither of the named parties will adequately present its position. These third parties participate in the form of an *amicus curiae* (friend of the court) brief. The appellate court determines whether to accept requests by a party to participate as an *amicus*. As an example of an *amicus* participation, none of the cases challenging racially segregated public schools came from Georgia, so the state did not participate in the hearing that led to the 1954 decision. The Supreme Court, recognizing the explosive nature of its order that racial segregation in public education could not be justified, scheduled a second hearing to explore how its ruling should be implemented. At this second round, the court invited Georgia and other states that operated segregated schools but had not been sued in the cases that culminated with *Brown* v. *Board of Education* to explain what issues then anticipated in desegregating their schools.

BASES FOR JUDICIAL DECISIONS

At both the trial and the appellate level, judges give great deference to previous court decisions. This reliance on precedent, which is also often referred to with the Latin term *stare decisis* ("let the decision stand"), promotes consistency among trial courts and over time. While courts are not prohibited from reversing precedent, they rarely do; however, consider that when the U.S. Supreme Court declared segregated schools to be unconstitutional, it overturned a 58-year-old precedent.

Contending parties in an appeal point to different lines of precedent when urging the judges to find for their client. Consequently, judges usually have some latitude in how to resolve a case. Studies of the factors that influence appellate judges' decisions have concluded that the judges' ideology and partisanship play important roles. For this reason, when chief executives get to name judges, they almost invariably select individuals from their own party. In 2005, for the first time, a Republican governor got to name a member to the supreme court.

Judges, of course, are also bound by the state and federal constitutions. While they can interpret these documents, they cannot render decisions that clearly conflict with either. Judges also interpret statutes, but these have less weight than the constitutions. Indeed, judges can find that statutes conflict with either the federal or state constitutions, and, exercising the power of judicial review, they can declare a statute to be unconstitutional. Should a state court judge declare a federal statute to be unconstitutional, this would likely trigger an appeal by the losing party to the U.S. Supreme Court for an interpretation.

Appellate courts have their decisions published. Decisions by the supreme court of Georgia appear in a set of volumes entitled the *Georgia Supreme Court Reports*, while the *Georgia Appeals Reports* contain decisions from the court of appeals. Opinions rendered by trial courts in Georgia are not published in bound volumes.

The majority opinion rendered by an appellate court carries the greatest weight as precedent. Sometimes, a justice or justices will agree with the decision rendered by the majority but follow a different line of reasoning to get to the same conclusion. If they write up their rationale, this is called a concurring opinion. Judges who disagree with the ultimate finding of the majority can file a dissenting opinion in which they lay out their reasons for coming to a conclusion opposite that reached by the majority.

JUDICIAL SELECTION

Since 1984, judges (other than probate judges) have been selected through nonpartisan elections. The Democratic-controlled legislature made this change after Republicans began to win some judgeships in metropolitan Atlanta. The move to change the positions from partisan to nonpartisan coincided with a decision to elect the judges at the time of the primary. Fewer voters turn out for primaries than general elections, and the primary electorate is disproportionately composed of committed partisans. When the Democratic Party could claim the loyalties of most Georgians, choosing judges at the time of the primary increased the likelihood that Democratic jurists would be selected. As with other offices in Georgia, a majority vote is needed for selection. This meant that when no candidate received a majority, the decisive election would coincide with the party runoffs, three weeks after the primary. In 2005, the Republicans in the General Assembly shifted judicial selection back to the general election but kept the judges nonpartisan. The net effect was to have a non-partisan judicial ballot, but to vote that ballot on high-turnout general election days that favored Republican turnout, instead of on low-turnout primary election days that might favor Democrats.

While the choice of judges is officially done through the ballot, in reality, approximately two-thirds of Georgia's judges initially come to the bench via an appointment. In some instances, a new position has been created to deal with a growing caseload. The 24-member Judicial Council evaluates the number of cases handled by each circuit and recommends to the legislature when a new judgeship is in order. Other judges are appointed when their predecessor resigns in mid-term. The governor makes the appointments and, unlike in the federal system where Senate approval is necessary, the legislature is not involved.

While the legislature does not participate in judicial selection, Governor Jimmy Carter did create an administrative unit to help with the process. The Judicial Nominating Commission (JNC), appointed by the governor, screens prospective appointees. The JNC membership is heavily skewed towards attorneys but includes a few lay members. During Governor Roy Barnes' term, JNC chair Buddy Darden made temporary appointments of local notables to the panel that would interview candidates for a judgeship in their area. To be considered for a judicial vacancy, attorneys can be nominated by someone else or submit their own names. After interviewing candidates, the JNC forwards three to five names to the governor who selects from that short list. Recent governors have used their appointments to increase racial and gender diversity on the bench.

Appointments to the appellate bench can trigger a series of advances. Appointing a superior court judge to an appellate court creates the opportunity to fill the superior court position. That vacancy may be filled by a state court judge, which creates yet another vacancy. So a single vacancy may give a governor three appointments.

Georgia judicial elections usually involve no opposition. Even superior court judges who attract opposition win almost 90 percent of the time.[1] In 2006, only seven of the 63 superior court judges seeking reelection faced opponents, and only one lost. In smaller circuits, attorneys hesitate to oppose a sitting judge since if the attorney loses, he or she will have to continue to practice before the incumbent who probably did not appreciate the challenge. In urban circuits, where an unsuccessful challenger would less often come before the incumbent judge, the lack of attention voters give to judicial contests often dissuades prospective opponents. Judges most often attract challengers in the first election after their appointment to the bench. In several instances, an applicant whom the governor passed over runs successfully against the individual selected to fill the vacancy. Appellate court judges are more likely than trial judges to attract opposition. Fear of alienating a judge before whom an attorney may subsequently appear is less a factor since appellate decisions involve multiple judges. Moreover, the prestige of being an appellate judge makes these positions much more attractive.

Most Georgia judges serve until death or retirement. For members of the appellate courts, retirement is mandatory at age 70. Judges on trial courts often retire but continue to work part-time hearing cases.

---

[1]Charles S. Bullock III and Karen Padgett Owen, "Alternative Paths to the Bench," Presented at the Georgia Political Science Association, Savannah, GA, November 13–15, 2008.

Over the last couple of decades the bench has become more diversified. In 2008, 36 women served as judges of superior courts and another 25 sat on the bench of state courts. Twenty African American judges presided over superior courts and another eleven, along with two Latinos and one Asian American sat on state court benches.

JUDICIAL CONTESTS BECOME MORE POLITICAL

Traditionally, judicial elections were low-key affairs because candidates cannot discuss the kinds of issues that dominate legislative contests. Judicial candidates could not talk about their preferences or how they would rule in cases that might come before them. Staking out positions on issues would create the grounds for asking that a judge be removed when a case involving the issue came before that judge. Traditionally, challengers could not criticize a sitting judge for previous decisions. The only assessment of judicial qualifications might come from a survey asking members of the bar to rate the candidates.

The nature of high-profile judicial contests in Georgia changed once the U.S. Supreme Court gave its okay to more traditional campaigning for judgeships. In 2004, candidates closely associated with Christian conservatives challenged a member of the supreme court and ran for a position on the court of appeals. Supreme Court Justice Leah Sears drew an opponent supported by Republican Party activists, who considered some of her decisions too liberal.[2] She had angered Governor Perdue when she sided with the state's attorney general, who ignored the governor's order to drop an appeal involving a Democratic gerrymander of the state Senate. As discussed earlier, a federal court had ordered the state to redraw several of the districts, which worked to the advantage of the GOP. Democratic Attorney General Thurbert Baker appealed the case to the U.S. Supreme Court where the trial court decision was overturned.

The court of appeals contest involved three serious candidates, with Mike Sheffield being the most conservative. He was also the least well funded and seemed to rely heavily upon support from religious conservatives.

A controversial element in these two elections was a scorecard developed by the Christian Coalition. This group supports religious conservative values and had prepared scorecards rating the policy stands of members of the General Assembly and Congress for a decade. A conservative attorney developed a questionnaire that the Christian Coalition sent to candidates for these two judicial spots. The questionnaire asked candidates whether they agreed with a series of decisions rendered by the U.S. Supreme Court. Only Sheffield and the challenger to Supreme Court Justice Sears responded. The Christian Coalition disseminated these candidates' responses and indicated the unwillingness of their opponents to participate. The decision to respond to the questionnaire and

---

[2]Paul Bennecke, who managed the challenge to Justice Leah Sears, stepped down from his position with the state Republican Party.

the fact that these responses agreed with the preferences of many Christian conservatives proved insufficient to elect either candidate. Sears' challenger attracted only 37.7 percent of the vote, while the conservative candidate running for court of appeals got about 20 percent of the vote.

Another distinctive element in the court of appeals election was the amount of money spent by one of the unsuccessful candidates. Prior to 2004, judicial campaigns attracted little attention except among members of the bar. Losing candidate Howard Mead, who had been on the staffs of governors Zell Miller and Roy Barnes, spent more than $3 million, most of which came from his personal funds.

In a rare defeat of a sitting judge in 2008, Karen Beyers challenged an incumbent superior court judge because of his courtroom demeanor. The challenger criticized the longtime incumbent for being arrogant and disrespectful.[3]

JUDICIAL MISCONDUCT

Georgia judges must face the electorate every four years. The potential for removing those who become senile or act in nonjudicious ways rests with the electorate. As already noted, however, reelection defeats are infrequent.

Georgia has a commission that handles complaints against judges. In 1995, Georgia's Supreme Court removed a Fulton County state court judge for "an intolerable degree of judicial incompetence, and a failure to comprehend and safeguard the very basics of our constitutional structure." According to the supreme court, the judge frivolously issued arrest warrants, failed to appear for court, appeared when she had indicated she would not, and, it was discovered after her removal from her chambers, had case files for other courts that she previously had denied possessing.

Another state court judge resigned after an Atlanta television reporter tracked him to a bar and watched him spend an afternoon drinking. When the reporter approached the judge and suggested that he was too drunk to drive and should call a cab, the judge got in his SUV and roared away. Since he frequently presided over drunk driving cases, the furor surrounding these reports prompted him to resign.

JUDICIAL OFFICERS

The district attorney represents the state or local government in felony trials. If a county has a state court that hears misdemeanor cases, the prosecutor is the solicitor. District attorneys and solicitors are elected on partisan ballots to four-year terms.

Recently, Georgia established a statewide system for providing criminal defense to the indigent. Previously, some counties had their own systems with attorneys specializing in defense work while in other counties, the responsibili-

---

[3]Patrick Fox, "Beyers Scores Upset over Winegarden for Judgeship," *Atlanta Journal Constitution* (November 6, 2008), D6.

ties went to new members of the bar seeking to establish a practice. In some other smaller counties, representation of indigent criminal defendants rotated among members of the local bar. The new system makes public defenders state employees paid with tax dollars. The bar association supported the legislation creating this program. One motivation for this innovation was concern that a judge might find that one or more jurisdictions did an inadequate job of meeting the provision of the U.S. Constitution that guarantees criminal defendants the right to counsel. Another factor may have been that this program provides jobs with good benefits to a large number of attorneys.

Criminal defendants generate little public sympathy and, as a result, the program has received grudging support. This became clear when a high-profile murder trial threatened to bankrupt the system. Millions of dollars went to defend Brian Nichols after he grabbed a deputy sheriff's gun and killed a judge and others in the course of escaping from the Fulton County courthouse. The 2008 budget crisis resulted in funding being cut by 40 percent, prompting some counties to resume the practice of hiring outside attorneys to handle cases—work for which one claimed she earned only $2 per hour.[4]

CONCLUSION

Georgia has two appellate courts, and each county has a superior court with general trial jurisdiction. Some counties have state courts that try misdemeanor cases. Judges compete in nonpartisan elections, although the bulk of them arrive on the bench after being appointed by the governor. Recent years have seen an increase in the diversity of the bench.

Key actors in the judicial system other than judges are the prosecutors who represent the state and public defenders who handle the cases of indigent defendants.

---

[4]Bill Rankin, "Public Defenders Denounce Flat Fees," *Atlanta Journal Constitution* (July 27, 2008), D1, D10.

CHAPTER 8

Local Government

In American politics, attention is most often focused on major office politics. National campaigns attract media coverage and generate voter enthusiasm, and these campaigns structure alternatives on political issues. But it is at the local level, in county, city, and school board politics, that most lives are affected day to day. This chapter describes the function and politics of local government in Georgia, with a primary focus on two types of creatures: counties and municipalities (towns and cities).

To understand the powers exercised by local governments, one must understand the relationship between local governments and the state. The relationship is set forth in Dillon's Rule, articulated by Justice John Dillon, which holds that local governments are creatures of the state and as such receive their authority from the state rather than directly from the people. This distinguishes local governments from states in the context of the U.S. Constitution, which does not address the concept of local government. Under Dillon's Rule, the authority of a local government is confined to powers explicitly granted to it by the state, or implied in the explicitly granted power, or powers essential to meeting their "declared objectives and responsibilities" as local governments. Local governments have no special standing as entities, as do the states or individuals; therefore, local governments can be created and dismantled by the state.

COUNTY GOVERNMENT

States create counties to act as administrative districts for the purpose of instituting state authority. According to the Carl Vinson Institute's Ed Jackson, the first mention of a county in Georgia is in 1735, in a map referencing Savannah County, and since then, numerous efforts by first colonial and then later state government resulted in the growth of the number of counties, from 24 in 1800 to 137 by 1875. The number of counties reached a constitutionally mandated maximum of 145 (defined by a 1904 constitutional amendment).

Pressure to create new counties led to an amending of the constitution specifically to create a new county—Ben Hill County—and thus began the practice of making counties by amending the constitution. Roughly one new county a year was created until the number reached 161 in 1924, when Peach County was formed from portions of Macon and Houston Counties. When Campbell and Milton counties teetered on the brink of bankruptcy during the Great Depression and were consolidated into Fulton County, the number of counties was reduced to the current 159. The 1945, 1976, and 1983 Georgia constitutions set a cap of 159 counties, which is a problem for legislators who would like to resurrect Milton County, in Fulton County north of the Chattahoochee River.

Of all the states in the Union, only Texas has more counties than Georgia. County creation was popular in Georgia for many reasons, but the primary one was that many of the state functions were centered in the county. The state legislature was apportioned on a county basis, so creating new counties created new legislative seats for ambitious politicians. The creation of the county also created a variety of other elective offices, most notably the sheriff, who was responsible for many executive functions in county government; county and superior courts, which would require judges; and the identity of one town or city in the county as county seat and the need to build a county courthouse with the resultant contracts and profits to flow from its construction.

Clarke County is among those that experienced subdividing. Watkinsville was the county's original seat. The University of Georgia ended up in Athens in part because Watkinsville had a tavern, and it would not do to have the state college in the same town as a tavern. As the home of the university, Athens grew, while Watkinsville stagnated as a small cotton-market town, and in 1871 Athenians convinced the legislature to move the county seat to their city. Watkinsville, disappointed over the loss of status and anticipating an economic boom from regaining a county seat, petitioned the legislature to create a new county out of western Clarke County, with Watkinsville as its seat. The legislature fulfilled their hopes in 1875 by creating Oconee County, while Clarke County shrank to become the state's smallest county in square miles.

COMMISSIONERS

County commissioners serve as the policy-making authority for the county, adopting ordinances and resolutions and crafting regulations pertaining to county government and county property. Originally an "inferior court" or court ordinary governed each county. As reported by Ed Jackson, these courts consisted of "five justices [and] had jurisdiction in judicial matters not entrusted to the superior court. The inferior court also had some administrative authority (e.g., providing for construction of county courthouse and other public buildings, levying taxes, and overseeing maintenance of county roads)." These courts functioned as a probate court or chancery court, dealing with wills, issues of custody and guardianship of minors, and issuing marriage licenses. These latter functions were transferred to a "court of ordinary" by the 1851 state constitution. A 1974 constitutional amendment renamed the "ordinary" as the "probate judge." Until 1984, Towns and Union counties still had government under the office of the probate judge.

BOX 8.1

Athens

The city of Athens was established in 1801 on land purchased for the construction of the University of Georgia. Situated on the Oconee River at the edge of Indian country, Athens grew with the university. In 1990, the city of Athens and Clarke County voted by referendum to create a consolidated city-county government. Unified Athens-Clarke County is Georgia's fifth-largest city and the Athens Metropolitan Statistical Area (MSA) also includes Madison, Oconee, and Oglethorpe counties and has approximately 175,000 residents.

The Unified Athens-Clarke government is a mayor-commission form of government, with a mayor elected at large and ten commissioners. A manager who reports to the mayor and commission oversees day-to-day operations. Eight of the commissioners represent single-member districts, while two others are elected from "superdistricts" that encompass districts 1–4 or 5–8, respectively. Voters districts 1–4 and 5–8 also vote to elect one additional member from the super districts, so each citizen is actually represented by two councilors. Most of the university campus is located in commission district 4; however, student housing is split among districts 3, 4, and 7.

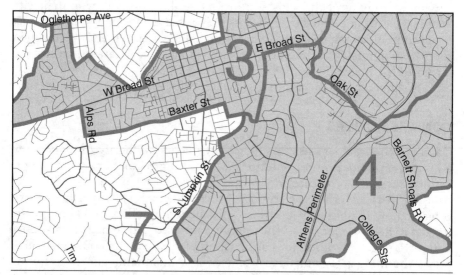

Source: Athens-Clarke County, www.athensclarkecounty.com/documents/maps/districts.gif (accessed September 7, 2009).

The 1868 state constitution empowered the courts ordinary "powers in relation to roads, bridges, ferries, public buildings, paupers, county offices, county funds and taxes, and other matters, as shall be conferred on them by law." But, it also authorized the legislature to create county commissions and "to define their duties." Harris County had the first commission in 1869, and within a decade, half of Georgia's counties used commission government. No constitutional requirement for the number of commissioners existed, and in 1879 the legislature authorized the first "sole commissioner" county government in Forsyth County. The sole commissioner format with the commissioner not only overseeing administrative activities but also promulgating local ordinances is unique to Georgia. Supporters of this arrangement tout its efficiency, while critics worry about placing so much power in the hands of one person. Usage of sole commissioners, once widespread (Cobb and DeKalb had this format until after the middle of the twentieth century), persists in fewer than a dozen counties.[1] Bleckley County survived a voting rights challenge that went to the U.S. Supreme Court to retain its sole commissioner government.

Currently, county commissions have from one to 10 members, with five being the most common number. Although traditionally most commissioners ran at large, as a result of challenges brought under Section 2 of the Voting Rights Act, counties now typically elect at least some commissioners from districts, although the chair may be elected countywide.

In smaller counties, the chair of the commission may function as the CEO of county government overseeing day-to-day activities. In more populous counties, a manager appointed by the commission heads up the executive branch, while the commission and its chair adopt the budget and establish the procedures under which the county government functions.

Constitutional Officers

Every county elects at least four officials. The clerk of the superior court maintains court records for the county and helps the judges with their paperwork.

The probate judge, as noted above, fills the historic role of the ordinary, dealing with property deeds, minor guardianships, wills, and marriage licenses. Probate judges also have the historic role of supervising elections. Counties now have an election supervisor and a board of elections, although in small counties the probate judge usually doubles as the election supervisor.

The sheriff is the primary law enforcement officer in most counties, charged with both keeping the peace and keeping the jail. Counties can create police departments to supplement the sheriff, but the sheriff cannot be replaced. Historically, sheriffs often dominated county politics, sometimes using the power of their badge to accumulate both power and economic

---

[1]Today, Bartow, Bleckley, Chattooga, Murray, Pickens, Pulaski, Towns, Union, and Walker counties use sole-commissioner governments.

gain.[2] The endorsement by the sheriff could sway voters and was particularly prized during the days of the county unity system.

The tax commissioner maintains the tax records of the county, receives tax returns, and collects and pays out tax receipts to state and local governments.

Many, but not all, counties also elect a coroner and a surveyor. Increasingly, urban counties have replaced the elected coroner with a medical examiner who is a physician.

CONSOLIDATED GOVERNMENT

Five Georgia counties have consolidated county-municipal government with the cities and towns in their borders. Consolidation requires authorizing local legislation and approval by a vote of the residents of the county. Georgia's first experience with city-county consolidation came in 1970, when Columbus and Muscogee County united. In 1990, Athens and Clarke County merged,[3] followed by Augusta and Richmond County (1995), Cusetta and Chattahoochee County (2003), and most recently Georgetown and Quitman County (2007).

Supporters promote consolidated government as a means to eliminate duplication of services and personnel and thus a way to save money. For example, the consolidated government has one police department. Consolidation may also extend city services to the suburbs or if residents outside the city had contracted for services, they receive these services at less cost because they now fund them through taxes. Opponents balk at the increased taxes levied on the new residents of the city to cover the costs of these additional services.

MUNICIPAL GOVERNMENT

Charters and Home Rule

Georgia cities get their fundamental law in charters granted by the legislature through local legislation. Charters describe a local government—the institutions, the officers, how elections will be conducted, and how decisions will be made. A charter indicates the scope of the municipality's powers and spells out its physical boundaries. In some states, city boundaries may not spill across county lines, though in Georgia, cities are able to—for example, the City of Atlanta is located in both Fulton and DeKalb counties. The tiny city of Royston spreads into three counties.

Georgia uses the "special charter act" approach, which requires the legislature to draft a separate charter for each municipality. This approach has the benefit of allowing custom tailoring of city charters; however, because the act is adopted by the legislature, it places the city at the mercy of the legislature for its scope of powers.

---

[2]The power of a south Georgia "high sheriff" is chronicled in Melissa Fay Greene, *Praying for Sheetrock* (New York: Addison-Wesley, 1991).

[3]Winterville, in Clarke County, chose to not participate in the consolidated government and continues as an independent municipality, with residents receiving county services from Clarke County.

BOX 8.2

Services That a Georgia Municipality May Provide

Air quality

Construction codes

Electric/gas utilities and street lighting

Libraries

Parks and recreation

Pension systems for municipal employees

Planning and zoning

Police and fire protection

Public health facilities

Public housing

Public transit

Stormwater drainage and sewage collection

Street construction and maintenance

Terminal/dock/parking facilities

Waste collection and disposal

Water purification and distribution

Since 1995, in order to be considered a municipality, a city or town must meet the following conditions:

perform at least three services from a prescribed list (see Box 8.2)

hold at least "six regular, officially recorded public meetings" per year

hold regular municipal elections

Failure to meet these three criteria can result in the revocation by either the state, or after 10 years of inactivity, by a vote of the electorate. Immediately after adoption of these requirements, a number of tiny towns lost their charters for not providing enough services.

Recently, several new cities in the Atlanta-area have gotten charters. The culmination of the prolonged effort to make Sandy Springs a city opened the way for the incorporation of all of north Fulton County, along with a new city in south Fulton. In 2008, the spate of incorporations spread into DeKalb County with the incorporation of Dunwoody.

Types of Municipal Government

As of 2007, Georgia has 535 incorporated municipalities. These cities and towns (the only two types of municipalities incorporated in Georgia) can take four forms: strong mayor-council, weak mayor-council, council-manager, and commission.

The mayor-council forms of government assign the executive function to the mayor and put policy-making authority in the hands of the elected council. Strong mayor-council governments place full responsibility for the functioning of the city in the hands of the mayor. Mayors hire and fire department heads including professional city managers and fulfill other functions such as implementing policy, crafting a budget, and fulfilling ceremonial roles. Depending on the charter, a strong mayor may have the authority to veto council ordinances and have other powers of appointment such as to local boards and commissions. The policy-making authority is invested with the council, including the ability to approve, change, or reject budgets, and when mayors veto, the council may have the authority to override the veto, much as a legislature can with a governor.

By contrast, in a weak mayor-council government, the mayor's authority is limited to carrying out largely ceremonial functions. Responsibility for hiring, firing, and making appointments and contracting decisions is either shared with the council or entirely delegated to the council.

The council-manager form invests primary executive function in the hands of a professional city manager who is hired by the city. This manager oversees the implementation of policy decisions made by the council. Council-manager government traces its origins to the late-nineteenth century "good-government" reforms designed to rid local governments of partisanship and ward politics. Instead of public policy being the product of favor granting and patronage, local government would adopt a corporate model with an elected board hiring a professional manager to oversee day-to-day operations, much like a chief executive officer. Council-manager governments usually have a ceremonial mayor, either elected citywide or chosen from among the council. The mayor may serve as an equal, voting member of the council. The council hires the professional city manager to run city government.

Commission government chooses a council at large from the entire municipality. The commission is headed by a chairman selected from the body, usually rotating on an annual basis. Each commissioner then takes on responsibility for overseeing a particular department of government—public safety, for example. The commission form of government is common to counties of Georgia.

Special Purpose Districts

In addition to cities and counties, the state also allows for the creation of special purpose districts. Special purpose districts provide multiple services but do so for one principle function, typically related to development, redevelopment, or reclamation of land and property within the district's jurisdiction. In Georgia, special purpose districts are limited to Central Business Improvement Districts (CBIDs), which may be established to redevelop or improve existing downtowns, and Local Independent Authorities (LIAs). LIAs include Downtown Development Authorities, for central business districts; Development Authorities, required for counties and municipalities; Resource Recovery Development Authorities, also required for counties and municipalities; Land Bank Authorities; and Urban Residential Finance Authorities. Local authorities are financed via revenue bonds, though CBIDs do have the authority to levy property taxes subject to approval by commercial landowners and business owners in the district.

BOX 8.3

Milledgeville

From 1807 to 1868, Milledgeville was the state capital of Georgia. The Reconstruction government relocated the government to the emerging economic, administrative, and communication center of the state, Atlanta.

Current Milledgeville is the county seat of Baldwin County and is home to three institutions of higher learning. The 2000 census set the city population at just over 18,000, but 2007 estimates place the number closer to 20,000. Typical of many of middle Georgia's cities and towns, the population is roughly equally divided between Anglo whites (49.9 percent) and African American (47.7 percent).

Milledgeville uses a mayor-council form of government, with the mayor elected at large and seven city councilors elected from districts. Three of the seven councilors are African Americans. The city also employs a professional city manager.

In 1861, Georgia's secession convention met at what is today called the Old Capitol Building and took Georgia out of the Union. Georgia voters had voted a convention to consider secession on January 2. Convening on January 16, 297 delegates conferred for four days. On January 19, 1861, they reported an ordinance of secession and voted 208–89 to secede. The ordinance was signed in a public ceremony on January 21. The Convention remained in Milledgeville until March 2, revising the state constitution to include an explicit guarantee for slave holding and also granting exclusive authority to amend the state constitution to a convention instead of the legislature.

Sources: William W. Freehling and Craig M. Simpson, eds., *Secession Debated: Georgia's Showdown in 1860* (New York: Oxford University Press, 1993); Michael P. Johnson, *Toward a Patriarchal Republic: The Secession of Georgia* (Baton Rouge: Louisiana State University Press, 1977).

Takings and Property Rights

One of the most important responsibilities of local government is the regulation of the use of property. In exercising these powers, local governments may clash with traditional notions—particularly strong in the South—that a landowner has unfettered authority to use property as he or she wishes without government interference. Georgia's constitution grants county and municipal governments zoning authority, though the legislature can dictate the procedures to be followed in zoning.

Some of the most controversial decisions taken by local governments involve requests by landowners to change the uses to which they can put their property. Changing the zoning from agricultural or large-lot residential to permit higher density residential (apartments, condominiums, or single-family residences on smaller lots) or development for commercial use can increase the value of the property many times over. Landowners justify rezoning requests by contending that changing the use of the property will permit new development that, once completed, will generate more revenues through sales taxes or higher property assessments. The rezoning will also provide housing, services, and/or job opportunities. Opponents point to the existing land-use plan and urge authorities to adhere to the vision it sets out. They may also claim that the jurisdiction lacks the infrastructure needed to handle the growth that would result should the rezoning request be granted. Before allowing new development, opponents will argue, the community should put in place the road improvements, water and sewage capacity, and schools needed to handle the anticipated growth.

Zoning policy has played important roles in the politics of several suburban counties. A frequent pattern is for local authorities in rural areas to initially encourage all kinds of growth. While some citizens have wanted to keep their communities unchanged, larger numbers jump at the opportunity to get rich quick by selling their land to developers or speculators. In time, some of those who move into the new developments become concerned that unconstrained growth is threatening the features that made the area attractive—features such as uncrowded schools, lack of traffic congestion, and open spaces. These concerns may stimulate a "smart growth" reaction that results in replacing pro-growth members of the county commission, as happened a few years ago in Cherokee and Gwinnett counties. The smart- or slow-growth commissioners may be replaced in a subsequent electoral cycle as developers fund the campaigns of candidates more sympathetic to their interests.

Property owners whose rezoning requests are denied can go to court, where they must prove that the benefits to the public are insufficient to warrant the landowner's inconvenience. To have a zoning decision reversed in court, opponents must prove "fraud, corruption, or manifest abuse" by the zoning board or city or county commission. The standard for standing (the ability to bring a case) is also high, as opponents must have a "substantial interest" and be an "aggrieved citizen."[4] To meet this standard requires more than aesthetic nuisance or inconvenience effects (traffic, for instance); opponents must show a loss of property value or intrusion of externalities—noise, odor, loss of privacy.

A second major local property rights issue is the exercise of eminent domain by state and local governments. The state has the authority to seize and condemn property, subject to compensation, in order to promote a necessary public policy objective—the construction of a highway or acquire the site for a new school, for example. This practice became controversial in 2005 when the U.S. Supreme Court ruled in a case from New London, Connecticut, that the state's power of eminent domain permitted the condemnation of private property so that it might be redeveloped by another private party in order to provide greater tax revenue to the government.[5]

Georgia's legislature had explored broadening eminent domain to make it as extensive as in Connecticut. The backlash set off by the *Kelo* decision prompted Georgia legislators to backtrack from plans to expand eminent domain authority, and instead, they explicitly excluded the practice upheld by the Supreme Court. When the state or local government engages in a "taking," it must meet specific criteria, with the benefits to the public exceeding the detrimental effect on the property owner.

LOCAL PUBLIC OFFICIALS

County government, much like the General Assembly, has achieved greater descriptive representation. Once the preserve of white, Democratic males, county commissions and the ranks of constitutional officers now have scores of black, Republican, and female members. Women and African Americans have also increased their numbers on school boards, most of which now choose members in nonpartisan elections.

Republicans now dominate the governments in many suburban counties. African Americans hold seats on the collegial governing bodies of most jurisdictions in which blacks constitute at least a quarter of the population and dominate local governments in majority-black communities. Women have come to dominate some county offices.

Changes in Local Politics: Party

Georgia counties and cities handle partisanship differently. Partisan elections are used to select the vast bulk of county officials, with the major exception

[4]*Cross v. Hall County*, 238 Ga. 709, 235 S.E.2d, 379 (1977).
[5]*Kelo v. City of New London* 545 U.S. 269 (2005).

being members of boards of education, many of whom are selected on non-partisan ballots. In contrast, most cities elect mayors and council members in nonpartisan elections. Macon still has partisan elections and is a major exception.

How far have Republicans come? In 1989, a total of 153 Republicans held elective county offices, which constituted 5.8 percent of these offices. Of those, 63 were county commissioners (8.1 percent of total) and a dozen were sheriffs (7.5 percent of total). By 2007, those numbers climbed to about 500 Republican Party elected officials with 300 county commissioners (38 percent of total) and about a quarter of the county constitutional offices, including 40 sheriffs (25 percent of total).

Early Republican office holding in local government was mainly in the counties of metropolitan Atlanta, Columbus, Augusta, Macon, and Savannah. Republicans first emerged as majority office holders in Cobb and Gwinnett counties on the north side of Atlanta, and also in rural, traditionally Republican Fannin County on the North Carolina border. Some of the counties in which Republicans enjoyed their initial successes have returned to the Democratic fold. The influx of minority residents shifted county population demographics, and the accompanying increase in minority voter participation dominated county politics. As identification with the GOP has become widely acceptable among white voters throughout Georgia, Republicans have won local posts in counties far from urban centers, and currently they tend to dominate local governments in suburban counties such as Columbia (suburban Augusta), Oconee (suburban Athens), Forsyth, Paulding, and Coweta (suburban Atlanta). As of 2007, Republicans held all the seats on 30 county commissions and constituted a majority on 32 other commissions. Democrats filled all commission seats in 57 Georgia counties. Republicans dominated commissions in suburbia and much of north Georgia, while the Democrats' greatest strength on commissions was found in core urban counties and in the Black Belt of middle Georgia.

Changes in Local Politics: Race

Republicans realized substantial gains in office holding, but these gains pale compared to the dramatic rise of black political empowerment in local office. In 1969, there were a total of 15 black local elected officials in Georgia, only four of whom served as county officials. Two decades later, Georgia had 425 total black local elected officials, including 102 county commissioners and 81 board of education members. By 1998, the numbers for black elected officials had climbed to 513 elected officials, with 93 county commissioners and 107 board of education members. Early black office holding in local government was mainly in the Atlanta metro area and in parts of the state where black voters were able to constitute locally elected majorities and take advantage of district formats for electing local commissioners. Table 8.1 shows the growth of black office holding through time.

TABLE 8.1   African American Local Office Holders, 1969–2001

Year	County	Municipal	School Board
1969	4	8	3
1970	3	15	7
1971	6	20	8
1972	7	32	10
1973	9	42	28
1974	9	72	31
1975	12	89	36
1976	13	115	43
1977	18	132	41
1980	23	149	43
1981	23	151	55
1984	29	170	58
1985	58	179	57
1987	94	229	73
1989	102	242	81
1991	103	257	84
1993	105	266	95
1997	99	290	104
1999	93	302	99
2001	102	293	118

Source: Appropriate issues of the *National Roster of Black Elected Officials* (Washington, DC: Joint Center for Political and Economic Studies).

Black commissioners constituted the majority on eight county commissions as of 2008 and held 22 percent of the commission seats statewide. As of 2007, African Americans held 23 percent of 908 county school boards and constituted a majority on 18 boards.

Changes in Local Politics: Gender

Three constitutional offices have become the domain of women who now constitute a majority of the superior court clerks (111), tax commissioners (107), and probate judges (86). Women rarely get selected to be sheriff, coroner, or surveyor, although there has been some growth in these offices over the last generation. The state's largest county, Fulton, had a black female sheriff during the 1990s.

As of 2007, Georgia had almost 100 women serving on county commissions. While this is only about one-eighth of the total, it more than doubles the number of women commissioners serving during the 1980s. Although still a small minority, women hold more than 70 seats on county school boards.

LOCAL REVENUES

Traditionally local governments in Georgia relied heavily on property taxes. These are based on the assessed value of the property so that as property appreciates in value, the taxes on it increase. Even when the value of property remains constant, the taxes can increase if the local government raises the rate of taxation, called the millage rate. Property taxes are especially unpopular because they must be paid in a lump-sum, often near the end of the calendar year, when family budgets are being squeezed by holiday purchases.

Georgia counties have a source of revenue that citizens find more acceptable than property taxes. Both counties and school districts have been authorized to add an additional cent to the 4 percent sales tax collected by the state. These additional pennies collected on most purchases are commonly referred to as Special-Purpose Local-Option Sales Tax (SPLOST). Before a local government can levy a SPLOST, it must specify the project to be funded with the revenue collected and secure public approval in the form of a referendum. School districts have used SPLOST money to construct new schools and to expand existing ones. County SPLOST funds have gone for road improvements, parks, and public buildings. A SPLOST continues in effect until the projects for which it was levied have been paid for. Usually, as a local jurisdiction approaches the point at which enough money has been collected to pay for a set of projects, a new referendum is held to fund a new set of projects. Because the SPLOST is collected at the rate of one penny per dollar, voters seem not to be as sensitive to its collection as to the property tax. Moreover, the public seems to like the idea that they know precisely what the money will be used for, and this allays distrust of decisions made over the expenditure of other revenues. For these reasons, voters approve the vast majority of SPLOST proposals put before them.

The Speaker of the House, Glenn Richardson, spent much of the year leading up to the 2008 session pushing a plan to eliminate the property tax. Local governments successfully opposed the Speaker's proposal since, had it taken effect, they would lose control over their funding levels and become dependent on the state for their funding. Once convinced that his efforts to eliminate local property taxes could not succeed, Richardson sought to freeze property assessments, which would eliminate one way to increase property taxes. This effort also failed.

Another change that failed in the 2008 session involved a constitutional amendment that would allow local governments to collect an additional penny (a new type of SPLOST) earmarked for transportation projects. In light of growing public complaints about Atlanta traffic, reports that Atlantans have some of the longest commutes in America, and evidence that a bridge inspector had been certifying the safety of bridges without doing the necessary inspections, this new tax proposal drew widespread support. The business community got behind the idea since increasing speculation suggested that Atlanta's phenomenal growth (most

Georgians now live in the Atlanta metro area) might grind to a halt as a result of gridlock. The House approved the constitutional amendment, but in the closing minutes of the legislative session, the proposal came up three votes short in the Senate.

THE URBANIZATION OF GEORGIA: BALKAN ATLANTA

Most Georgians live in one of the nation's major metropolitan areas; they do not, however, live in large cities. Densely populated Georgia is largely unincorporated—59 percent of the population does not live in an incorporated city, town, or village but instead receives all local services from county government. And, as indicated in Table 8.2, even those persons who live in an incorporated city or town largely live in small towns. Only 12.1 percent of Georgians live in a city with a population of more than 100,000, and just 5.6 percent live in a city of 50,000 to 100,000. Most Georgians living in incorporated towns instead live in places with fewer than 50,000 residents, and over 8 percent live in places with fewer than 10,000 residents.

Of the 534 municipalities in Georgia, 239 have fewer than 1,000 residents, while only five have more than 100,000 residents, and only one (Atlanta) has more than 200,000, according to the 2007 census estimates (Table 8.3). Taken together with the dozens of small Georgia counties with populations of less than 25,000, this extreme application of federalism places local government very close to most Georgians and creates numerous opportunities for both office holding and self-governance.

Atlanta is the governmental and economic center of Georgia. Originally founded as Terminus in 1837, the area was settled subsequent to the Cherokee removal and the opening of northwest Georgia to whites. In 1843, Terminus was rechristened Marthasville, and then four years later arrived at the name Atlanta. In 1868, the state capitol was moved from Milledgeville to Atlanta.

The decades-long effort of Bill Hartsfield to establish Atlanta as a center for aviation was at the heart of an effort to propel this small industrial city to the forefront of national and later international attention.

TABLE 8.2   Distribution of Georgians by Population of City or Town

Under 1500	155,879	1.66%
1500–5K	384,577	4.11%
5–10K	281,834	3.01%
10–25K	777,703	8.31%
25–50K	559,482	5.97%
50–100K	526,372	5.61%
Over 100K	1,141,424	12.10%

TABLE 8.3   The Twenty-Five Most Populous Cities in Georgia in 2007

Place	2007 Census Estimate	2000 Census	Percent Change	Rank 2007	Rank 2000
Atlanta	519,145	416,474	24.65	1	1
Augusta-Richmond County	192,142	195,182	**-1.56**	2	2
Columbus	187,046	186,291	0.41	3	3
Savannah	130,331	131,510	**-0.90**	4	4
Athens-Clarke County	112,760	100,266	12.46	5	5
Macon	93,076	97,255	**-4.30**	6	6
Roswell	87,312	79,334	10.06	7	8
Sandy Springs	83,166	84,986	**-2.14**	8	7
Albany	75,825	76,939	**-1.45**	9	9
Marietta	67,021	58,748	14.08	10	10
Warner Robins	60,392	48,804	23.74	11	12
Johns Creek	59,580	60,671	**-1.80**	12	11
Alpharetta	49,662	34,854	42.49	13	13
Smyrna	49,534	40,999	20.82	14	15
Valdosta	47,567	43,724	8.79	15	14
East Point	42,940	39,595	8.45	16	16
Rome	36,463	34,980	4.24	17	17
Gainesville	34,818	25,578	36.12	18	22
Peachtree City	34,516	31,580	9.30	19	18
Dalton	33,401	27,912	19.67	20	20
Kennesaw	31,613	21,675	45.85	21	27
Hinesville	30,504	30,392	0.37	22	19
Douglasville	30,098	20,065	50	23	31
Lawrenceville	28,969	22,397	29.34	24	25
Newnan	28,857	16,242	77.67	25	37

Atlanta won the battle with Louisville and Birmingham to emerge as the First City of the South, in no small part due to its mild climate, relatively benign national image on race relations, and right-to-work laws that attracted industry.

Atlanta currently uses a mayor-council form of government. There are 15 councilors, of whom 12 are elected from districts throughout the city and the remaining three are elected at large. The mayor possesses a veto of council legislation, but it can be overridden by a 10-vote majority.

The first African American mayor of Atlanta, Maynard Jackson, was elected in 1973. Previous white mayors of the city going back to the 1940s, such as Bill Hartsfield and Ivan Allen, had enjoyed the support of black voters and had been elected by biracial coalitions. As the black population approached majority in the 1960s, black politicians sought the mayor's office in their own right and took with them the support of black voters. Every mayor since 1973 has been an African American, including former congressman and United Nations Ambassador Andy Young (1981–89); Maynard Jackson again (1989–93); Bill Campbell (1993–2001); and Atlanta's first female mayor, Shirley Franklin (2001–present). In 2005, Franklin was reelected with over 90 percent of the vote.

The estimated population of the city of Atlanta is 519,145, while the surrounding Atlanta metropolitan statistical area has a population of 5,626,400. Only 9.22 percent of the Atlanta metro population actually resides within the city limits. Atlanta is only the thirty-third largest city in the United States, but it ranks tenth for metropolitan population.[6] Metropolitan Atlanta covers over 8,000 square miles and incorporates 28 of the state's 159 counties. The metropolitan area also includes over 140 incorporated municipalities.

The growth of Atlanta in the past half-century is mostly the story of the growth of the suburbs. Nine counties report growth of at least 500 percent since 1960, led by Gwinnett's incredible 1,683 percent growth, from a town county of 43,000 persons to a sprawling super-suburb of over three-quarters of a million persons. The five counties in Atlanta's Standard Metropolitan Statistical Area (SMSA) in 1960 have a net gain of almost 2.5 million people. According to the U.S. Census Bureau, in 2007 Georgia ranked first in the number of 100 fastest-growing counties in the United States with eighteen. Four of the 10 fastest-growing counties in the United States were in Georgia, including Forsyth (up 61.5 percent since 2000), Paulding (up 56.7 percent), Henry (up 55.9 percent), and Newton (up 54.9 percent).

One consequence of this growth is an incredible concentration of population and, potentially, political power in Atlanta's suburbs. In 1960, Gwinnett County was home to 1.1 percent of the state's population; as of 2007, it is 8.3 percent. Cobb County was 2.9 percent in 1960 and is now 7.4 percent. In the meantime, Fulton added a half-million people but slipped from just under 15 percent of the state's population in 1960 to 10.6 percent in 2007, while DeKalb climbed from 6.5 percent to just 7.9 percent.

As indicated in Figure 8.1, the city of Atlanta's share of the state population steadily increased through 1960 and then started to taper off. Initially, this

---

[6]The top 10 metropolitan areas in the United States by population are: New York-Newark-Bridgeport (21,976,224); Los Angeles-Long Beach-Riverside (17,775,984); Chicago-Naperville-Michigan City (9,725,317); Washington-Baltimore-Northern Virginia (8,211,213); Boston-Worcester-Manchester (7,465,634); San Jose-San Francisco-Oakland (7,228,948); Philadelphia-Camden-Vineland (6,382,714); Dallas-Fort Worth (6,359,758); Houston-Baytown-Huntsville (5,641,077); and Atlanta-Sandy Springs-Gainesville (5,626,400).

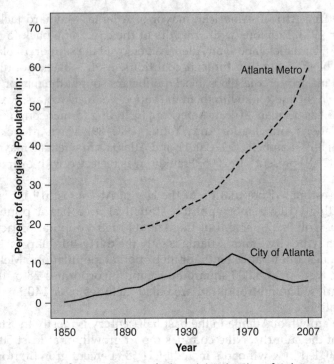

FIGURE 8.1 Percent of Georgia's Population Living in City of Atlanta and Surrounding Environs, 1860–2007

was an actual loss of population through the 1980s. The city reversed the population-loss trend by 2000, but growth outside of the city limits far outpaced any gains in the city. As indicated in Figure 8.1, through 1960, the population of Atlanta and its surrounding suburban environs was split roughly 50-50. Since then, the suburban and ex-urban counties that make up metro Atlanta have exploded, adding population at an exponential rate compared to the core city (see also Table 8.4).

The diversity of the city of Atlanta is a product of decades of black in-migration, white flight, and regentrification by affluent and educated whites seeking an urban lifestyle. In the city of Atlanta, 52.6 percent of residents are black or African American, while a third are Anglo whites, and 6.5 percent are Latinos. The white population has actually been increasing since 2000, as young and affluent whites seek to shorten their commutes. Atlanta has the fastest-growing white population of any major U.S. city. Gary Gates reports that Atlanta also has the third-largest gay and lesbian population of any major U.S. city, an estimated 12.8 percent of all residents.[7]

---

[7]Gary J. Gates, *Same-Sex Couples and the Gay, Lesbian, Bisexual Population: New Estimates from the American Community Survey* (The Williams Institute on Sexual Orientation Law and Public Policy, UCLA School of Law October, 2006).

TABLE 8.4 Population Growth in Atlanta MSA Counties, 1960 and 2007

County	Population 1960	Population 2007	% Change	Total Change	State % 2007	State % 1960
Gwinnett	43,541	776,380	1,683.10	732,839	8.29	1.10
Forsyth	12,170	158,914	1,205.80	146,744	1.70	0.31
Fayette	8,199	106,144	1,194.60	97,945	1.13	0.21
Henry	17,619	186,037	955.80	168,418	1.99	0.45
Paulding	13,101	127,906	876.30	114,805	1.37	0.33
Cherokee	23,001	204,363	788.50	181,362	2.18	0.58
Rockdale	10,572	82,052	676.10	71,480	0.88	0.27
Douglas	16,741	124,495	643.60	107,754	1.33	0.42
Cobb	114,174	691,905	506.00	577,731	7.39	2.90
Dawson	3,590	21,484	498.40	17,894	0.23	0.09
Clayton	46,365	272,217	487.10	225,852	2.91	1.18
Barrow	14,485	67,139	363.50	52,654	0.72	0.37
Newton	20,999	96,019	357.20	75,020	1.03	0.53
Coweta	28,893	118,936	311.60	90,043	1.27	0.73
Walton	20,481	83,144	305.90	62,663	0.89	0.52
Pickens	8,903	30,488	242.40	21,585	0.33	0.23
Bartow	28,267	92,834	228.40	64,567	0.99	0.72
Carroll	36,451	111,954	207.10	75,503	1.20	0.92
DeKalb	256,782	737,093	187.00	480,311	7.87	6.51
Butts	8,976	23,759	164.60	14,783	0.25	0.23
Pike	7,138	17,204	141.00	10,066	0.18	0.18
Jasper	6,135	13,660	122.60	7,525	0.15	0.16
Heard	5,333	11,387	113.50	6,054	0.12	0.14
Haralson	14,543	28,718	97.40	14,175	0.31	0.37
Fulton	556,326	992,137	78.30	435,811	10.60	14.11
Spalding	35,404	62,826	77.40	27,422	0.67	0.90
Lamar	10,240	16,961	65.60	6,721	0.18	0.26
Meriwether	19,756	22,748	15.10	2,992	0.24	0.50
Statewide Total	**3,943,116**	**9,363,941**	**137.40**	**5,420,825**	**100**	**100**

Most persons who live in the Atlanta area (and who usually call themselves Atlantans) do not live in the city, but in the numerous suburbs and exurbs of the city. Most of these persons do not even live in incorporated municipalities, but instead mainly reside in unincorporated areas served by county government. This high degree of decentralization is not unique among major metropolitan areas, but the Atlanta metro is more decentralized in terms of governmental structure than any major urban area. Atlanta will

BOX 8.4

Edge Hill

The smallest city by population in Georgia is Edge Hill. Located on two-tenths of a square mile along state highway 171-S near Carters Lake in southern Glascock County, Edge Hill was incorporated in 1939 and has a population of 36 persons as of 2007. According to the U.S. census, there are 11 households in the city and the population is 97 percent Anglo white and 3 percent Native American. Compared to the rest of Glascock County, the residents of Edge Hill are affluent, with a median household income of nearly $60,000, or twice that of the rest of the county.

continue to remain small because of an inability to annex. The city itself is ringed by other municipalities and for years was unable to move north because of an agreement with Fulton County that the city would not expand toward Sandy Springs.

AN INSTANCE OF REGIONAL GOVERNMENT: MARTA

The delegation of local governing authority into so many municipalities in Georgia creates a variety of coordination problems. Planning is necessarily decentralized, and given the historic role of the county as the primary active sovereign in government, regional and state coordination confronts political and cultural barriers.

A primary area of contention is transportation policy. Roads are an old source of political power and even patronage, and the state for decades pursued a highway development program that rewarded the counties of rural lawmakers. Consequently, isolated low-growth communities often enjoyed the benefit of divided highways, while many of metropolitan Atlanta's commuters crept along on two- and three-lane roads to make their way to the major interstates. The state could not fund alternative transportation because the state constitution requires that motor fuel taxes only fund roads.

Local efforts at alternative transportation such as trains and buses were eschewed by suburban voters in Cobb, Gwinnett, and Clayton counties, all of which opted out of the regional mass-transit proposal of the early 1970s because of historic factors such as racism and suburban flight of the urban core. The rejection of the Metropolitan Atlanta Rapid Transit Authority (MARTA) proposal by Cobb voters was actually a step backward from the past, as Cobb's historic largest city, Marietta, had once been connected to Atlanta by a streetcar line.

A 1962 constitutional amendment paved the way for the creation of MARTA as a regional governmental authority, and in 1965, the state legislature authorized its actualization.

BOX 8.5

The Brain Train

The Brain Train is one of three proposed expansions of rail service in Georgia under the Georgia Rail Passenger Program (GRPP). Unlike MARTA, which is a traditional "closed" rail passenger system, the GRPP proposes to follow existing freight and passenger rail routes to provide service to outlying major cities within 75 miles of Atlanta. The Brain Train would connect Georgia Tech, Emory, and University of Georgia by tying into multimodal transportation hubs at both ends of the route and also including a dozen stops. The estimated cost is around $400 million.

Another route proposed by the GRPP goes from Atlanta to Macon, running along the Norfolk Southern line through Lovejoy, which enjoys the support of Clayton County (which once rejected MARTA) and also federal assistance.

The challenge to implementing these routes is coordinating support from local and national actors, as well as the rail industry, which controls the rail routes. The historic disinterest in rail service among Georgia state lawmakers offers little promise of coordinated state efforts, leaving nongovernmental organizations and local governments to move the rail initiative. For example, in 2006, the legislature prohibited the state DOT from spending money on commuter rail without direct legislative authorization.

In 1971, Fulton and DeKalb counties authorized a special 1 percent sales tax to fund MARTA. MARTA is still funded entirely by a 1 percent sales tax and rider fares and receives no state operating funds. At about the same time, Cobb, Gwinnett, and Clayton County voters refused MARTA. The rail system started construction in 1975 and initiated service four years later. The current rail system is 48-miles long with 38 rail stations and a daily ridership of almost a half-million passengers. The legislation authorizing MARTA requires that its revenue be split evenly between operations and capital improvement. The system has not expanded for several years, leaving it with a large capital reserve; instead, capital expansion funds have gone into system modernization.

MARTA is one of the largest governments in Georgia, with almost 5,000 employees, including a 300-person police force. MARTA is governed by a 14-member board of directors named by the City of Atlanta and Clayton, DeKalb, Fulton, and Gwinnett counties, plus ex officio members named by the state. Clayton and Gwinnett voted for the MARTA authorization but not funding, thereby allowing them to name board members while not contributing to funding. The general manager exercises day-to-day executive authority over the system. The state legislature monitors the finances of the system through a legislative oversight committee.

The major counties that rejected MARTA—Cobb, Gwinnett, and Clayton—now support countywide bus systems that connect to the MARTA system. And, while 78 percent of MARTA rail riders are African Americans who live mainly in Atlanta, peak-hour ridership on the Northside rail lines is predominantly white.

CONCLUSION

Georgia enjoys a tradition of strong and diverse local government. Until relatively recently, the state delegated most political power down into the counties, while also limiting the expansion and political power of major urban centers. The investment of political power in counties contributed to the proliferation of counties in the 19th century, and until the last part of the twentieth century the county was the principle mechanism for the exercise of the power. This political reality in a state that was still largely rural contributed to the emergence of the county as a source of personal and political identity.

The use of special charter mechanisms and local legislation rules in the Georgia General Assembly potentially constrained the ability of municipalities to form and exercise significant authority. The long-standing debate in metropolitan Atlanta over the incorporation of Sandy Springs stands as stark evidence of a county (Fulton) using the political power of its legislative delegation to prevent a community from attaining home rule. The willingness of the legislature to otherwise create cities, towns, and villages led to the proliferation of numerous municipalities.

The fragmentation of Georgia into numerous counties and cities has contributed to a dispersion of local political power in one of the largest urban centers in the United States. A municipal map of metro Atlanta looks like a crazy quilt of small incorporated and unincorporated areas, and each of these local government entities exercises varying authority and operates under several different models of municipal government. The consequence is that many problems confronted by the Atlanta metropolitan area and also other growing urban centers in Georgia involve coordination across several municipal governments. In some instances this fragmentation creates the benefit of competitive federalism, where residents can shop among several communities for one that offers the mix of cost, taxes, and services they desire. In other instances, fragmentation can delay addressing significant problems, or steer the availability of local services, as in the case of MARTA.

PART THREE

Agents of
Change

CHAPTER 9

Voting Rights in Georgia

Atlanta, a mecca for upwardly mobile African Americans, has been a central player in the continued pursuit of voting rights for all Americans. Georgia can point to substantial success in black political participation and the election of African American politicians. Such was not always the case. The pursuit of voting rights in Georgia is a political story of dramatic change. To understand contemporary Georgia politics, one must recognize what it inherited from Reconstruction.

GEORGIA AND DISCRIMINATORY VOTING PRACTICES

Starting almost immediately after the Civil War, Georgia implemented a series of policies and practices that impeded black political participation. Georgia initiated the poll tax (1871), which it made cumulative in 1877: past unpaid poll taxes accumulated and individuals had to pay the back taxes to vote.[1] Around the turn of the twentieth century, Georgia followed other southern states in adopting a literacy test, which required voters to demonstrate their ability to read and write; a property-owning requirement; an understanding clause; and a grandfather clause. In 1917, Georgia limited participation in the Democratic Party primary to white voters.[2]

Black voters unsuccessfully sought to vote in the Democratic primary in 1944 after the Supreme Court banned the white primary in Texas but were turned away, and it took another case to strike down Georgia's white primary.[3]

---

[1]Laughlin McDonald, Michael B. Binford, and Ken Johnson, "Georgia" in Chandler Davidson and Bernard Grofman, eds., *Quiet Revolution in the South* (Princeton: Princeton University Press, 1994).

[2]*See* Joseph Bernd and Lynwood Holland, "Recent Restrictions upon Negro Suffrage: The Case of Georgia," *Journal of Politics*, 21 (August 1959), 487–513; V. O. Key, *Southern Politics* (New York: Knopf, 1949), 620.

[3]*Chapman* v. *King*, 154 F.2d 460 (5th Cir. 1946).

Acting Governor M. E. Thompson vetoed a 1947 statute designed to maintain the white primary by taking the state out of the election business. The governor evidently agreed with the *Atlanta Constitution*: "We cannot much longer continue to subject Negroes to 'taxation without representation' or draft them to jeopardize their lives in defense of a democracy which denies them the right of franchise."[4]

Violence and intimidation accompanied efforts to restrict black voting into the mid-twentieth century. Political leaders such as Gene Talmadge explicitly suggested using violence to discourage black voting in the 1940s. Historian Kevin Kruse notes that in the July 1946 Democratic primary, where black voters contributed to Jimmy Carmichael's popular plurality (though Talmadge won the decisive county unit vote), threats of violence preceded the vote. Further, violence followed, and murdered blacks were accompanied by signs reading, "The First Nigger to Vote Will Never Vote Again" or similar sentiments, and locals observed coarsely, "This thing's got to be done to keep Mr. Nigger in his place."[5]

Even as blacks faced threats of violence in rural Georgia, African American participation increased in Atlanta. The black vote determined the outcome of a February 1946 special election for Congress in the Atlanta-based Fifth District. The word went out in black neighborhoods on the eve of the election to support Helen Mankin, a liberal member of the General Assembly. She won with over 1,000 votes from black Ward 3-B, the last box to come in. Black voters also flexed their muscles by joining upper-class Northside whites to create a "black-stocking-silk-stocking" coalition that elected Mayor Bill Hartsfield and, in 1953, put Dr. Rufus Clement on the school board, Georgia's first black officeholders since Reconstruction.[6]

Black voter registration rates remained low in Georgia into the early 1960s. The poll tax had been eliminated in 1945, but the literacy test and antagonistic local registrars discouraged black participation. In 1962, 27.4 percent of Georgia's nonwhite voting age population had registered to vote, compared with 62.6 percent of whites.[7] Only Alabama and Mississippi had lower rates of black registration than Georgia prior to the Voting Rights Act. As shown in Table 9.1, 30 heavily black Georgia counties had less than 10 percent of the age-eligible blacks registered in 1962. In four of these counties, fewer than 10 nonwhites had registered to vote.

GEORGIA AND THE VOTING RIGHTS ACT

The 1965 Voting Rights Act (VRA) singled out Georgia and six other southern states for special scrutiny. Section 5 of the new legislation applied to Georgia because a) it had literacy tests as a prerequisite for registering and b) less than half the voting age population had voted in the 1964 presidential

[4]Quoted in "White Primary," *Time*, July 17, 1944.
[5]Kevin Kruse, *White Flight* (Princeton: Princeton University Press, 2005), 24.
[6]Ibid., 38.
[7]U.S. Commission on Civil Rights, *Political Participation* (Washington: Government Printing Office, 1968), 238.

BOX 9.1

Barack Obama's Effect on Georgia Politics

Although Barack Obama failed to carry Georgia, coming up on the short end of a 53–47 percent split in the vote, his candidacy affected the state's politics. In anticipation of Georgia's presidential primary early in February, the Obama campaign set out to increase black registration. After scoring the most lop-sided victory in any state, Obama's volunteers continued registering African Americans. By the time that the registration books for the general election closed, 337,000 new blacks had signed up to vote. As evidence of the success of the registration effort, although the state has about twice as many whites as blacks, 10,000 more blacks than entered Georgia's electorate in 2008. By the time of the election, African Americans constituted 30 percent of the regis-trants, up from 27.2 percent four years earlier.

While registration is a necessary prerequisite for political influence, it means nothing if the newly registered fail to turn out. Prior to 2008, Republicans had a more effective get-out-the-vote operation than Democrats. Democrats overcame the GOP advantage when the Obama campaign opened 40 offices in Georgia. The staff for these offices included 53 paid personnel along with 4,800 trained volunteers. In contrast, John McCain had no offices in Georgia and ran his effort out of Tallahassee. Obama volunteers knocked on thousands of doors and called tens of thousands of households.

Campaigns like to get their votes sewn up early, so the Obama campaign encouraged its supporters to take advantage of absentee voting or the no-excuse early voting that, in 2008, for the first time, began 45 days before the election. These efforts resulted in African Americans casting 35 percent of all votes in the weeks prior to election day. A survey found that among Georgians who had voted by October 30, Obama led 55-to-40 percent.[1]

The advantage Obama enjoyed in early voting did not hold up as whites voted in much higher proportions than blacks on election day, so that the exit poll found that blacks cast 30 percent of all votes in the election—an increase of six percentage points over 2004. This surge in black participation did not deliver the state to Obama, but it helped Jim Martin deny a majority to incum-bent Senator Saxby Chambliss (R). The Democratic nominee for a seat on the Public Service Commission, Jim Powell also benefitted and had a narrow lead in a second contest set for a December runoff.

The Democratic Party might have reaped greater rewards down ticket had it slated quality candidates in state legislative districts represented by Republicans although having sizable black minorities. However, the 79 House districts and 21 Senate districts lacking a Democratic nominee included many of those with large black minorities. Democrats did manage to wrest four House seats away from Republicans in districts experiencing African American growth.

[1]kos, "GA-Sen: True Battleground," (Daily Kos), www.dailykos.com/storyonly/2009/10/31/124032/ 16/876/647988 (accessed September 1, 2009). This survey, conducted by Research 2000, must be taken with some degree of skepticism. Independent analysis shows that Research 2000 polls show a historic Democratic bias. Elizabeth A. Martin, Michael W. Traugott, and Courtney Kennedy. "A Review and Proposal for a New Measure of Poll Accuracy." Public Opinion Quarterly 2005 69(3): 342–369.

TABLE 9.1 Nonwhite Registration, 1962, 1967, and 2004 in Counties with Very Limited Black Registration in 1962

County	1962 % Nonwhite	1967 % Nonwhite	2004 % Black
Baker	1.90	71.70	76.50
Bleckley	3.30	20.80	55.40
Burke	6.50	41.80	73.50
Calhoun	6.00	24.60	55.80
Chattahoochee	0.90	7.20	35.10
Early	8.00	20.00	68.30
Echols	7.70	7.70	63.70
Fayette	2.20	5.70	118.20*
Glascock	0.30	6.00	59.40
Harris	8.50	36.10	69.30
Houston	9.80	54.80	69.40
Jeff Davis	6.20	65.00	76.90
Jefferson	5.90	54.90	71.90
Lee	1.60	55.00	65.00
Lincoln	0.20	47.60	67.70
McDuffie	9.20	41.40	61.60
Madison	5.60	26.40	57.80
Marion	3.40	17.40	83.40
Miller	0.60	19.90	72.00
Mitchell	7.50	29.70	52.90
Quitman	5.40	25.60	84.60
Seminole	0.90	33.90	66.90
Stewart	5.10	26.40	78.90
Sumter	8.20	46.70	65.80
Talbot	8.70	25.90	79.70
Terrell	2.40	53.90	65.00
Treutlen	4.60	62.10	74.30
Warren	8.40	63.70	73.70
Webster	0.90	26.80	76.50
Worth	7.80	25.80	59.00

*Fayette County has experienced an influx of African Americans since 2000, which is reflected in the registration data.

Source: U.S. Commission on Civil Rights, Political Participation (Washington, DC: U.S. Government Printing Office, 1968); sos.georgia.gov/elections/voter_registration/Turnout_by_ demographics.htm (accessed 09/05/2009).

election. States subject to Section 5 must secure approval of changes in election laws from either the U.S. Department of Justice or the District Court of the District of Columbia. The legislation authorized federal agents to go to covered jurisdictions to register prospective voters who had been turned away by local authorities and to monitor elections. Although initially scheduled to expire in 1970, Congress has extended Section 5 (most recently in 2006) until 2031.

The VRA had a dramatic impact in Georgia. In 1967, over half of Georgia's nonwhite voting age population had registered to vote. Within two years of enactment, registration rates for nonwhites increased in each of the 30 counties as shown in Table 9.1. In eight counties, a majority of nonwhite adults had signed up to vote. The last column in Table 9.1 shows that the barriers to participation having been breached, black registration remains widespread into the twenty-first century.[8]

Voter registration data from the U.S. Census indicate widespread and growing black voter registration since 1980. Table 9.2 shows that in 1980, 59.8 percent of adult African Americans reported having registered compared with 67 percent of the white voting age population. By 1990, black and white Georgians had closed the gap: 57 percent of African Americans and 58.1 percent of whites reported registering. Blacks reported registering at higher rates than others in four of the last six national elections.

A problem with self-reported political participation data, such as that compiled by the U.S. Census, is that respondents tend to give socially approved answers—some individuals who have not registered will tell a pollster that they had registered, and because of the heavy emphasis placed upon the civic duty of voting, a number of nonvoters will report that they went to the polls.[9] Georgia is one of five states that maintain voter participation data by race, making it possible to have more accurate registration data concerning race. Additionally, since 1996, Georgia's secretary of state has conducted a post-election audit of voter turnout by going through voter sign-in sheets and cross-checking that information against the registration data showing the voter's race. Unlike the figures provided by the Census Bureau, these are not estimates but actual counts. Data from the secretary of state indicate that black registrants increased by 225,000 between 1996 and 2004, from 24.4 percent of all registrants in 1996 to 27.2 percent by 2004. Efforts by the Barack Obama campaign to expand support resulted in 337,000 additional African Americans signing up to vote in 2008, so that by the time of the fall elections, blacks constituted 30 percent of the registrants.

In 2006, almost 43 percent of Georgia's black registrants participated in the general election. Elections in presidential years attract more participants, and,

---

[8]The one exception, Chattahoochee County, has low levels of both black and white registration because a large share of its adult population is stationed there at Ft. Benning. Many of these soldiers are probably registered back home.

[9]William T. Harbaugh, "If People Vote Because They Like To, Then Why Do So Many of Them Lie?," *Public Choice*, 89 (1996), 63–4.

TABLE 9.2 Reported Registration Percentages* by Race in Georgia, 1980–2004

	1980	1982	1984	1986	1988	1990	1992	1994	1996	1998	2000	2002	2004	2006
Black	59.80	51.90	58.00	55.30	56.80	57.00	53.90	57.60	64.60	64.10	66.30	61.60	64.20	57.90
White	67.00	59.70	65.70	60.40	63.90	58.10	67.30	55.00	67.80	62.00	59.30	62.70	63.50	62.10
Non-Hispanic Whites			—	—	—	—	—	—	—	63.10	61.00	65.30	68.00	67.90

*Percentages are calculated using the voting age population as the denominator.

Source: U.S. Department of Commerce, Bureau of the Census, *Voting and Registration in the Election of November 1980* (Washington, DC, U.S. Government Printing Office, 1982), and subsequent issues.

in 2004, 72.2 percent of the African Americans registered in Georgia went to the polls, where they accounted for just over a quarter of the ballots cast, indicating that blacks turned out at slightly lower rates than whites. Blacks flocked to the polls during the early voting period in 2008, and in the 45 days leading up to the election they cast 35 percent of the votes recorded. Their participation rate dropped off on election day, so that the exit polls show 30 percent of the ballots in the presidential contest coming from blacks, which would indicate that they participated at the same rate as the rest of the electorate.

Figure 9.1 shows the dramatic change in the primary electorate since 1990, when 90 percent of Georgians participated in the Democratic primary. In each of the five most recent primaries, the Democratic share of the vote has hovered between 53 and 55 percent of the total. The decline in the Democratic share resulted from whites moving massively to the GOP. The other trend shown in Figure 9.1 traces the increased influence of black votes in choosing Democratic nominees. In the early 1990s, African Americans cast fewer than a quarter of the Democratic ballots. From 2002 to 2006, fewer than half the Democratic primary votes came from blacks. Then, in the 2008 presidential primary, with Barack Obama on his way to a massive victory in

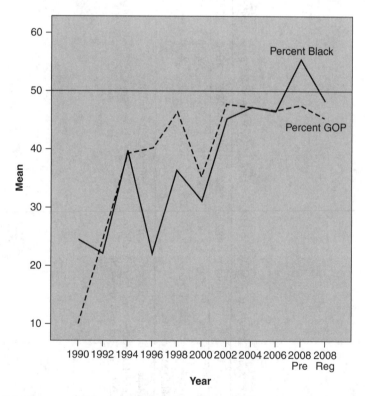

FIGURE 9.1 Race and Primary Participation Since 1990

Source: Data compiled by authors from materials gathered by the Georgia Secretary of State.

Georgia, blacks accounted for 55 percent of the Democratic electorate. Half a million more whites took Republican than Democratic ballots in the 2008 presidential primary. In the 2008 regular primary in July, whites outnumbered blacks by 6,200 votes in the Democratic primary as African American cast 48.2 percent of the ballots, with non-Hispanic whites accounting for 49.4 percent.

AFRICAN AMERICAN OFFICE HOLDING IN GEORGIA

The first blacks to win election in modern Georgia came from Atlanta, which is no surprise given the relative economic, social, and political success of African Americans in the city. When Congress adopted the VRA, only three Georgian African Americans held office. Figure 9.2 shows the number at an anemic 30 in 1969. The 1982 Voting Rights Act Amendments facilitated challenges to at-large electoral systems. The shift away from at-large to district systems in many cities, counties, and school boards resulted in an explosion of black representatives. By 1991, more than 500 African Americans held elective

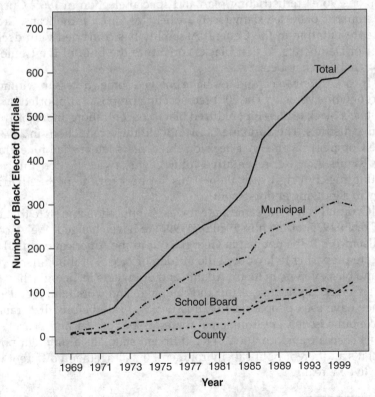

FIGURE 9.2   Black Elected Officials in Georgia, 1969–2001

Source: Data compiled by the authors from various volumes of the *National Roster of Black Elected Officials* (Washington, DC: Joint Center for Political and Economic Studies).

office. Current estimates indicate as many as 800 black elected officials, including four members of Congress, two statewide partisan officials, six statewide judges, 55 state legislators, and hundreds of local officials.

Georgia became the first southern state to elect an African American to Congress in the twentieth century when Andrew Young won the 44-percent-black Fifth Congressional District in 1972. In 1986, Atlanta councilman John Lewis defeated State Senator Julian Bond in the then-majority-black Fifth District to become the second black member of Congress from Georgia. The 1992 redistricting created two additional majority-black districts that sent state lawmakers Sanford Bishop and Cynthia McKinney to Congress. A decade later, Atlanta Senator David Scott raised the number of African Americans in Georgia's U.S. House delegation to four, equaling the largest number of black members to represent any state.

Electoral success in the state legislature came earlier for blacks. Leroy Johnson became the first modern black southern legislator in 1962, representing part of Fulton County. A second black would enter the 56-member Senate before initial passage of the VRA. In 2009, a dozen blacks served in the Senate. In the state House, the first seven African Americans arrived following the "one-person, one-vote" redistricting plan and special election in 1965. Currently, almost a quarter of the legislative seats are held by African Americans. Growing black representation in the General Assembly has coincided with declining number of Democrats so that blacks constitute the bulk of the Democratic caucuses in both chambers.

African American candidates have enjoyed some success in winning the support of white voters.[10] The 2001 redistricting proposal, supported by much of the state's black leadership, reduced black concentrations in majority black legislative districts. The Supreme Court upheld these reductions in 2003, only to have Congress reverse that decision three years later when renewing the Voting Rights Act. Representative John Lewis, twice beaten into comas protesting for civil rights, explained his support for the new redistricting strategy in a glowing endorsement:

"[Georgia] is not the same state it was. It's not the same state that it was in 1965 or in 1975, or even in 1980 or 1990. We have changed. We've come a great distance. . . . It's not just in Georgia, but in the American South, I think people are preparing to lay down the burden of race . . . I think many voters, white and black voters, in metro Atlanta and elsewhere in Georgia, have been able to see black candidates get out and campaign and work hard for all voters. And they have seen people deal with issues as, I said before, that transcend race: economic issues, environmental issues, issues of war and peace. . . . So there has been a transformation, it's a different state, it's a different political climate, it's a different political environment. It's altogether a different world that we live in, really."[11]

---

[10]Charles S. Bullock III and Richard E. Dunn, "The Demise of Racial Districting and the Future of Black Representation," *Emory Law Review* 48 (Fall 1999).

[11]Affidavit of John Lewis at 18, *Georgia* v. *Ashcroft*, 195 F. Supp. 2d 25 (D.D.C. 2002).

CONCLUSION

Black political participation in Georgia has climbed in all areas since the 1960s, in no small part due to the role of the Voting Rights Act. In the areas of voter registration, office holding, and in coalescing with white voters who support black candidates, impressive gains have been made that were unimagined in 1960.

Future prospects for black candidates depend in part on the future of the Democratic Party. White voters increasingly identify with the Republican Party, and since 1992, there have been few elections in which Republicans have not added to their ranks of elected officials. African Americans now hold more state legislative, congressional, and statewide constitutional offices than do white Democrats, but Democratic candidates, both black and white, increasingly fail to win elections at all levels. If these trends continue, African Americans may lose some of the statewide posts they currently have, as they did in 2006 when David Burgess lost his reelection bid for the Public Service Commission. Nevertheless, they are unlikely to lose congressional or state legislative seats in districts that have substantial black populations and may make additional gains as white Democratic incumbents step aside.

CHAPTER 10

Georgiamanders

Electoral rules often determine political winners and losers. The rules that condition redistricting are among the most important because they have the potential to disrupt the status quo. Disrupting established relationships may open the way for new interests to achieve influence in the legislature. The other side of that coin is that if new interests gain influence, it comes at the expense of those who previously dominated the process. Not surprisingly, those who have power fight to retain it and will seek to draw districts that maintain their dominance.

Until the onset of the redistricting revolution in the 1960s, white Democrats from rural communities dominated Georgia politics. With urban counties limited to a maximum of three seats in the House and (except for Fulton County) a senator only two of every six years, their legislators could *always* be outvoted by the far more numerous rural representatives. Beginning with the early 1960s, federal authorities have played a huge role in shaping Georgia's legislative districts, and these decisions have dramatically changed the composition of the Georgia legislature and the state's congressional delegation. At times, federal demands have been articulated by judges who, in some instances, have drawn the maps. At other times, the U.S. Department of Justice has reined in Georgia legislators and forced them to craft districts that enhance opportunities for minorities. Federal pressures have combined to increase the numbers of African American and Republican officeholders. As the numbers of these groups have grown, so has their ability to influence public policy.

ONE-PERSON, ONE-VOTE IN GEORGIA

The configuration of legislative districts can go a long way toward determining what interests in a state will have power. Rural Georgia maintained its control over state politics, even as the state began to change after World War II, by not redrawing districts to reflect population changes. Failure to adopt new districts, sometimes referred to as "the silent gerrymander," resulted in growing population disparities, especially since the most populous counties got only three seats in the state House, while even the least populous counties each got their own seat. The county unit system reinforced the inequality, since it gave rural voters disproportionate influence in the selection of statewide officials.

Before the 1960s, courts ignored redistricting activities, which they considered to be inherently political and, therefore, a "thicket" from which courts would never emerge unscathed.[1] In 1962, the U.S. Supreme Court departed from precedent, and, in a case from Tennessee, launched what has become known as the Reapportionment Revolution.[2] The Court pointed to the equal protection clause of the Fourteenth Amendment to demand that legislative districts have equal populations. In short order, urban dwellers successfully challenged Georgia's county unit system and the districts used for the congressional and state legislative districts.

The County Unit System

The 1917 Neill Primary Act used the Electoral College as a rough model for weighting votes in Democratic primaries for statewide and some congressional offices.[3] This arrangement for rural counties gave the Talmadge machine its power base, even to the extent of defying the majority will in the 1946 gubernatorial primary. In 1962, the courts ended the county unit system for violating the equal protection clause because votes in small, rural counties had a greater impact on election outcomes than the votes of urban residents.[4] The popular vote now determined nominations, which greatly enhanced the influence of the most populous counties and signaled the death knell for bossism in rural Georgia.

The General Assembly

Just as a relatively small share of Georgia voters could determine the outcome in statewide Democratic primaries, so also could far less than half of the state's population elect a majority of the legislature. Figures based on the 1950 census calculated that as little as 26.3 percent of the population could elect a majority of the state House.[5] Less than 27 percent of the population could elect a majority of the Senate, although in 1952, because of the rotational system, less than 6 percent of the population could have elected a majority of the Senate. In 1962, a federal court ordered Georgia to distribute seats in one chamber on the basis of population.[6] Because the rotational system prevented some senators from acquiring seniority and the power that accompanies experience, and because

---

[1]*Colegrove* v. *Green*, 328 U.S. 549 (1946).

[2]*Baker* v. *Carr*, 369 U.S. 186 (1962).

[3]Democratic Party leaders in each congressional district could decide whether to require a plurality or majority for nomination.

[4]*Sanders* v. *Gray*, 203 F. Supp. 158 (N.D. Ga. 1962).

[5]Manning J. Dauer and Robert G. Kelsay, "Unrepresentative States," *National Municipal Review* (December 1955): 572–4.

[6]*Toombs* v. *Fortson*, 205 F. Supp. 248 (N.D. Ga. 1962).

redistricting the House would require changing the state constitution, the legislature drew new Senate districts prior to the 1962 elections.

Fulton County had elected one senator under the old plan, but under the new one it chose seven. Leroy Johnson won a new district that contained much of Atlanta's black population to become the first African American elected to a southern legislature in modern times. The 1963 Senate also saw three Republicans join what had been a Democratic fraternity.

Two years later, the U.S. Supreme Court ruled that both chambers in a state legislature must be based on population.[7] In the state House, tiny Echols County had 133 times the weight of a Fulton County vote. To correct this inequality, Georgia redrew its state House districts and held special elections in 1965. As in the Senate, once urban counties got a fairer share of seats, some districts elected African Americans, while others selected Republicans. Seven African Americans and 23 Republicans entered the House following implementation of the equal population plans.

Congressional Districts

Having felled the county unit system and the malapportioned Senate, Atlanta-based plaintiffs turned their guns on the congressional districts. The 1962 congressional map appears in Figure 10.1; the population data appear in Table 10.1. District 5, which had the fewest counties—Fulton, DeKalb, and Rockdale—had the most people (823,680), more than twice the ideal district population for the state of 394,312. District 9 in northeast Georgia fell 30 percent below the ideal. Seven of the 10 districts were underpopulated by anywhere from −3.65 to −30.98 percent. The U.S. Supreme Court rejected the congressional district maps as a gross violation of the principle of one-person, one-vote.[8] In response, the legislature divided District 5 so that metro Atlanta got a second member of Congress.

RACIAL AND PARTISAN CONSEQUENCES OF REDISTRICTING

As a consequence of these decisions concerning districting practices for Congress and the state legislature, legislative districts must be adjusted to equalize populations after each census. Just as the redistrictings of the state legislature in the 1960s opened the way for the first African Americans to join those chambers, adjustments made following the 1970 census resulted in an African American joining Georgia's congressional delegation. As with many of the changes, however, it did not come easily. Andrew Young, an African American, had won the Democratic nomination in the Fifth Congressional District in 1970 but lost to the Republican incumbent. The legislature went out of its way to make Young's course difficult should he choose to run again in 1972, when they excluded his home from the newly designed District 5. While

---

[7]*Reynolds* v. *Sims*, 377 U.S. 533 (1964).
[8]*Wesberry* v. *Sanders*, 376 U.S. 1 (1964).

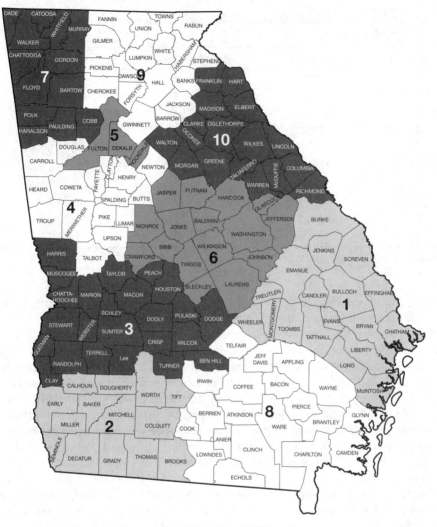

FIGURE 10.1   Georgia Congressional Districts, 1962

members of Congress need not live in their districts, it is easier for them if they do. Since Georgia is one of the states covered by Section 5 of the Voting Rights Act, it must get federal approval before implementing any new districting plan, and DOJ refused to clear the plan. This forced Georgia to produce a new plan that placed Young's home in the district. Young won the district and he and Houston's Barbara Jordan became the first African Americans elected to Congress from the South in the twentieth century.

Redrawing the state legislative districts also facilitated the election of additional African Americans and Republicans. The numbers of blacks in the state House rose from 14 to 19, while Republicans added five seats in the Senate and two in the House following population adjustments in the early 1970s.

TABLE 10.1   Population Deviations in the 1962 Georgia Congressional District Map

District	Population	Raw Deviation	Percent Deviation
1	379,933	−14,379	−3.65%
2	301,123	−93,189	−23.63%
3	425,254	+30,942	+7.85%
4	323,489	−70,823	−17.96%
5	823,680	+429,368	+108.89%
6	330,235	−64,077	−16.25%
7	450,740	+56,428	+14.31%
8	291,185	−103,127	−26.15%
9	272,154	−122,158	−30.98%
10	345,323	−48,989	−12.42%

Source: Wesberry v. Sanders, 376 U.S. 1 (1964).

With the 1980 redistricting, the trend of more urban and suburban state legislators with fewer representing rural Georgia continued. Again the federal government influenced Georgia's decisions about mapping. Section 5 of the Voting Rights Act has been interpreted to mean that a covered jurisdiction cannot reduce the concentration of minorities in a district that has become predominately minority. The 1980 census showed District 5 to be majority black by a very narrow margin. However, the district was substantially under-populated which necessitated adding population. The General Assembly plan increased African American population to 57 percent. However, the chair of the House committee dealing with the redistricting had made racist statements indicating his opposition to a majority-black district. Because of his racism, DOJ rejected Georgia's plan, even though it enhanced the likelihood that the district would elect an African American. Georgia had to redraw the Fifth District and bring south DeKalb County's growing black population into the district. This was done in order to meet DOJ's demand that the district be at least 65 percent African American. Wyche Fowler, a white Atlanta politician, succeeded Young when President Jimmy Carter named Young as the U.S. Ambassador to the United Nations. Fowler held on to the seat until 1986, when he ran for the U.S. Senate. The 5th District voters then elected John Lewis, a hero of the civil rights movement.

As it came time to draw new districts to reflect the population shifts of the 1980s, General Assembly leaders hoped to satisfy DOJ rather than expend the time and resources litigating an unacceptable plan. Toward that end, Zell Miller, when still lieutenant governor, had named Eugene Walker, an African American from DeKalb County, to chair the Senate redistricting committee. Walker and a number of others in the Legislative Black Caucus explored ways to create a second black congressional district. While it was possible to have one heavily black district in the Atlanta area, creating a second district with a black majority necessitated linking the black populations in at least three urban areas. The plan that Walker supported tied together the black populations in south DeKalb County, Augusta, and Macon. In the past, creating an additional black congressional district would almost certainly have satisfied DOJ. However, the Justice Department had a new perspective, which demanded that jurisdictions maximize the number of districts in which a minority group constituted a majority of the population.

In 1982, when Congress renewed Section 5 of the Voting Rights Act for an additional 25 years, it also rewrote Section 2. The new version of Section 2 eliminated the need to prove discriminatory intent and instead stipulated that if the status quo had the effect of making it more difficult for minorities to elect their preferences than it was for whites, then the existing system violated the Voting Rights Act. DOJ incorporated Section 2 into its review of Georgia's plan and concluded that it was possible to create not just one, but two, additional majority-black districts by stringing together African American populations in distant parts of Georgia.

After DOJ rejected two Georgia proposals, the General Assembly capitulated and devised a plan that retained a 62 percent black Fifth Congressional District for John Lewis. The plan added a 57 percent black district in southwest Georgia that extended a finger to pick up African Americans in Macon, and a 64 percent black district that stretched from DeKalb County eastward to the South Carolina line picked up Augusta's black population, and then extended a narrow neck along the Savannah River to pluck out 50,000 African Americans in Savannah. This configuration, as shown in Figure 10.2, resulted in the most extraordinary congressional map Georgians had seen. While the map that it replaced had split only three of Georgia's 159 counties, District 2 in southwest Georgia split 12 counties and District 11 split another eight counties. Both districts sent African Americans to Congress in 1992, with Cynthia McKinney becoming Georgia's first black congresswoman.

The post-1990 districting plans for the state House and Senate also failed to meet DOJ expectations and twice got rejected. The plans approved by DOJ resulted in 42 House and 13 Senate districts in which a majority of the population was black.[9] The 1992 elections increased the numbers of black legislators by four in the House and one in the Senate, as shown in Table 10.2.

Republicans also benefited dramatically from the new plans. Indeed, Republicans had allied themselves with black Democrats in pushing to increase the numbers of majority-black districts. Republicans realized that by aggregating African Americans into selected districts, the neighboring ones would become much whiter and, therefore, more likely to elect Republicans. The 1992 congressional elections began paying dividends for the GOP, which won four seats, twice as many as it had previously held in the twentieth century. Most of these seats would have remained Democratic had they not been bleached to create the majority-black Second and Eleventh Districts. Two

---

[9]Charles S. Bullock III, *The Georgia Political Almanac: The General Assembly 1993–94* (Decatur: Cornerstone Publishing, 1993), 27–8.

FIGURE 10.2   Georgia's Eleventh Congressional District, 1992

TABLE 10.2   African American Legislative Gains in the Wake of New District Plans

	Senate	House
1960s*	1	7
1975**	0	5
1983	2	0
1993	1	4
2003	−1	3

*The initial election following redistricting of the Senate came in 1962, while in the House it occurred in 1965.

**DOJ required a new plan with districts more favorable to blacks prior to the 1974 election.

years later, Republicans added three more seats, and in April 1995, Nathan Deal, the last white Democrat in the state's congressional delegation, defected to the GOP. This resulted in Georgia having eight white Republicans and three black Democrats in Washington. Republicans also made substantial gains in the state legislature. The 1992 election saw them increase their share of House seats by 50 percent, while adding four seats to the 11 they had in the Senate. The GOP surge in 1994, which may have been augmented by the redistricting plan, resulted in Republicans gaining another 16 seats in the House and six more in the Senate. After the 1994 elections, Republicans had record numbers of seats in both chambers, having doubled their number of seats in the Senate across two elections and increasing their House seats from 35 to 66.

The extraordinary districts drawn for Congress and shown in Figure 10.2 got challenged as racial gerrymanders. The Supreme Court ruled that the Eleventh District, which reached 290 miles from the Atlanta suburbs to Savannah, violated the equal protection clause of the Fourteenth Amendment. The Court acknowledged that in order to comply with Section 5 of the Voting Rights Act, it would be necessary for the legislature to take into consideration the distribution of the minority population. However, the court concluded that race had been the primary consideration in drawing the plan, and when the legislature gave priority to racial considerations in order to separate black and white voters by putting them in different districts, that violated the equal protection clause. Subsequently, the court found that the Second District had also violated the Federal Constitution.

The legislature failed to agree on a remedial congressional plan. The Senate preferred a plan with only one majority-black district, while the House tried to maintain three majority-black districts. When the legislature proved unable to come up with a new map, the federal court in Augusta stepped in and drew a map based on the one used during the 1980s. Since the earlier map had only one majority-black district, that is all that the court put into the map used for the remainder of the 1990s.[10]

The court plan reduced Representative Cynthia McKinney's Eleventh District from 64 to less than 40 percent black. Representative Sanford Bishop's southwest Georgia district went from 57 to 39 percent black. While McKinney loudly proclaimed that this new map would result in her defeat, she handily beat back the challenge from three whites in the Democratic primary and easily won reelection in November. Bishop also had no trouble turning aside white challengers both in the Democratic primary and the general election.

The new maps, by reducing the black percentage in two previously majority-black districts, increased the black proportion in neighboring districts. Representative Charlie Norwood (R) had to compete in a district that

---

[10]The DOJ challenged the court plan, arguing that there should be at least two majority-black districts. The Supreme Court rejected that contention noting that DOJ had previously rejected Georgia's plans with two black districts. The court held that the benchmark against which it was appropriate to compare the new plan was the last legal one, which was the plan drawn in the early 1980s and that plan had only one majority-black district. Consequently the new plan with only one majority-black district did not constitute retrogression. The case was *Abrams* v. *Johnson* 521 U.S. 74 (1997).

had increased from 18 to more than 40 percent black. Republicans often find it
difficult to win districts more than 30 percent black but Norwood turned back
a challenger 52 to 48 percent to retain his seat in 1996.

The General Assembly redrew the state House and state Senate districts
since, in drawing these to satisfy DOJ demands, they had given racial considerations priority over every other factor. This resulted in 37 majority-black
House districts and 12 majority-black Senate districts. These new maps did
not reduce the number of black legislators.

REDISTRICTING IN A NEW CENTURY

In 2001, the Democratic majority that had controlled the General Assembly for
more than 12 decades faced its most daunting challenge. The fastest-growing
parts of the state tended to be Republican, while areas with slow or no growth
favored Democrats. More troubling, most voters statewide, beginning with
1996, had preferred Republicans in both state House and Senate elections, as
shown in Table 10.3. Democrats had managed to retain majority status in the
two chambers only as a result of the current districting plan. A plan that more
fairly represented the growth areas would almost certainly enable
Republicans to take control of the legislature. The threat of a GOP majority
gave the Legislative Black Caucus (LBC) a very different perspective on redistricting than in the 1990s, when many in the LBC strongly supported efforts
to maximize the number of seats likely to elect African Americans. If

TABLE 10.3   Republican Shares of Votes and Seats in General Assembly
Elections (All Numbers Are Percentages)

	Senate		House	
	Votes	Seats	Votes	Seats
1992	40	27	—	29
1994	45	38	—	37
Redistricting of both chambers				
1996	52	39	51	41
1998	51	39	53	43
2000	55	43	52	42
Redistricting of both chambers				
2002	55	46	52	41
Redistricting of both chambers				
2004	57	61	57	53
2006	67	61	59	59

Source: Computed by authors from official election returns. See Georgia Secretary of State,
Georgia Election Returns, available at www.sos.georgia.gov/ELECTIONS/election_results/
default.htm (last visited September 5, 2009).

TABLE 10.4   The Reduction in Black Adults in Majority-Black Districts in the 2001 Senate Plan

District Number	Percent Black Adults 2000	Percent Black Adults 2001	Change
2	60.30	50.31	−9.99
10	70.30	64.14	−6.16
12	55.30	50.66	−4.64
15	61.60	50.87	−10.73
22	63.10	51.51	−11.59
26	62.30	50.80	−11.50
35	75.60	60.69	−14.91
36	60.00	56.94	−3.06
38	76.30	60.29	−16.01
39	54.40	56.54	+2.14
43	88.40	62.63	−25.77
55	71.90	60.64	−11.26

Source: Compiled by the authors.

Republicans took over the legislature, LBC members, all of whom were Democrats, would lose positions of power and leadership, such as committee chair or vice chair.

All but two LBC members supported plans designed by the desperate Democratic Party. These plans shifted some blacks from majority-black districts to shore up the electoral positions of endangered white Democrats. This evidence is clearest in the Senate. At the time of the 2000 census, a dozen Senate districts had more black than white residents. Some of these, in part because of the ratcheting effect imposed by Section 5, had become overwhelmingly black. As shown in Table 10.4, the average black Senate district became 10 percentage points whiter in the 2001 plans. Helping to convince LBC members to support these plans was research done by political science professor David Epstein, which estimated that in a district in which blacks made up about 44 percent of the voting age population, an African American candidate would have a 50-50 chance of election.[11] In a 50 percent black adult district, Epstein estimated the probability of electing the candidate preferred by the black population to be 75 percent. As Table 10.4 shows, each of these districts retained a majority-black adult population.

In addition to judiciously spreading the black population in order to help white Democrats, the 2001 districting plans sought to undermine Republicans by frequently forcing two incumbents to compete in the same district. Eliminating senior Republicans deprived the GOP of experienced leadership.

---

[11]Expert report of David Epstein at 16–17, *Georgia* v. *Ashcroft*, 195 F. Supp. 2d 25 (D.D.C. 2002) .

In order to offset their declining support in the electorate, Democratic legislators drew districts that soaked up Republican voters by over-populating
GOP districts frequently by as much as 4 percent and sometimes by as much as
4.99 percent. With the same objective of promoting Democratic fortunes,
Democratic voters got spread thinly, with their districts being underpopulated,
frequently by 4 percent and sometimes by as much 4.99 percent. Democrats
hoped that their approach would not simply maintain their current strength
but would increase their ranks in the Senate by five seats and pick up as many
15 seats in the House. They also hoped to win seven of the state's 13 congressional seats, a substantial gain over the three seats they had held since 1995.

The audacious Democratic plan had some success. It did not produce the
gains that Democrats hoped for, but it did yield a 30-to-26 majority in the
Senate along with 108 of the 180 House seats and five congressional seats. The
Senate victory proved short-lived, however, when Sonny Perdue, the first
Republican governor since 1872, convinced four Democrats to change parties,
thereby giving Republicans a 30-to-26 advantage in the upper chamber. The
2002 elections, like the three previous ones, resulted in the Republicans winning a greater number of votes statewide in both House and Senate districts,
although in neither chamber did they win the majority of the seats.

Republicans went to court to challenge the districting plans for the new
century and prevailed in their attack on the state House and Senate plans.
When asked to explain the population deviations in these plans, Democratic
leaders said that they wanted to minimize the loss of seats by the city of
Atlanta and south Georgia, two areas that had grown less rapidly than the
state as a whole. The court went back to a decision handed down more than 40
years earlier to remind the legislature that favoring one area of the state over
another in districting plans was unconstitutional.[12] When the legislature
failed to take corrective action, the court drew new maps, and where the population deviation had been as much as plus and minus 4.99 percent from the
ideal population, the court's plans narrowed deviations to +1 and −1 percent.
The court plans also eliminated the bias in favor of Democrats. The new plans
resulted in Republicans winning 34 seats in the Senate and 95 House seats.

The special master retained by the court to help with redistricting took care
not to endanger any African American legislators, who retained 39 House seats
and increased to 11 the number of Senate seats. African Americans have continued to make gains in subsequent elections, so that in 2008 they numbered 44 in
the House and 12 in the Senate. Republicans could now count two of the black
representatives, and both chambers had more black than white Democrats.

After Republicans gained control of the state House in 2004 they redrew
the congressional maps. Their primary objective was to add Republicans to
the west Georgia district represented by Phil Gingrey (R), whose district
Democrats had drawn with the expectation that it would elect a Democrat.
The Republican map made Gingrey more electorally secure, with a district
that cast 71 percent of its votes for Bush in 2004. Republicans also had, as a

---

[12]*Larios* v. *Cox*, 300 F. Supp. 2d 1320 (N.D. Ga. 2004).

secondary goal, making the Eighth District, which centered on Macon, more Republican, in the hope that Democratic incumbent Jim Marshall might be defeated. Marshall escaped defeat in 2006 by a margin of less than 2,000 votes.

REDISTRICTING AND PARTISANSHIP

In addition to increasing the ranks of African American legislators, redistricting has often promoted Republican fortunes. With GOP strength concentrated in growth areas, when adjustments get made to equalize populations, they pick up seats. As Table 10.5 shows, Republicans added Senate seats after each redistricting. In the House, gains came less consistently although Republican ranks grew following four of the six new maps. Their biggest gain came in 2005, when the courts replaced the Democratic gerrymander, and in 1965, when the House for the first time adopted a one-person, one-vote plan. The loss of four seats in 2003 demonstrates the efficiency of the Democratic gerrymander.

REGIONAL SHIFT IN POWER

Prior to the redistricting revolution, north and south Georgia had equal numbers of state Senate districts, since the two regions have equal numbers of counties. But with population as the basis for allocating seats, the southern half of the state has consistently lost representation. Under the current plan, drawn by the courts to replace one in which Democrats tried to cushion the blow to the southern part of the state, only 15 of the 56 Senate districts are largely located in south Georgia. This loss of almost half of its seats reduces the region's ability to influence legislation. This may become especially important if the prolonged drought persists, since thirsty Atlanta will try to take increasing amounts of water, which will result in less going downstream to water the fields of south Georgia farmers. Generally, the shift of seats from rural areas, especially south Georgia, to the suburbs around the cities in the northern part of

TABLE 10.5 Republican State Legislative Gains in the Wake of New District Plans

	Senate	House
1960*	3	22
1973	2	7
1983	2	0
1993	4	17
2003	2**	−4
2005	4	23

*The initial election following redistricting of the Senate came in 1962, while in the House it occurred in 1965.

**Republicans won two additional seats in the election. Within days of the election, four Democrats switched to the GOP.

the state enhances the likelihood that public policy will be more responsive to the needs of suburbanites. One manifestation has been growing support for proposals to cut taxes. The tax burden falls heavily on affluent suburbanites, while benefits have been allocated to rural and central city residents. With the beneficiaries of many programs now having less representation in the General Assembly, they have been unable to forestall tax-cutting measures.

THE FUTURE

Georgia has continued to grow more rapidly than most of the nation and projections show the state gaining a fourteenth seat in Congress after the 2010 census. Currently, Republicans control both chambers of the state legislature and the governorship. If a Republican wins the governorship in 2010 and if Republicans maintain their majorities in the legislature, which is almost certain, then for the first time ever the GOP will be in position to draw the maps for the state immediately after a reapportionment. It is likely that the plans for the state legislature will become more favorable to Republicans than the current maps, which were drawn by unbiased judges. It is also likely that if Republicans control the redistricting process, they will ensure that the new congressional district tilts in their favor. Republicans might also try again to adjust the boundaries of Jim Marshall's middle Georgia district in order to take it away from the Democrats.

CONCLUSIONS

While the Voting Rights Acts have played critical roles in opening the political process for African Americans, the requirement that districts have equal populations has also contributed to the increased numbers of black legislators both in Georgia's congressional delegation and in the General Assembly. In the early days of the one-person, one-vote requirement, shifting seats to urban areas facilitated the election of the initial black legislators, since urban areas tended to be more tolerant than rural communities. As Georgia's black population has become increasingly urbanized, the proportion of representation of urban areas in legislative bodies has enhanced black representation.

Republicans, like African Americans, have tended to concentrate in urban areas, particularly suburban communities. Both groups benefited both in the 1960s and in more recent years from requirements that districts have equal populations. However, Democrats demonstrated in 2001 how the equal population requirement could be generally honored and yet Republicans discriminated against. As Table 10.4 shows, Republicans won majorities of the popular vote for legislators years before overcoming Democratic gerrymanders and getting a share of seats more commensurate with their popular support.

Redistricting has contributed to the greater diversity in the makeup of Georgia's legislative contingents. It has also resulted in increased attentiveness to the policy concerns of urban and suburban Georgia, to the detriment of those of rural Georgians.

PART FOUR

Linking the Public to the Government

CHAPTER 11

Political Parties

Political parties aggregate interests in the American political system, where, with only two major parties that contest elections, each appeals to a broad range of voters. This is in contrast to nations that have numerous parties, each one of which appeals to a narrow set of interests.

It is sometimes said that a modern democracy could not exist without political parties since they structure the choices available for voters and provide cues to help many voters determine whom to support. Especially for voters, who pay relatively little attention to politics or who must express choices for minor offices about which they know nothing, the linkage between the voters' party preference and the party label provides invaluable information.

Frank Sorauf identifies three levels at which parties are active. There is the party in the electorate, the party as an organization, and the party in government.

PARTY IN THE ELECTORATE

Georgia does not require that voters indicate a partisan preference when registering. Consequently, there are no "official" figures on the numbers of Democrats, Republicans, or supporters of third parties. Nonetheless, most voters, if asked, will indicate that they see themselves as having a partisan preference, and it is survey data or exit polls that provide estimates of partisan loyalties in Georgia.

Even in the absence of registration data, it is obvious that the ranks of Democrats have declined while the numbers of Republicans have increased over time. Exit poll data reported in Table 11.1 show that between 1992 and 2006, the strength of the two major parties reversed. In 1992, 42 percent of the general election voters identified themselves as Democrats, while 34 percent identified with the GOP. Fourteen years later, the percentages had reversed, and 44 percent of Georgia's voters identified themselves as Republicans, with only 32 percent Democratic. Georgia had become far more Republican than the nation as a whole, since the 2006 exit poll showed the United States to be

TABLE 11.1 Partisanship of Georgia Voters. 1992–2008

	1992	1994	1996	1998	2000	2004	2006	2008
Democrats	42	40	38	40	41	34	32	38
Republicans	34	36	34	37	37	42	44	35

Source: Exit polls.

38 percent Democratic and 36 percent Republican. Obama's appeal which brought record numbers of African Americans to the polls coupled with disgust with the Bush administration reversed the trend and in 2008, Democrats outnumbered Republicans by 38 to 35 percent.

In recent years, neither party could claim the loyalty of most Georgia voters. To succeed, statewide candidates of either party must appeal to voters not affiliated with their party. The need to appeal to more than just their own partisans should dissuade candidates from taking extreme positions. Democrats who adopt positions far to the left or Republicans who take stands on the far right will have difficulty attracting support from the Independents who hold the key to statewide elections.

A few Georgians support third parties. Libertarians contest most statewide positions but not many other offices. The Libertarian Party is recognized as a party in Georgia, so its candidates automatically appear on the ballots, where they usually draw less than 4 percent of the vote. Other parties have had little success gaining ballot access because to qualify as a new party requires a petition signed by 5 percent of the registered voters. According to the organization, Ballot Access, no third-party candidate for the U.S. House has appeared on a Georgia ballot since 1943.

A few candidates have run as members of the Green Party, which has not qualified as a party in Georgia, so its candidates are not identified as such on the Georgia ballot. In the special election held in 2000 to fill the vacancy caused by the death of Senator Paul Coverdell, a Green Party candidate attracted less than 1 percent of the vote. No candidates' party identification appeared on the ballot since this was a special election. In that same 2000 election, Green Party presidential nominee Ralph Nader did not appear on the Georgia ballot and therefore, could secure only write-in votes.

PARTY ORGANIZATION

Democrats and Republicans each have a chairperson who is elected at the state party convention, although during the decades of Democratic control of Georgia, the governor, who acted as titular head of the party, handpicked the chair. In 2008, women led both parties. The day-to-day operation of the party is largely left in the hands of an executive director. Each party has a small permanent staff. Responsibilities for these party workers include press relations, grassroots activities, liaison with and campaign assistance for state legislative candidates, and coordination with national party organizations. In the party that controls the governorship, some of the personnel at the state headquarters have worked on the successful gubernatorial campaign.

Both parties have units in most counties, with small rural counties being the ones in which a party may lack an organizational presence. County party organizations typically meet once a month. During election years, the local party helps promote the candidacy of its nominees for local, legislative, and statewide offices. Both in anticipation of the primary and later during the general election season, candidates attend meetings of county parties to inspire the faithful and to recruit campaigns workers. Prior to the primary, the party generally avoids showing favoritism among candidates competing for its nominations.

Only recently have local party committees become active year round. During the era of the solid Democratic South, the local party in many counties was much like a mushroom—invisible most of the time and becoming active only under the proper climatic conditions, that is, the immediate onset of an election. As weak as the Democratic Party tended to be during the one-party era, Republicans were even weaker—they did not even come alive at election time in most communities.

Parties today have far less influence over setting election rules than Democrats did prior to the adoption of Georgia's first election code in 1964. Until regularized by the state, county Democratic committees set the date for the primary election and determined whether the nomination would be by a majority of the vote or a plurality. The local party could change the rules for the elections in the county in order to give an advantage to its preferred candidates. Typically these were the incumbents, so challengers often found the deck stacked against them.

Today in some college communities, Young Democrat and College Republican chapters play important auxiliary roles. These campus organizations, vehicles through which many students first become politically active, provide a ready source of eager workers for campaigns which, in turn, gives an incentive for candidates to attend meetings of these student organizations and to offer financial support. Many alums of College Republican and Young Democrat chapters go to work in congressional offices, as lobbyists, or with political operatives. Governor Perdue's initial campaign drew heavily on recent graduates, with all but two of the 18 paid staff still in their 20s.[1]

Organizations that confront repeated setbacks have a strong incentive to innovate. The Republican Party grew frustrated because of its inability to translate the successes of Richard Nixon and Ronald Reagan into increased numbers of officeholders in Georgia's congressional delegation and state legislature. As a step towards winning more offices, Republicans began to identify constituencies in which the electorate had indicated a willingness to vote Republican in presidential and statewide contests. In these promising

---

[1]Carlos Campos, "College Kids Worked Hard and Cheap," *Atlanta Journal Constitution* (January 13, 2003), B10.

BOX 11.1

Jared Thomas: Republican Young Gun

Some students acquire so much campaign experience while in college that upon graduation they take on clients and run campaigns. Jared Thomas successfully managed a state senate campaign while a University of Georgia undergrad. Two years later, he ran a campaign that saw Tom Price win an open seat in the U.S. House. In 2006, Thomas's string of successes ended when his candidate for lieutenant governor lost the Republican nomination. Thomas's career has taken a new direction, although he remains in politics. He leads the Georgia Chapter of Americans for Prosperity, a conservative interest group.

districts, Republican leaders at the state and local levels sought to recruit attractive candidates.[2] Districts in which the party found attractive candidates received a disproportionate share of the financial resources. This targeting paid off in the 1990s, as Republicans expanded their share of officeholders dramatically.

In addition to identifying promising situations and funding candidates in these districts, parties provide a range of services to incumbents, challengers, and competitors for open seats. The assistance provided includes training in the skills of campaigning for the novices. Parties also do opposition research to prepare challengers to take on incumbents more effectively. While parties can no longer raise massive amounts of soft money, they can urge more financially endowed legislators to share some of their wealth with hard-pressed, underfunded colleagues.

Parties have been especially effective in get-out-the-vote (GOTV) activities designed to ensure that voters likely to support the party's nominees follow through and cast ballots. But before that takes place, volunteers or people hired by the party do door-to-door or telephone surveys to determine which voters are inclined to support their party and the issues that concern the voters. This information is then used closer to election day to guide the distribution of mail so that voters get information showing how the party and its nominees address their top policy concerns. In the days just before the election, voters who have been identified as likely supporters get telephone calls or home visits from activists to remind them of the date of election and urge them to participate. Since 2002, the GOP "72-hour campaign" has mobilized conservative Georgians. In 2002, Ralph Reed, formerly the political director for Pat Robertson's Christian Coalition, headed the Georgia GOP and helped refine the techniques that proved successful in getting Republicans to

---

[2]Charles S. Bullock III and David J. Shafer, "Party Targeting an Electoral Success," *Legislative Studies Quarterly*, 22 (November 1997): 573–84.

the polls. Republicans have also done mailings encouraging supporters to vote absentee.

In 1998, Georgia Democrats had an effective GOTV campaign directed at black voters. Prerecorded telephone messages from Bill Clinton and Representative Cynthia McKinney encouraged black voters to come to the polls in order to thwart Republican efforts to impeach the president. Georgia voters indicate their race when registering, so Democrats knew which households to target.

PARTY IN THE GOVERNMENT

Party is the primary dividing line in the General Assembly. As we noted in our previous discussion of the Georgia General Assembly, the majority party organizes the chamber, takes the best committee assignments, and controls the flow of legislation. While party cohesion in the General Assembly is less rigid than in the British Parliament, it is nonetheless the best predictor of how a legislator will vote on controversial issues.

In the executive branch, the constitutional officers recruit their key staffers from among members of their own party. Individuals who have sensitive policy responsibilities especially will come from the elected officials' party. While it is typical for elected officials to surround themselves with fellow partisans, there are some exceptions. In 2005, for example, Governor Perdue hired a new press secretary. When interviewing for the job, Heather Hedrick revealed to the governor that she was engaged to marry Democratic Representative Rob Teilhet. Trusting that Hedrick could separate her professional life and her personal life, Perdue hired her.

While Georgia elects judges on nonpartisan ballots, the judiciary is far from insulated from partisan concerns. Since approximately two-thirds of the judges come to the bench initially as a result of an appointment, the vast majority of those who get tapped to fill a vacancy belong to the governor's party. During his reelection bid, the *Atlanta Journal Constitution* revealed that Governor Barnes had seemingly made a practice of choosing his judicial appointees from among lawyers who had contributed to his campaign.

CONCLUSION

During the last generation, the relative fortunes of Democrats and Republicans have reversed. The generations-long control of Georgia by Democrats finally came to an end, and Republicans now occupy most elected positions above the local level, where Georgia's many rural counties continue to be in the hands of Democrats. Of Georgia's 15 statewide officials elected on partisan ballots, 12 of those serving in 2009 belonged to the GOP. The 2008 exit polls show that Democrats outnumbered Republicans, at least among those who vote in general elections, although with almost a quarter of the electorate claiming to be Independents, neither party has the loyalty of most Georgians. The GOP successes are, at least in part, due to having a more active party organization. Republicans, as the newer party, had to develop techniques for recruiting candidates and mobilizing voters at a time when Democrats continued to coast on a heritage that attracted the best candidates and the bulk of the electorate; for decades the only path to a political career led through the Democratic Party. After suffering more than a decade of almost uninterrupted setbacks, Democrats, led by Jane Kidd, the daughter of Governor Ernest Vandiver (1959–63), find themselves having to play catch-up.

CHAPTER 12

Interest Groups

The First Amendment in the Bill of Rights guarantees "the right of the people peaceably to assemble and to petition the government for a redress of grievances." This guarantee provides the basis for the organization of individuals into groups that seek policy outputs, goods, and services from the government. As the economy has become more complex and as people have gotten more free time, the number and variety of groups making demands on government have proliferated. Some groups represent people in their capacity as workers, while others represent people in their recreational interests. Some groups represent interests based on ideology and others, interests based on religion. Still other groups represent people who have similar characteristics such as foster children or veterans.

Examine any facet of government, and one is likely to find groups concerned about the decisions rendered by that unit. Several hundred groups in Georgia carefully monitor the activities of the General Assembly and try to block actions harmful to their group, while urging the legislature to take steps promoting the group's interests. Other groups seek to influence executive branch decisions by asking the governor or other constitutional officers to intervene on their behalf or by trying to win public contracts for goods or services. Still other groups may pursue their goals through the courts by filing test cases or challenging the actions of governmental actors or private entities.

TYPES OF GROUPS

Given the vast array of group interests, no effort will be made to catalog all those active in Georgia politics. Such an attempt would probably fail, and therefore, here we will only identify some of the major types of participants. Groups that promote economic interests are among the most important for many citizens, since they can determine financial rewards and thus what kind of life a person leads. Examples include the Medical Association of Georgia, which represents doctors, and the Georgia Trial Lawyers Association, which represents attorneys. Professional organizations representing attorneys, doctors, and various other professions, such as hairdressers and dental hygienists, seek authority from the state to regulate those who can practice the profession. Often, the state will turn over to these professional organizations the licensing prerequisites, such as the administration of the bar exam, which must be passed by aspiring lawyers.

In the sphere of public education, one finds the Professional Association of Georgia Educators, the Georgia Association of Educators, and the Georgia affiliate of the American Federation of Teachers. These education groups, along with the American Association of University Professors, encourage the legislature to improve and expand facilities and to increase the salaries of educators, and maintain or expand the benefits packages available.

In some states, labor unions are powerful political forces, providing much of the funding for Democratic candidates and demanding in return that the state do business only with unionized shops and that it protect the right of unions to organize. Georgia, however, is a right-to-work state, which makes unionization difficult. While organized labor in Georgia supports Democrats, this is not nearly as potent a force as in a number of Midwestern and Northeastern states.

The Chamber of Commerce in various guises is a major force, representing business interests in Georgia. There is an office of the U.S. Chamber of Commerce along with the Georgia Chamber of Commerce. In addition, many communities have their own local chambers. Both the U.S. and Georgia chambers have lobbying operations in Atlanta. These organizations seek to promote a probusiness climate. This often means lower taxes, vigilance against legislation that would make labor union organizing easier, and government subsidies to encourage businesses to locate or expand in Georgia.

While the Chamber of Commerce supports businesses generally, numerous other probusiness entities have narrower scopes. For example, trade associations represent realtors, family druggists, neighborhood grocers, and undertakers. Even more specialized lobbying efforts promote individual businesses like Georgia Power, Delta Airlines, and Coca-Cola. Conflicts can arise when actions generally supportive of business threaten a particular sector or company. Another type of group represents avocational concerns of subsets of the public. In 2005, the General Assembly came under heavy lobbying from a set of south Georgians who wanted to repeal legislation that banned using dogs to hunt deer.

Another set of groups represents environmental concerns. A major player in this policy area is the Sierra Club, which often takes the lead in trying to protect natural resources from development. A frequent ally is the Georgia Conservancy.

Ideological groups run the entire range of the spectrum. On the left, the American Civil Liberties Union steps forward to protect the rights of unpopular minorities, using litigation as its primary mode of operation. Laughlin McDonald, one of the nation's leading voting rights litigators, has spent decades in the courtroom challenging regulations that he believes dilute the political influence of minorities.[1] Other ACLU attorneys vigilantly protect freedom of expression.

On the other end of the ideological continuum, the Christian Coalition promotes a wide range of conservative goals. The Christian Coalition is a grass-roots organization that urges political action by its members and others who agree with its positions. The Coalition examines the voting records of legislators and distributes scorecards rating those legislators in terms of the frequency with which they support positions favored by the Coalition. The Coalition also distributes questionnaires to candidates and then publishes the results of the responses they receive to selected items on their questionnaires. While these questionnaires do not indicate the position favored by the Coalition, its supporters have no trouble when reviewing one of the Coalition's voter guides in determining which candidates to support. In some years, the Coalition claims to have distributed more than a million copies of its voter guides. Legislators who have fared poorly on Coalition scorecards or voter guides—and these have almost always been Democrats—have been outraged, fearing that, given the name of the organization, some of their constituents might interpret them as being poor Christians.[2]

Access to abortion continues to be an issue in Georgia politics. Georgia Right to Life anchors the conservative end of the spectrum. To receive this organization's endorsement, candidates can support abortion only to save the life of the mother. Not surprisingly, this organization has sought to roll back the current availability of abortions. The leading voice in efforts to maintain current access to abortion is Planned Parenthood.

While the current concerns of groups vary widely and they may pursue them in a number of contexts, lobbying the legislature is the most frequently used approach.

Lobbying

More than 1,400 lobbyists representing more than 5,000 interests have registered with the Georgia Ethics Commission.[3] This averages about six lobbyists per legislator, which is the third highest in the South behind Florida (12 lobbyists per legislator) and Texas (8 lobbyist per legislator).[4] In 2006, the combined expenditures reported for Georgia lobbying activities, exclusive of the compensation earned by lobbyist exceeded $1.2 million.[5] Many lobbyists'

---

[1]McDonald is the author of *A Voting Rights Odyssey: Black Enfranchisement in Georgia* (Cambridge: Cambridge University Press, 2003), a volume that details many of his efforts in Georgia.

[2]Charles S. Bullock, III and John C. Grant, "The Christian Right and Grass Roots Power," in Mark J. Rozell and Clyde Wilcox, eds., *God at the Grass Roots: The Christian Right in the 1994 Elections* (Lanham, MD: Rowman and Littlefield, 1995).

[3]Pete Robinson, "Lobbying and Lobbyists at the Georgia General Assembly," *James* 4 (November 2008): 10.

[4]projects.publicintegrity.org/hiredguns.chart.aspx?act=lobtoleg (accessed June 10, 2008)

[5]projects.publicintegrity.org/decs/hiredguns/legLobbyist_graphic.html (accessed June 10, 2008)

backgrounds fit one of several profiles. One is the full-time lobbyist who is an employee of a corporation, such as AT&T, or an organization, such as the Georgia Association of Realtors. A second type is a contract lobbyist who works for multiple clients much as an attorney would. GeorgiaLink, which counts as clients national interests like American Express along with Georgia entities such as the City of Atlanta and the Georgia Hispanic Chamber of Commerce, illustrates this type. Contract lobbyists may charge clients an hourly rate plus expenses, and, since they have multiple clients, must be careful to guard against conflicts of interest. Some interests sign yearlong contracts and pay a retainer in the $2,000 to $6,000 per month range.[6] A third type of lobbyist represents nonprofits, which typically have limited budgets. Yet another type would be the individual who represents a government agency. In 2002, some 200 lobbyists for state agencies like the Board of Regents and the Secretary of State spent $17 million seeking to influence legislative outcomes.[7] Initially, Governor Perdue had sought to ban lobbying on behalf of government agencies since most of their efforts are directed at expanding the agency budget.

The various kinds of lobbyists have different resources available to them as they go about making their cases. Contract lobbyists and those who work for large corporations or trade associations have expense accounts that can be used to host legislators in expensive restaurants and provide them with tickets to sporting events. Some lobbyists regularly bring in breakfast or lunch to feed the members of a committee or the workers in the office of a legislative leader. Organizations host receptions to which all legislators are invited, with the one sponsored by the Savannah Chamber of Commerce, which features fresh seafood, being a favorite. Groups that depend heavily on favorable decisions by a particular committee will host a dinner for committee members and staff. Lobbyist entertaining is so prevalent that one legislator noted, "If you haven't gained 15 pounds during the session, you're not doing your job," to which a lobbyist responded, "If you're not careful, you could gain 50 pounds."[8]

Lobbyists report the amounts spent on individual legislators. During the 2006 session, each of five powerful legislators had more than $7,500 in expenditures showered on him.[9] In one recent year, 86 percent of the expenditures reported by lobbyists went for meals and entertainment.[10] Lobbyist spending has grown dramatically in recent years and now totals more than $1 million per year (see Table 12.1). Even when the legislature is not in session, lobbyists spend money on legislators, so that during the latter half of 2003, the amount totaled almost $100,000.[11]

---

[6]Tom Crawford, "Georgia Lobbyists: Here's the Buzz," *Georgia Trend* (January 2006).

[7]James Salzer, "State Spends $17 Million for Lobbying Legislature," *Atlanta Journal Constitution* (March 24, 2002), A1.

[8]Ben Smith, "Way to Legislators' Hearts," *Atlanta Journal Constitution* (February 8, 2004), C6.

[9]Ann Hardie, "The $1 Million Lobby," *Atlanta Journal Constitution* (February 2, 2006), F1.

[10]Jim Tharpe and Nancy Badertscher, "Lobbies Spend a Million in 2004," *Atlanta Journal Constitution* (February 2, 2005), B1.

[11]Smith, "Way to Legislators' Hearts," F1.

TABLE 12.1   Top Lobbying Operations in Terms of Expenditures During the 2005 Session

Savannah Chamber of Commerce and Convention and Visitors Bureau	$51,078
Georgia Power Company	$31,654
Georgia Beverage Association	$22,525
Georgia Chamber of Commerce	$22,076
Georgia Municipal Association	$22,022
Augusta Metro Chamber of Commerce	$21,220
Technology Leadership Coalition	$19,747
Board of Regents, University System of Georgia	$16,437
Home Builders Association of Georgia	$13,698
Georgia Oilmen's Association	$13,466
Total for all groups	$745,432

Source: Dick Pettys, "$750,000 Spent on Lawmakers during Session," *Athens Banner Herald* (April 11, 2005), A8.

Corporate or contract lobbyists provide campaign contributions to candidates and often help their clients decide on how to distribute campaign funds from the organization's political action committee. A lieutenant governor alerted those trying to influence the General Assembly that, "It is going to be necessary for organizations who want to be successful in their lobbying efforts to be involved in helping candidates not only financially, but also helping them through their campaigns through voluntary efforts."[12] Some lobbyists for trade association or professional organizations double as the executive director for the group.

In contrast, those who work on behalf of nonprofits can provide little more than information and stories—stories that may appeal to consciences of legislators. Their pleas to legislators to help handicapped children or the elderly are not made on golf courses or in luxury suites high above professional or collegiate sporting events. Those who lobby for state agencies are also precluded from making campaign contributions. Some of them can offer interesting trips to legislators or tickets to collegiate games. Lobbyists seek to present information to decision makers in order to influence the vote on legislation.

Because of the provision of gifts and benefits, it is often perceived that lobbyists are buying the votes of legislators. Both lobbyists and legislators vehemently deny this and claim that the only return received for campaign contributions or other benefits is access. Those who have supported the legislator in the past get to have face time, during which they can explain their perspectives. If the legislator has no strong feelings about what is being requested and if it does not appear that the constituents would care one way or the other, the legislator will likely accede to the lobbyist's request.

[12]Lucy Soto, "Lobbyist's Letter Reveals Rawness of Fund-Raising," *Atlanta Journal Constitution* (November 29, 1999), C1.

In addition to establishing direct contact with legislators, lobbyists may also use intermediaries. One effective tactic is to have a contributor to the legislators' campaign make the contact or to have people from the legislator's district appeal for support. Throughout the legislative session, people come to the Capitol, some individually and others in groups, trying to influence legislators' votes. Sometimes the numbers of citizen lobbyists becomes so great that it makes navigating the halls of the Capitol difficult. During the heated debate over a constitutional amendment to ban same-sex marriages, advocates on the opposing sides became so aggressive that legislators tried to avoid going through the halls of the Capitol. Lobbyists for other concerns would go through the halls holding up their distinctive lobbying badges in order to avoid being accosted by the representatives representing either gays or religious conservatives.

Lobbyists play an especially important role in the General Assembly. Because of limited staff and other research resources (see Chapter 5 on the General Assembly), lobbyists become major sources of information to help legislators make intelligent decisions. As legislators become more sophisticated, lobbyists must provide rationales, rather than simply tickets and good times, to convince legislators to support their requests. The lobbyists may offer the results of research conducted by their organization. Under ideal conditions in which all sides are adequately represented in the policy process, legislators will receive the best information available from the opposing sides on an issue. Even under conditions in which all sides do not have comparable resources to present information, a lobbyist may be constrained in the degree to which he or she would exploit the situation. As any lobbyist will readily acknowledge, their most valuable resource is their credibility. A lobbyist who misleads a legislator will soon be out of work because the legislator, upon discovering the deception, will loudly criticize the offending lobbyist, who will no longer be trusted within the legislature.

Another frequent objective is to convince a department head to award a contract to the lobbyist's client. With Georgia's annual budget of approximately $20 billion, the state purchases vast amounts of numerous commodities and services. Traditionally, these kinds of decisions about policy or purchases were influenced by exchange of favors and, at least occasionally, outright bribery or kickbacks. With the increasing scrutiny of the press and the tightening of ethics legislation, the exchange of information is becoming more important, while the provision of meals and tickets has become less important.

Not surprisingly, efforts expended by lobbyists help shape public policy, although often their influence is around the edges. As one senior member of the profession observed, "In this business, average is good. Not getting hurt is good. You don't try to hit home runs; you try to hit singles. You try not to give up too many hits."[13] Elaborating on the defensive as opposed to offensive efforts, another experienced hand said that 90 percent of his efforts focused on preventing harm to his clients.

---

[13]Crawford, "Georgia Lobbyists: Here's the Buzz."

BOX 12.1

Rules for Succeeding as a Lobbyist

Understand the political process. "A lobbyist who is not an avid student of government will not last very long." Pete Robinson

Become familiar with the political actors and their interests. Know the key actors in the area of your concern.

Have full command of the concerns and activities of your client and understand how these relate to the political system so that you can explain your position clearly and concisely.

Learn the rules and norms that govern the behavior of legislators, bureaucrats and judges.

Commit the ethics rules to memory.

Understand the constraints under which those whom you seek to lobby operate. Recognize the demands of their constituents, their political party, their sense of right and wrong.

"Do not take yourself too seriously." Pete Robinson

A recommendation made by Jasper Dorsey, a well-respected lobbyist for Southern Bell to a protégé is, "There is room for only one ego—and it's not yours." Dick Yarbrough

NEVER MISLEAD A LEGISLATOR. "Embarrass a legislator once, and a lobbying career can be undone. This principle of integrity is, if anything, more important today than ever. Your word is your bond, and information truly is power." Chuck Clay

Do not promise more than you can deliver.

"Personal relationships are still important, but knowledge is key." Chuck Clay

Never threaten a legislator. They don't like it, and you are unlikely to be able to carry out the threat.

Show the legislator the benefits for him or her that will come from supporting your position.

Adapted, with some direct quotations, from Pete Robinson, "Lobbying and Lobbyists at the Georgia General Assembly," *James* 4 (November 2008), 10; Dick Yarbrough, "Lobbyists are Important, Necessary and Sometimes True Gentlemen," *James* 4 (November 2008), 12; Chuck Clay, "Georgia's Top Lobbyists and Associations," *James* 4 (November 2008), 20–25. Robinson and Clay are former legislators; they and Yarbrough have been active in Georgia politics for decades.

WHO BECOMES A LOBBYIST?

Very few young people have lobbying as a career goal. Instead, lobbyists drift into the profession after doing something else. Some lobbyists are attorneys and take on lobbying as simply another venue in which to represent their clients. Those who do corporate lobbying have often worked for the corporation in some other capacity, perhaps doing public relations, before it is discovered that they have skills as a lobbyist. Still others learn lobbying the old fashion way—they become understudies to existing lobbyists. By working with an established lobbyist and watching how that individual practices the craft, these recent college graduates acquire the skills. Some of Atlanta's largest law firms now have their own lobbying operations. For example, Troutman Sanders brought in as a separate unit a lobbying operation headed up by former Senate Majority Leader Pete Robinson and his partner Robb Willis. Perhaps the most politically oriented law firm in Atlanta, McKenna, Long, & Aldrich, counts among its members former Governor Zell Miller; U.S. Representative Buddy Darden; Keith Mason, who was formerly Governor Miller's executive secretary; and Eric Tannenblatt, who served in a capacity similar to Mason's with Governor Sonny Perdue.

Still others go into lobbying after serving in the legislature. Retirement or defeat may set a legislator up to try to influence public policy in a different way. By one recent count, 41 former legislators had registered to lobby the institution in which they once served.[14] This ranked eighth in the nation and third in the South behind Texas (70) and Florida (60), which had the most in the nation.

THE IMPACT OF THE CHANGE IN PARTY CONTROL ON LOBBYING

Many of Georgia's premier lobbyists believed, as did most voters, that Governor Roy Barnes was sure to win reelection in 2002.[15] The lobbying corps contributed generously to the Barnes reelection campaign and largely ignored challenger Sonny Perdue. Because of the aggressiveness of Barnes's fundraising campaign and his pressures on lobbyists not to hedge their bets by giving token amounts to Perdue, a number of lobbyists would not even return phone calls from the challenger. Consequently, when Perdue upset Barnes, the new governor owed nothing to most lobbyists. Rumors circulated around the Capitol that the new governor had a list of lobbyists with whom he would not interact. Into the uncertainty surrounding the change in governors stepped a number of ambitious Republicans. These new lobbyists included some who had served in the General Assembly and experienced GOP campaign activists. They sought to win business away from established firms by pointing out the quality of their ties to the leaders of Republican Party that now controlled both the governorship and Senate. "If you want to have any input to the governor or in the Senate," they warned, "you need to hire us."

Not only did change in partisan control open the door for new lobbying enterprises, it also shifted the relative balance of influence between certain

---

[14]projects.publicintegrity.org/decs/hiredguns/legLobbyist_graphic.html (accessed June 10, 2008).

[15]Much in this section draws on Charles S. Bullock III and Karen L. Padgett, "Partisan Change and Consequences for Lobbying," *State and Local Government Review* 39 (2007): 61–71.

established interests. For example, under Speaker Murphy, his fellow trial lawyers enjoyed favored status. The Judiciary Committee, comprised almost exclusively of lawyers and chaired by a series of Murphy confidants, had wide-ranging responsibilities and often received sensitive legislative proposals whose subject matter would seem to be outside the scope of a committee focusing on judicial matters. Moreover, the Judiciary Committee received several types of proposals strongly opposed by the bar. For example, the committee held up tort reform proposals that would limit the pain and suffering damages awarded to accident victims—and thus the contingency fees for successful plaintiffs' attorneys. In addition, Murphy led efforts against proposals to bar legislators who were also attorneys from representing private clients before state boards and to grant prosecutors the same number of jury strikes as defense attorneys in criminal cases.

During the Barnes administration, trial attorneys had a fellow member atop the executive branch, and they showed their appreciation with generous and enthusiastic support for his reelection. During a three-month period, attorneys gave Barnes almost $1 million, more than 20 times what they gave Perdue.[16] During his four-year term, Barnes received contributions totaling more than $3.4 million from more than 3,400 attorneys.[17] The total contributions from each of several large Atlanta law firms exceeded $100,000. In the wake of Barnes's defeat and the GOP takeover of the Senate, Georgia trial lawyers recognized the peril confronting their interests and, in anticipation of the 2004 elections, they devoted unprecedented attention to recruiting candidates for the legislature. They even recruited trial attorneys who would run as Republicans since, like most groups, they had a single dominant interest—the defeat of tort reform. If a legislator were willing to oppose tort reform, the trial lawyers could support that individual regardless of party. A group too closely linked to one party can become vulnerable should the party they support lose, which happened to trial lawyers in 2005. Once Republicans completed gaining control of state government, they enacted tort reform that capped recoveries for pain and suffering from a single defendant at $350,000.

The change in control also strengthened the hand of conservative religious groups that are among Republicans' strongest supporters. Sadie Fields, head of the Christian Coalition, enjoyed unprecedented access to the governor and legislative leaders. The new Republican leadership rewarded the Religious Right, which had played such an important role in ousting Democrats, by passing legislation that Democrats bottled up in the legislature. At the top of the list of priorities for religious conservatives had been abortion restrictions, and the first session controlled by Republicans passed

---

[16]Rachel Ramos, "Lawyers Keep Barnes' Funds Brimming" *Fulton Daily Report* (October 17, 2002), 1, 7.
[17]Richard Whitt, "Big Bucks Rain on Barnes' Campaign," *Atlanta Journal Constitution* (October 14, 2002), B8.

a "Woman's Right to Know" bill. This required that a woman seeking an abortion be counseled about the alternatives and wait one day after first approaching an abortion provider before having the procedure. Another change required that an underage girl be accompanied by a parent before getting an abortion. Previously a young girl needed only to have an adult present. The leader for Georgia Planned Parenthood, acknowledged that her organization had never been as poorly positioned vis-à-vis the General Assembly.

The passing of the old regime required lobbyists to work harder regardless of whether their positions found favor with the new majority. In the past, if a lobbyist lined up the support of the Speaker of the House, the lieutenant governor, and the governor, the probability of success approached 100 percent. Indeed, in the House, if Speaker Murphy actively supported the proposal, he would help run interference and might even detail one of his lieutenants to help secure enactment.

Under the Republican legislative leadership, a greater number of legislators gained influence in the decision process. In 2003, lobbyists complained that they had to work much harder because they had to contact so many more legislators. Lobbying in Georgia had become more like that in the national Capitol, where the lobbyist has to repeat the reasons behind the position taken by the organizations he or she represents to a seemingly endless list of legislators. In 2003, some Georgia lobbyists remarked with surprise that even freshman wanted to have input, and their views had to be considered.

ETHICS REFORM

Republicans, who felt that the Democratic majority bent the rules for partisan advantage, repeatedly called for ethics reform. Sonny Perdue pledged that should he become governor, ethics reform would be a top item on his agenda. In his initial State of the State Address, he made ethics reform a high priority. The Republican-dominated Senate passed the governor's ethics proposals but, like much of Perdue's program, they died in the Democratic House. Once Republicans took control of both chambers, they adopted portions of the Perdue package. The new legislation required that lobbyists reveal sources of income that paid them more than $10,000 annually. New electronic reporting forms were devised for lobbyists' expenditures. The law imposed a one-year cooling-off period before legislators, constitutional officers, and state agency heads could begin lobbying. Democratic critics noted that the governor did not include his office in this effort to delay the immediacy of a revolving door.

During the 2002 gubernatorial campaign, the *Atlanta Journal Constitution* reported that many of the individuals appointed to the state bench by Governor Barnes had made campaign contributions to him. The 2005 legislation prohibited contributions to a governor's reelection fund from those seeking a judicial appointment.

While the General Assembly took action on Governor Perdue's ethics proposals in 2005, his fellow Republicans balked at enacting the entire package. The governor's ethics proposal had also limited the value of gifts or meals provided by lobbyists to legislators to no more than $50, a provision to which Speaker of the House Glenn Richardson (R) objected. House Minority Leader DuBose Porter (D) could not resist the opportunity to twit the majority with the disparaging observation that, "This bill went from a choir robe to a g-string—that's all it covers." To this, the majority leader responded by noting that the night before, the Democratic leader had attended a dinner sponsored by a lobbyist that had the following menu: "Appetizer: broiled crab cake. Entree: 18 oz. New York Strip Steak. Dessert: key lime pie, and there was a $39 bottle of wine sitting on the table. 'Mr. Porter, you're talking out of one side of your mouth and eating out of the other. If you keep doing that, that g-string's not going to fit.'"[18]

Regulating Lobbying

Georgia requires that lobbyists register with the Ethics Commission and identify their clients. The state allows a wider range of expenditures than federal law or some other states permit. Some states prohibit all expenditures on behalf of legislators. In Georgia, however, while lobbyists must report the amount spent on legislators, there is no cap on the amount. The House defeated Governor Perdue's proposal to limit meals and gifts to $50. And while Perdue sought to limit some aspects of lobbyists' expenditures, he accepted $200,000 from AT&T to help pay for his inauguration ball.[19] The Center for Public Integrity, which evaluates state lobbying regulations, ranks Georgia as tied for the eighteenth best. Among weaknesses identified by the Center are the absence of a cooling-off period between the time a member leaves the legislature and embarks on a lobbying career, and of a requirement that lobbyists reveal what they are paid.

CONCLUSION

Interest groups play an especially important role in the Georgia legislature because of the dearth of staff. Lobbyists provide vital information that helps legislators assess the proposals on which they must vote. The shift in partisan control has opened the way for lobbyists with ties to the GOP, and this has contributed to different interests being advantaged than succeeded when Democrats controlled the legislature. Georgia permits lobbyists to provide legislators with a variety of benefits so long as these are reported,

---

[18]Sarah Ann Galle, "A Season of Change: A Glimpse into the Changes of the Georgia House of Representatives During the 2005 Legislative Session," unpublished manuscript.
[19]James Salzer, "The Surf, the Sand. The Life of Lawmakers," *Atlanta Journal Constitution* (September 9, 2007), A12.

and representatives of economic interests as well as those retained by public entities ply legislators with food, drink and tickets to events.
Representatives of concerns with few financial resources have to rely on the
power of their arguments to bring legislators around to their positions.
Those who wear the lobbyist badge around the Capitol come from various
backgrounds, and some work for public affairs firms while others are employees of the interests they represent.[20] Still others run one- or two-person
operations, while some who speak for society's less fortunate work largely
as volunteers.

---

[20]Legislators, lobbyists, interns, aides and reporters all wear distinctive badges when the General
Assembly is in session.

CHAPTER 13

The Electoral Process

For many years, Georgia's electoral politics was strictly an intramural affair played out among Democrats. Candidates competed for the Democratic nomination, and those who succeeded attained public office, usually without general election competition, since Republicans rarely offered competing slates. The first Republican primary for governor did not occur until 1970. In most elections from 1900 to 1950, not a single Republican ran for a Georgia congressional seat, and Republicans seeking legislative or local offices were also rare.

Now both parties have heated primaries for open positions at the state level. In many counties and legislative districts, however, one-party politics persists. Some urban counties, as well as rural ones with large percentages of African Americans, have so few Republicans that meaningful competition takes place in the Democratic primary. In many suburban counties, the opposite situation prevails. Democrats rarely put forward candidates, and those who run provide little competition to the winners of the Republican primary.

PRIMARIES

Although the Democratic primary no longer controls access to public office as it did for most of the twentieth century, primaries remain important for candidate selection since they winnow the fields of Democrats and Republicans to one for each party. Partisan primaries take place in the summers of even-numbered years, after candidates qualify for office in late April. Georgia is an open primary state, which means that voters do not indicate a partisan preference when registering, which allows them to participate in either party's primary. When appearing at the polls, the voter can select either party's ballot.

Georgia is one of fewer than 10 states that require a majority vote for nomination. Although many cities use runoffs, the states that have this practice are in the South and have a history of Democratic dominance. In the past, requiring a majority vote ensured that a small faction within the Democratic Party could not win office with a narrow primary plurality. When no candidate gets a majority in the primary, the top two finishers compete in a runoff three weeks after the primary. While a voter can opt to participate in either party's primary, a voter who voted in one party's primary cannot participate in the other party's runoff, since the two stages are considered to be part of a single decision process.

The candidate who leads in the initial primary moves on to win the nomination in the runoff approximately 70 percent of the time.[1] Instances in which the runoff reverses the order of finish for the top two candidates most often occur in elections for high visibility offices such as governor and senator. Moreover, the security of the frontrunner is less when he or she has eked out a narrow plurality in the primary. Incumbents unable to secure a majority in the initial primary lose runoffs more frequently than do challengers or the leading candidates in contests for an open seat.

Primary participation has changed dramatically since 1990, as reported in Table 13.1. In that year, Democrats cast 90 percent of the ballots; in recent years they have struggled to get more voters to the polls than the Republicans. As the Democratic primary electorate has shrunk, it has become

TABLE 13.1   Partisan Primary Turnout

Year	Total	Democratic	Republican	Percent Registered Turnout
1990	1,171,131	1,053,013	118,118	43.50
1992	1,151,971	875,149	276,822	40.10
1994	761,371	463,049	298,322	25.80
1996	1,182,168	717,302	474,866	33.70
1998	905,383	486,841	418,542	23.70
2000	960,414	613,884	340,001	26.70
2002	1,102,611	575,533	527,078	28.60
2004	1,418,838	731,111	671,961	35.40
2006	912,358	485,748	426,610	21.40
2008 Pres.	2,014,544	1,056,251	958,293	44.90
2008 Reg.	1,011,199	552,651	458,548	21.30

Source: Computed by authors from official election returns. See Georgia Secretary of State, Georgia Election Returns, available at http://www.sos.georgia.gov/ELECTIONS/election_results/default.htm (last visited September 5, 2009).

---

[1]Charles S. Bullock III and Loch K. Johnson, *Runoff Elections in the United States* (Chapel Hill: University of North Carolina Press, 1992).

blacker. The African American share of the Democratic primary vote has doubled since the early 1990s and now comes close to equaling the white vote. The growth in the black share of the primary vote increases the likelihood of nominating African Americans and liberals of any race. In the presidential primary of 2008, more blacks than whites took Democratic ballots and Barack Obama beat Hillary Clinton by more than a 2:1 margin. With few Georgians identifying themselves as liberals, choosing liberals to lead Democrats into the general election makes their election difficult in much of the state.

Declining turnout constitutes another change visible in Table 13.1. Obviously fewer voters now select Democratic nominees. While participation in GOP primaries has grown, Republican contests do not attract as many people as voted in the Democratic primary in 1990. Primary voters do not provide a reliable sample of the attitude distribution in the public. Those who turn out in primaries tend to be strong partisans and therefore are less likely to be moderates. Thus the risk becomes that Democrats will nominate candidates too liberal for most Georgians, while Republicans might select candidates to the right of most Georgians.

PRESIDENTIAL PRIMARY

Every leap year, Georgians can participate in another primary. Since 1972, Georgia has chosen delegates to the national party conventions via a presidential preference primary held early in the spring. In most counties, the only item on the ballot will be the candidates seeking their party's presidential nomination. With so little to be determined appearing on the ballot, participation in the presidential preference primary remained relatively small until 2008.

In 2008, Georgia, like many other states, experienced record participation in the presidential primary, as reported in Table 13.2. Democrats attracted more than a million voters, with Barack Obama winning the largest percentage he received in any state. The Republican side also witnessed record turnout, with Mike Huckabee polling 34 percent, narrowly defeating John McCain, who got 32 percent, and Mitt Romney with 30 percent. In

TABLE 13.2   **Participation in Recent Presidential Primaries**

Year	Democrats	Republicans
2000	284,431	643,188
2004	616,541	161,374*
2008	1,056,251	958,293

*Nomination uncontested

Source: Computed by authors from official election returns. See Georgia Secretary of State, Georgia Election Returns, available at www.sos.georgia.gov/ELECTIONS/election_ results/default.htm (last visited September 5, 2009).

both parties more voters came to the polls in 2008 than in 2000 and 2004 *combined.*

Georgia, along with other southern states, sought to increase the region's influence in the presidential selection process by establishing the first Super Tuesday. In 1988, southern states held their presidential primaries on the same date, hoping to encourage the Democratic candidates to spend more time campaigning in the South and to adopt positions more in line with the moderate to conservative stands taken by southern Democrats. The southern leaders who instituted Super Tuesday also hoped that situating the region's presidential primary early in the selection process—an approach called front loading—would increase the likelihood that their party would nominate a candidate from their region, someone like Georgia Senator Sam Nunn. Southern Democratic leaders had become concerned that the presidential nominees offered by their party were too liberal to compete effectively in the South. The blowout losses suffered by George McGovern (1972) and Walter Mondale (1984) had endangered Democrats down ticket.

The effort to enhance the South's influence in selecting the Democratic nominee failed in 1988 because the creators of Super Tuesday overlooked two significant changes. They did not anticipate the presence of an African American candidate, Jesse Jackson, who united black support and won a plurality in Georgia and the other Deep South states. Contributing to the Jackson success was another factor overlooked by the creators of Super Tuesday: no longer did white southerners uniformly vote in the Democratic primary. With the Republican presidential nomination also being hotly contested, many southern conservatives opted to vote in the Republican primary. That decision made the Democratic primary electorate still more liberal and less likely to support Al Gore, the one white southerner in the contest.

Although the Democratic strategy failed in 1988, as another liberal northerner, Michael Dukakis, won the nomination but failed to carry any southern states in the general election, Georgia sought to enhance its influence in the 1992 selection process. Under the urging of Governor Zell Miller, the state moved its presidential primary forward one week, becoming the first southern state to vote. Miller's friend and fellow southern governor, Bill Clinton, bounced back from a second place finish in New Hampshire to win convincingly in Georgia. Other southern states followed Georgia's lead.

Recently, Georgia's influence in the selection process has diminished substantially as other, larger states have also engaged in front loading. In 2008, Georgia moved its primary up to February 5, only to be eclipsed by balloting taking place on the same day in New York, Ohio, and California, each of which has far more delegates to the national conventions.

GENERAL ELECTIONS

The general election comes in November of even-numbered years. Every general election involves a selection of all members of the General Assembly and members of the U.S. House. The selection of constitutional officers and

BOX 13.1

General Election Runoffs

Nine states have vote thresholds, and these usually require candidates to get a majority of the vote in order to win a nomination. Georgia has a similar requirement for primaries, but unlike other states, it also requires candidates to win the general election with a majority of the vote. Failure to poll a majority necessitates a runoff between the top two vote getters.

When Democrats dominated Georgia politics, the general election majority-vote requirement rarely came into play. But as Republicans gained strength, the presence of a Libertarian or independent candidate on the ballot increased the possibility that no one would get a majority.

General election runoffs remain infrequent, but since 1992, five statewide partisan contests have needed a second vote to pick a winner. In 1992, Senator Wyche Fowler came up 17,379 votes short in his bid for reelection. In the runoff, former Peace Corps director and state senator Paul Coverdell overcame a 35,000 vote deficit to upset the incumbent by 16,238 votes. Since Coverdell had needed a runoff to win the GOP nomination, he had to compete in four elections to make it to the Senate. The same election saw the first Republican ever elected to the Public Service Commission (PSC) win an open seat in a runoff.

In the wake of the Fowler defeat, the Democrat-dominated legislature changed the vote threshold to require only 45 percent of the vote to win a general election. This lower threshold enabled Max Cleland to win a Senate seat in 1996 with 48.9 percent of the vote.

Republicans believed that had the majority-vote requirement been in effect, they would have repeated the 1992 experience and overtaken Cleland in a runoff. Once Republicans took control of state government in 2005, they resurrected the majority-vote standard. In the next election, the higher threshold paid the GOP a dividend as the Democratic incumbent on the PSC led the field with 48.8 percent of the vote. In the runoff, the Republican challenger won with 52.2 percent.

The majority-vote requirement came into play again in 2008, but this time it gave each party a second chance to reverse the fate of the initial vote. Senator Saxby Chambliss (R), like Wyche Fowler, led in the general election in his effort to secure a second term but fell 9,200 votes short of a majority. In the other contest, Democrat Jim Powell led former PSC member Lauren "Bubba" McDonald by 23,000 votes, but neither major party candidate reached 48 percent.

During the month leading up to the Senate runoff television advertising intensified, pre-recorded calls filled voice mails, and many Georgians got more pieces of campaign mail than Christmas catalogues. In the end, Republicans did the better job of getting their core constituents back to the polls, and Chambliss and McDonald won with 57 percent of the vote. The 2008 runoffs repeated what has become a pattern of Republicans victories.

vote for president occur on a four-year cycle but Georgia, like most states, selects statewide constitutional officers so as not to coincide with the presidential election. Separating the election of governor and other constitutional offices from the choice of a president will make the electorate more attentive to the issues raised by the state candidates in the years that they appear on the ballot.

As a result of separating the state from the national elections, fewer Georgians express preferences for the leaders of the state than for president. Participation rates in the off-year elections invariably fall well below those in the presidential years. Even though a greater number of Georgians participate in the presidential elections, in both presidential and off-year elections, Georgia has one of the lowest rates of participation in the nation. The 2006 turnout of 2.1 million was less than 60 percent of the 3.9 million Georgians who voted in 2008.

Georgia is unique in requiring a majority to win a general election. The need for a runoff becomes a possibility if a Libertarian or independent candidate competes along with a Democrat and a Republican. In 2008, statewide runoffs decided the winners of the U.S. Senate seat and a seat on the Public Service Commission. Republicans have proved much more successful than Democrats in getting their supporters to return to the runoff that comes four weeks after the general election. No Republican has lost a statewide runoff. In the 2008 Senate runoff, Saxby Chambliss (R) won with a 57 percent landslide after coming up 18,000 votes short of a majority in November.

MUNICIPAL ELECTIONS

Georgia cities follow the logic that results in the separation of state and national elections. That is, municipal elections take place at times separate from the election of state and county officials, as well as the president. Most municipalities elect their mayors and council members in odd-numbered years. Most Georgia municipal officers, unlike state officials and most county officers, compete in nonpartisan elections. This may be yet another reason for separating the choice of municipal officials from the choices of higher officers.

SPECIAL ELECTIONS

Elections at times different from those offices discussed above may become necessary to fill vacancies caused by the death or resignation of an officeholder. The governor calls special elections to replace public officials and chooses one of two formats. One option is to hold a conventional party primary and runoff with general election to follow. The other option, which is more often selected since it eliminates at least one election and therefore saves money, uses an open primary with a runoff to determine the officeholder if no candidate polls a majority.

Special elections are often scheduled to deal with financial matters such as a bond referendum or, more frequently, a referendum to levy a local sales tax. Counties and school boards can levy an additional one-cent sales tax to fund capital projects. Thus a school board may propose an additional special local option sales tax (SPLOST) to pay for the construction of new school facilities or the rehabilitation of existing ones. At the county level, a SPLOST may be proposed to pay for highway projects or the construction of public buildings. If the local electorate approves the tax, it will be added to the 4 percent state sales tax and will be collected until it retires the bonds sold to pay for the new facility.

REGISTRATION

Traditionally, registering to vote could be done only at the county courthouse with the probate judge. The Motor Voter Act made registration in Georgia and elsewhere in the nation easy. One can sign up to vote when getting a driver's license or by going to the local library or various government offices. Especially in election years, voter registration drives are held on campuses and in shopping centers. Even simpler is to download the voter registration form from the Internet. In 1945, Georgia became the first state to allow 18-year-olds to register and vote.

THE ACT OF VOTING

As recently as 2000, Georgia counties used four different major types of ballots. Many counties used an optical scan system. Particularly in urban areas, balloting took place using punch cards like those that caused the confusion and delayed the Florida vote count in the 2000 presidential election. Also widely used were voting machines, lever-operated contraptions about the size of a large refrigerator. Although these had not been manufactured in decades, they generally gave a reliable count and would not permit overvoting, which involves expressing preferences for more than one candidate for a position. Two counties voted the old fashioned way by marking paper ballots with pencils.

After the embarrassment suffered by Florida with its punch card ballots and questions about whether a voter had expressed a preference by sufficiently punching out a chad on the ballot, Georgia's Secretary of State Cathy Cox launched her own investigation of Georgia voting. She discovered that a larger percentage of Georgia voters than Florida voters who had gone to the polls had failed to register a legal preference. Anticipating that she and Georgia might get sued, Secretary Cox convinced the legislature to authorize a uniform electoral system for the state. She opted for a touch-screen voting system, using technology similar to that involved in ATM banking transactions. Georgia spent $54 million to become the first state to have touch-screen voting statewide.

Almost immediately, critics fretted that hackers could manipulate the voting machines. They urged that the system be retrofitted to provide a paper receipt that could be reviewed in case of a recount. Secretary Cox rejected this idea because of added expense. A survey done at the University of Georgia found 93 percent of the voters had confidence in the voting process, an increase of 20 percentage points over the old system. Although calls for a paper trail continue, thus far the state has taken no steps to modify or replace its voting machines.

Voting in Georgia again became the center of controversy and litigation in 2006, when the legislature required that voters produce photo identification in order to vote. The change tightened the types of identification accepted by poll workers from 17 to seven and required a government-issued photo identification. Representatives of the elderly, blacks, and the Democratic Party went to court to enjoin implementation of this change. They asserted that their clients were less likely to have a driver's license, the most widely available form of acceptable identification. Research has shown that these groups are less likely to have a drivers's license or the identification card issued by the state for nondrivers.[2] The state offered to make an ID card available at no charge to anyone who lacked a driver's license. After years of legal wrangling, the photo ID requirement passed muster in both the federal and state courts. At the federal trial, plaintiffs failed to produce a single voter who lacked an acceptable ID or testified that it would be impossible to get one. In 2009, the General Assembly considered adding another precondition for registering which would require that new voters prove that they are U.S. citizens.

PARTICIPATION BY ETHNIC GROUPS

Georgia is one of only five states in which voters indicate their race or ethnicity when registering to vote. Until 2001, the options were limited to *white*, *black*, and *other*. Now, in addition to the traditional categories, other options are *Asian American*, *Native American* and *Latino/Hispanic*. For the last couple of rounds of elections, Georgia has reasonably accurate figures on the number of registered voters by ethnicity. Moreover, by reviewing the sign-in sheets from the polling places, it is possible to determine the number of actual voters by ethnicity. Table 13.3 shows the make up of the Georgia electorate as of the 2006 general election. At that time, about 66 percent of the registered voters were white and 27 percent were black.[3] Whites turned out at a higher rate than any of the other groups, so that they cast almost 73 percent of all votes. Note that although all of the constitutional statewide offices were on the ballot, turnout in the 2006 general election eclipsed participation in the 2008 presidential primary by only about 100,000 votes.

---

[2]M.V. Hood III and Charles S. Bullock III, "Worth a Thousand Words?: An Analysis of Georgia's Voter Identification Statute," *American Politics Review*, 36 (July 2008): 555–79.

[3]Efforts of the Obama campaign succeeded in registering large numbers of African Americans so that by the time of the 2008 general election, blacks constituted 30 percent of Georgia's registrants, while whites were below 63 percent.

TABLE 13.3   Registered Voters and Turnout as of the 2006 General Election

Race	Registered	Voted	Percent Turnout	Percent Total
2006				
African Americans	1,198,259	512,495	42.80	24.00
Whites	2,963,854	1,553,839	52.40	72.90
Latinos	43,514	11,608	26.70	0.50
Asian Americans	43,245	11,347	26.20	0.50
Other/Unknown	158,316	41,674	26.30	2.00
Total	4,407,288	2,130,963	48.40	100.00
2008				
African Americans	1,560,419	1,182,509	75.80	30.10
Whites	3,258,454	2,522,294	77.40	64.10
Latinos	73,375	43,717	59.60	1.10
Asian Americans	62,591	36,382	58.10	0.90
Other/Unknown	244,132	149,486	61.20	3.80
Total	5,198,971	3,934,388	75.70	100.00

Source: Computed by authors from official election returns. See Georgia Secretary of State, Georgia Election Returns, available at www.sos.georgia.gov/ELECTIONS/ (last visited September 5, 2009).

Although Barack Obama did not win Georgia's electoral votes, the enthusiasm surrounding his campaign carried over to the Peach State as registration rose by a sixth over 2006 to 5.2 million. Many of the new registrants contributed to a record turnout of more than 3.9 million. More than three-fourths of the black and white registrants cast ballots. The excitement among African Americans resulted in an unprecedented turnout with their share of voters (30.1 percent), slightly exceeding their share of the registrants and equaling the black share of the adult population. As the share of ballots cast by blacks rose from 24 to 30 percent, the proportion coming from whites fell by almost 9 percentage points. Because relatively few minorities vote for Republican candidates, as the Georgia electorate becomes more diverse, the share of the white vote needed for GOP candidates to win statewide increases.

Campaign Finance

As with the rest of the nation, the cost of campaigning has grown dramatically. In 2002, Roy Barnes spent $20 million in his unsuccessful reelection bid. In that same year, a state Senate contest saw the four competitors spend more than $1 million. The successful candidate spent more than three-quarters of a million dollars to win a post that pays $17,000 per year. Contests for the state legislature now regularly cost more than six figures. Contested elections for Congress invariably cost more than a million dollars. In Georgia's most hotly contested

2006 congressional race, in which John Barrow retained his seat by fewer than 900 votes, he spent $2.27 million, while the loser, former Representative Max Burns, spent $2.17 million.

Campaign Consulting

For major elections such as governor or senator, campaign consulting firms around the nation bid for business in Georgia. One of the most visible campaign advisors, James Carville, and his partner at the time Paul Begala, achieved national attention when they managed Zell Miller's 1990 gubernatorial campaign. They helped Miller develop his appeal: a promise to institute a statewide lottery, the proceeds from which would go to support collegiate scholarships and a pre-kindergarten program for four-year-olds. Miller introduced his successful advisors to Bill Clinton, and they managed his 1992 presidential campaign.

Increasingly, campaigns for state legislature and even local offices rely on professional assistance, and candidates for these offices turn to local operations. Among the most visible has been Ralph Reed's Century Strategies. After Reed stepped down as political director for Pat Robertson's Christian Coalition, he returned to his native Georgia, where he established a campaign consulting and lobbying operation. His firm has been involved in a number of contests both in Georgia and around the nation. While Century Strategies works campaigns across the region, a younger generation of professionals concentrates on Georgia races. On the Republican side Clint Austin, Joel McElhannon, Marty Klein, and Mark Roundtree manage multiple campaigns of candidates who compete for offices local to statewide. The Democratic side has Billy Joyner, Gunner Hall, Page Gleason, and Bernita Smith. Campaign consultants offer a cafeteria listing of services. They can provide general strategy, polling assistance, fundraising help, and assistance in message crafting, designing mail pieces and in putting together a volunteer organization.

Ayres, McHenry & Associates, a national Republican polling operation, made its mark in Georgia and for many years was located in Atlanta before moving to Washington, DC. Democrats often turn to Beth Shapiro and Associates, an Atlanta-based pollster. Insider Advantage, headed up by former legislator Matt Towery, is the leading independent pollster currently located in Georgia.

CONCLUSION

Georgia, like other states, has a variety of elections with statewide officials competing at the presidential midterm, while local elections tend to be divorced from either presidential or statewide contests. Any of these election cycles, except for the presidential primary, which occurs in the spring of leap years, can be followed by a runoff. In some presidential years, Georgians have had as many as five major elections in which to participate, and in some localities additional elections have occurred to vote on referenda like a SPLOST levy. Jim Martin (D), who ran unsuccessfully for the U.S. Senate, competed in four contests in 2008: Democratic primary, Democratic runoff, general election and general election runoff.

While some observers have suggested that Americans tend to vote at lower rates than citizens of other countries in part because of voter fatigue produced by the multitude of elections, interest surrounding the 2008 presidential election resulted in Georgians turning out in record numbers both in the presidential primary in February and in the general election in November. Georgia's electorate has become increasingly diverse and in 2008, African Americans registered and voted in unprecedented numbers. The much-litigated photo ID requirement for voting in person seemed not to deter many voters in 2008. It remains to be seen whether the dramatic increase in participation will persist or if the appeal of Barack Obama had a unique impact.

CHAPTER 14

Education Policy

Education is the largest single budget item in the state of Georgia. Consequently, policy affecting common and higher education is arguably the most important issue before the General Assembly, as these items represent the greatest use of the public's money. The history of public education cannot be disentangled from the economic and racial history of the state; indeed, it is in many ways representative of the progress of Georgia since the eighteenth century and is also indicative of the consequences of institutional and political continuity in the state since the Civil War.

CONTEMPORARY EDUCATION IN GEORGIA

Georgia currently has 181 public school systems, of which 159 are county systems. Consolidation has dramatically reduced the number of school districts, which once numbered over 300. Approximately, one in every three schools in Georgia is in a rural setting.[1] Such schools continue to serve as a basis for community identity and often are the only local facility providing cultural opportunities or community gathering places. In this sense, the role of these schools has changed a little in the last century. Local school districts are headed by appointive superintendents and elected school boards. Prior to 1996, some local school superintendents were elected, and some local school boards were appointed by county grand juries.

There are also nearly 600 private schools or academies in the state, enrolling over 115,000 students. There were also 65 charter schools accredited from 1993 to 2004, with 37 in operation as of the fall of 2004.[2] As of January 2009, the Georgia Charter Schools Association identified 43 member schools.[3]

---

[1] Alice Sampson, "Rural Education" *The New Georgia Encyclopedia,* http://www.georgiaencyclopedia.org/nge/Article.jsp?id=h-2616 (October 1 2009).

[2] *Georgia Charter Schools,* "Facts at a Glance, August 2004," http://www.doe.k12.ga.us/_documents/schools/charterschools/charter_stats.pdf (October 1 2009).

[3] *Georgia Charter Schools,* "Directory of Schools," http://www.gacharters.org/directory-of-schools/ (October 1 2009).

BOX 14.1

Enrollment and Staffing

The Georgia public education system enrolls over one and a half million students in primary and secondary schools and employs nearly 100,000 teachers, 9,000 support professionals, and 7,000 administrators. The teacher-to-administrator ratio is 13.9:1; the student/teacher ratio is 16.5:1. According to data reported by Mewborn in 2007, 2002 enrollment in the public schools in Georgia was 53 percent white, 38 percent black, and 5.5 percent Latino. The Latino figures have nearly doubled in seven years. Enrollment as of March 2009 is 48 percent white, 38 percent black, and 10 percent Latino.

Source: Georgia State Department of Education, www.doe.k12.ga.us.; *New Georgia Encyclopedia,* "Public Education (PreK-12)" (by Denise Mewborn), www.georgiaencyclopedia.org/nge/Article.jsp?id=h-2619 (September 15, 2009).; Georgia Department of Education, 2009. School Year 2008–2009 Enrollment by Gender, Race/Ethnicity and Grade (PK-12), accessed at app3.doe.k12.ga.us/ows-bin/owa/fte_pack_ethnicsex.display_proc.

Approximately 32,000 students are currently homeschooled in Georgia. And, about 60,000 four-year-olds are enrolled in public pre-kindergarten (pre-K) programs funded with money from the lottery, and another 20,000 low-income children take part in Head Start programs. Both pre-K and Head Start programs are administered by Bright from the Start: Georgia Department of Early Care and Learning (formerly known as the Office of School Readiness).

Georgia has three schools for students with special needs, including the Georgia School for the Deaf in Cave Spring, the Georgia Academy for the Blind in Macon, and the Atlanta Area School for the Deaf (AASD) in Clarkston. The first two academies listed are residential schools founded in the mid-nineteenth century, while AASD was started in 1972 as a day-school program for deaf children in the metropolitan area.

The average annual per-pupil expenditure for 2007–2008 was $8,965.[4] About 40 percent of funding comes from local property taxes, with the balance coming from state appropriations. Local schools may also elect to raise money using special-purpose local-option sales taxes (SPLOST). The tax must be approved by the public in referendum, and the one-cent tax can only apply to capital improvements and outlays or the retirement of capital debt.

The Georgia Department of Education (DOE) was created in 1870. At present, the department has 380 full-time employees and interacts with local school systems employing nearly 120,000 persons. The department is headed by the elected state superintendent of education, who reports to the 13-member state board of education, appointed by the governor, with one member from each Georgia congressional district. Oversight is conducted

[4]*Administrative Technology: Georgia Department of Education.* app.doe.k12.ga.us/, (September 5, 2009).

by permanent House and Senate Education Committees. The department houses offices with diverse functions related to every aspect of education and student well being (see Box 14.2). DOE responsibilities include curriculum design and reform, textbook adoption, student assessment, student safety, nutrition, and transportation.

BOX 14.2
Organization of the Georgia Department of Education

Administrative organization

1. Office of Standards, Instruction and Assessment
   Division of Standards Based Learning
   Division of Innovative Instruction
   Division of Assessment and Accountability
2. Office of Finance and Business Operations
   Account Services
   Budget Services
   Facility Services
   Financial Review
   Internal Support
   Pupil Transportation
   School Nutrition
3. Office of Policy and External Affairs
   Charter Schools
   Communication
   Human Resources
   Policy
   State Schools
4. Office of Education Support and Improvement
   Learning Support
   Migrant Education
   School Improvement
5. Office of Technology Services
   Instructional Technology
   Information Technology
6. Standardized Testing
   Criterion-Referenced Competency Tests
   End-of-Course Tests
   Georgia High School Graduation Test
   Georgia Alternate Assessment
   Georgia Writings Assessments

Source: Compiled from information at Georgia State Department of Education website, www.doe.
k12.ga.us.

COMPLETION AND DROPOUT RATES AND ACADEMIC PERFORMANCE

The dropout rate is the number of students who leave school to join the military, take a job, give birth, are incarcerated, or fail out. General equivalency diploma (GED) students count as dropouts. Completion refers to the rate at which ninth graders graduate four years later. Georgia's completion rate from ninth to twelfth grade is around 73 percent. Georgia's average Scholastic Aptitude Test (SAT) score in 2003 was 984, while the national average was 1026. The SAT is more broadly administered in Georgia than in many other states, likely contributing to the lower average score. Mewborn points out that in 2002, 54,000 of the 72,000, or about 75 percent, of Georgia high school graduates took the SAT, while just 1,900 of 32,000, or about 6 percent, of Iowa graduates took the SAT.[5] In 2009, 71 percent of Georgia seniors took the SAT, while ACT participation rose by about 8 points.[6] Georgia's highly diverse student population also contributes to the lower SAT average, according to the College Board, which administers the SAT.

THE EVOLUTION OF PUBLIC EDUCATION IN GEORGIA

Georgia mandated public education in the original state constitution of 1777. The creation of universally accessible public education would take more than a century. The first public high school opened in 1783, in Augusta, but it was not until 1915 that the state provided a high school anywhere in Georgia for African American students.

The first effort at creating a statewide comprehensive system of education for the children of free white residents did not occur until 1858, and implementation was delayed by the Civil War. The first legislative session after the Civil War called for the creation of a free public education system in 1866, and the 1868 constitution mandated a "thorough system" for "all children of the state" regardless of race, and established a poll tax and a whiskey tax to fund the schools, thus simultaneously introducing sin taxes and Georgia's first discriminatory voting device. The Republican Reconstruction government in 1870 instituted the system structure, and with the return of Redeemer Democratic government in 1872, the system was implemented. This system, however, did not provide any state funding for black schools in the racially segregated system.

EDUCATING THE FREEDMEN

Starting in 1829, it was a crime in Georgia to educate an enslaved person. Subsequent to emancipation demand for literacy education by Georgia blacks was overwhelming. From 1866 to 1874, the number of freed blacks in schools increased from 8,000 to 20,000 persons.

---

[5]Denise Mewborn, "Public Education (PreK-12)" *New Georgia Encyclopedia,* www.georgiaencyclopedia .org/nge/Article.jsp?id=h-2619 (September 15, 2009).

[6]Jessica Jordan, "Georgia SAT scores drop in 2009" *Gainesville Times,* www.gainesvilletimes.com/ news/archive/22728/ (August 31, 2009).

BOX 14.3

"Advances" in Education in Georgia Since World War II

1945: Constitution explicitly mandates segregated schools, thereby making explicit what had been fact for eight decades.

1949: Uniform nine-month school year becomes mandatory.

1951: Three-penny sales tax is passed to fund schools.

1954: *Brown* v. *Board of Education* overturns the *Plessy* v. *Ferguson*'s separate-but-equal segregation standard. Georgia revives the states' rights doctrine of nullification and interposition and declares the decision "null and void" within the state.

1957: The legislature passes a law allowing the state to terminate funding to integrated schools and permitting the governor to close integrated schools.

1959: First major divisions over integration occur in the state, as progressive Atlantans battle to keep state funding even if their schools integrate. Simultaneously, many of the same Atlantans fight to maintain a "community schools" standard and to resist efforts to integrate neighborhoods in order to maintain de facto segregation.

1960: Sibley Commission recommends maintaining funding of integrated public schools.

1961: First Atlanta high schools integrate, as does the Georgia higher education system.

1963: Schools in Savannah, Athens, and Brunswick integrate.

1970: Georgia enjoys the most integrated schools in the United States after concerted effort by federal authorities to compel integration.

1985: Quality Basic Education Act is passed.

1993: HOPE scholarship fund takes effect.

2001: A+ Education Reform Act is passed.

Source: 2008–2009 Education Policy Primer, "Education in Georgia" www.gpee.org/2008–09-Education-Policy-Primer.126.0.html (September 3, 2009).

Local black populations started to educate themselves at the grassroots, with local schools established as early as January 1865. Private freedman's aid societies created additional schools by the summer, and with the creation of the Freedman's Bureau by Congress in March 1865, funding was available for renting of school facilities and to provide books and transportation for teachers. The national government did not provide salary or other operation costs. State tax dollars were not appropriated for freedman's schools.

BOX 14.4

Homeschooling

From 1975 to 2005 the number of children homeschooled in Georgia increased from 10,000 to 35,000. Students who are homeschooled are held to the same standards of achievement and attendance as other students who attend traditional public schools or private academies. The motives for homeschooling are numerous—medical and religious reasons, concerns about the safety or quality of education in public schools, or even the belief that some students learn better outside the traditional classroom environment that typifies industrial and post-industrial-era education. Homeschooled children are required to engage the same basic curriculum of science, math, social studies, and language arts as students in traditional schools. At least four and a half hours of instruction are required per day for 180 instructional days. These students are subject to the standardized tests and evaluation mechanisms mandated for students in regular schools.

Source: www.ghea.org/pages/resources/stateLaw.php (November 10, 2008) and Ga.code.ann. §20–2–690(c)(5).

Of almost 600 teachers in freedmen schools, only one in five were Georgia natives. One in four teachers was African American. The Freedmen's Bureau ceased funding for schools in 1870, approximately the same time that Georgia started to fund white (but not black) public education. The private aid societies directed their efforts to educating black teachers and developing urban centers of higher learning, such as the colleges that subsequently became the Atlanta University complex.

Early in the Reconstruction period, Georgia mandated segregated schools but even these were underfunded. Salaries and infrastructure support were lower in the black than white schools. With a few exceptions, local districts did not create black secondary schools until well into the twentieth century. The first public state college for blacks was not established until 1891, with the creation of Georgia State Industrial College (now Savannah State University).

EARLY EDUCATION REFORM

The nineteenth century witnessed little commitment to public education in Georgia. As illustrated by the example of the freedmen, local education was a local responsibility especially in black communities, and given the lack of resources and capacity in those communities, the efforts were rudimentary at best. Georgia's commitment to universal education came late, only really starting in the early twentieth century.

Georgia first made school attendance compulsory for all children between the age of eight and 14 in 1916. The state Board of Education was established in 1937. Until the early 1950s, Georgia only required an eleventh-grade education to attain a high school diploma.

From the 1950s through the end of the 1960s, most education debates revolved around preserving segregated schools. With the ultimate success of federal efforts to compel integration in the late 1960s, Georgia policy makers devoted greater efforts to improving public education. School funding soon came to command a majority of the state budget.

THE SIBLEY COMMISSION

The Sibley Commission was created in 1960 by Governor Ernest Vandiver to confront the growing reality of challenges to segregated schools in Georgia. Elected subsequent to the *Brown* decision and also the controversial integration of Little Rock Central High School in 1957, Vandiver campaigned on the promise that "no, not one" student would set foot in an integrated school were he elected to succeed segregationist Marvin Griffin as governor. However, by 1963 when Vandiver gave way to Carl Sanders, some public schools in Georgia and also the public higher education system of Georgia had integrated.

Governor Vandiver had promised to follow the policy lead of Virginia's political boss, Harry Byrd, who urged massive resistance among southern whites which would culminate by closing public schools confronted with integration. In 1960, confronted with a federal court order to desegregate the Atlanta public schools, Vandiver and his chief of staff, attorney Griffin Bell, asked state representative George Busbee (later governor from 1975 to 1983) to introduce legislation creating a Committee on Schools to examine the integration question. The commission, chaired by noted attorney John Sibley, gathered public sentiment toward integration.

The Sibley Commission sought to generate support for a "local option" approach to integration. Holding 10 hearings across the state, the commission sought to minimize the record in favor of massive resistance while encouraging a solution that would allow the option of symbolic desegregation at the discretion of local boards. Most witnesses still favored massive resistance, but the commission recommended acceding to desegregation while minimizing its scope within the districts.

The following January, after a federal order integrated the University of Georgia (UGA), the legislature repealed a ban on funding integrated schools. Christopher Allen Huff at UGA notes that the actions of Sibley Commission did prevent violence in desegregation in Georgia. However, he also contends that the Commission provided a blueprint for local white school boards to stave off desegregation.[7]

---

[7]Christopher Allen Huff, "The Sibley Commission" *New Georgia Encyclopedia,* www .georgiaencyclopedia.org/nge/Article.jsp?id=h-2617 (September 15, 2009).

BOX 14.5

Title I Funding

Title I funding is a federal education program that directs additional funds to local school districts for enhanced instructional development based on need, as measured by enrollment in the free or reduced-price lunch program. The basis for assessing economic need is poverty of the student population based on eligibility for free and reduced-price lunches. This is an example of using a proxy measure of need to assess the likelihood that other aspects of student development are not met at home. According to UGA's Denise Mewborn, the benefits and design of Title I are enjoyed by over half of the state's schools, to provide supplemental instruction in order to elevate student achievement. If half of the students in a school meet eligibility standards, Title I funds can be used for all students; if not, then funding can only be used to assist students not performing up to state standards.

Source: *New Georgia Encyclopedia*, "Public Education (PreK-12)" (by Denise Mewborn), www.georgiaencyclopedia.org/nge/Article.jsp?id=h-2619 (September 15, 2009).

QBE: THE QUALITY BASIC EDUCATION ACT

A former state legislator, Governor Joe Frank Harris, acting in concert with then state Senator Roy Barnes, advanced the 1985 Quality Basic Education Act (QBE) during his first term in office. The main thrust of QBE was to attain some degree of parity in funding for rich and poor school districts. Until QBE, the state had funded schools on a per-pupil basis with no consideration of the capacity of local systems to contribute to the quality of schools. Some school systems, such as those in the Atlanta suburbs, enjoyed more property tax revenue and therefore, had greater fiscal capacity to provide a quality education. Urban districts faced shrinking tax bases, while rural schools had insufficient revenues, and also, by tradition, had not adequately funded local education, in part due to the legacy of segregation. The QBE provided additional funds to schools that committed to increase local funding under a program called "local fair share."

QBE was not just free money. Suburban lawmakers sought to tie funding to pupil and teacher performance standards. The state instituted a complex funding formula based not on head-count, but rather on effort. This concept, termed the student full-time equivalent standard, tied funding to the amount of time students spent in the classroom, thereby promoting full-time attendance in underperforming districts.

The act also raised the minimum pay for teachers, introduced one of the first merit pay systems in the South, and increased funding for continuing education and accreditation of teachers.

QBE established a core curriculum—the Quality Core Curriculum (QCC)—that was the standard for Georgia public schools until 2003. QCCs were revised in 2003, when an external audit of the system criticized the curriculum for a lack of rigor. The revision, called the Georgia Performance Standards (GPS), went into effect in 2005 and was based on a primary core in English, math, physical science, and social sciences.

Assessment was performed on primary education students using the Criterion-Referenced Competency Test, based on standards and objectives from the 1985 Quality Core Curriculum and its revisions. Secondary students must complete both a core curriculum and pass the Georgia High School Graduation Test (GHSGT) to obtain a diploma, and standard End of Course Tests (EOCT). The EOCTs have been administered in certain high school subjects since 2004. Students in grades 3, 5, 8, and 11 must take written assessment tests.

THE LOTTERY AND HOPE

Zell Miller's political ambitions in Georgia had been thwarted by ongoing battles with old establishment Democrats. A former staffer for Governor Lester Maddox, the longtime lieutenant governor had failed in his 1980 effort to displace Herman Talmadge in a primary runoff. His ongoing battles with Speaker Tom Murphy had contributed to factionalism in the state Democratic Party, and it was generally believed that Murphy would do whatever it took to defeat Miller in the 1990 gubernatorial primary to succeed Murphy's protégé, Governor Joe Frank Harris.

Miller, however, managed to undergo another of his many political reinventions and staked his entire campaign on the creation of a lottery for education. Throughout the 1980s, states had experimented with lotteries. A major disappointment for lottery supporters, who hoped that the new revenue would benefit education, had been that lottery revenues were substituted for other appropriations to education programs. This act of substituting lottery revenues for other revenues in the general appropriation meant that no enhancement of education funding was realized.

The Miller proposal, which vaulted him to a runoff election victory over Atlanta Mayor Andy Young and a general election win over state Representative Johnny Isakson, was to dedicate lottery revenue to new education programs. Georgia voters approved the lottery by constitutional amendment in 1992, and in 1993, the lottery became reality in Georgia. Georgia learned the hard lessons of other states and limited lottery money to three new programs. The most popular and the one that has gotten the bulk of the lottery dollars has been the Helping Outstanding Pupils Educationally (HOPE) scholarships, which pay tuition to Georgia public colleges and universities along with a stipend for books for students who made a "B" average in a college prep curriculum. Other uses of lottery proceeds have funded pre-kindergarten schooling for four-year olds and upgrades to connect classrooms to the internet.

RECENT EFFORTS: A+ EDUCATION REFORM ACT AND NO CHILD LEFT BEHIND

HB 1187 was passed by the Georgia legislature and signed by Governor Roy Barnes on April 25, 2000. The act set caps on maximum class size, mandated school attendance for six-year-olds (all persons ages 6 to 16 must attend school) and most controversially, abolished tenure for public school teachers. In the area of school governance, A+ created an office of Education Accountability (now the Office of Student Achievement) and mandated use of the Criterion-Referenced Competency Test (CRCT). It also required each school to create an advisory board called a School Council, which consisted of two parents, two students, two teachers, two business people from the community, and the principal. The council serves as a sounding board on any matter of school policy or performance. The legislature restored tenure in 2003 and modified the class size caps after Governor Barnes failed to win reelection.

At the national level, the federal 2001 No Child Left Behind Act (NCLB) mandates student testing across a core skills set and uses those results to assess school progress. When schools fail to provide adequate yearly progress or cannot provide a safe environment, parents can request transfer to more successful schools. Persistently failing schools can be subject to personnel and administrative reorganization.

"TOUGH TIMES"

Governor Sonny Perdue came forward with a recommendation to fundamentally alter education in Georgia. In the summer of 2008, Perdue appointed a commission, the Tough Choices or Tough Times Working Group to examine the recommendations of the Tough Choices education initiative, a product of the New Commission on the Skills of the American Workforce. The group produced its recommendation in the spring of 2009 and advanced a variety of proposals to restructure primary, secondary, and community college education to improve the efficiency and performance. This proposal constitutes a dramatic change in public education in Georgia and in many ways represents the shifting of political power into the growing suburban counties.

The core of the proposed reform is based on creating a flexible public education system that minimizes inefficiency in advancing students toward their educational or vocational potential. The working group recommended altering the secondary education system to allow students to progress down a vocational or educational path when they are ready and argued that students who have demonstrated sufficient mastery to move on to college-level work by the eleventh grade be allowed to do so, instead of wasting "time and resources on school work that is not productive." To accommodate this goal, the working group recommended rigorous Advanced Placement courses, dual enrollment in college, or allowing qualified eleventh graders to leave high school early. In addition, the state will need to develop an assessment standard to determine that students are ready to move on.

In the long term, the commission recommended the creation of a comprehensive community college system either by "merging the technical colleges and two-year colleges so there is a seamless entry point for all students" or creating and enforcing a mechanism for the easy transfer of students between the two systems. The group also proposed a new mechanism for funding these programs that allows money to follow students. Consistent with the national sponsors of tough choices, the group also recommended exploring public/private partnerships to fund "demonstration sites" for implementing the AP, dual enrollment, and early departure options for students.

The second major recommendation of the group was to recruit and retain "World-Class Teachers" through a variety of mechanisms, including distance learning options; aggressive recruitment; rebranding primary and secondary education as a profession on par with law, medicine, and higher education; and creating a culture to attract and retain quality teachers.

The commission suggested that teacher training shift toward core subject matter expertise instead of pedagogy and that a more competitive model of teacher training be encouraged in the teachers' colleges. Alternative models of certification, including the Teach for America model, should be aggressively pursued, and the group recommended an assessment system that ascertains the "value added" of teacher efforts toward students. The group also recommended altering compensation to allow for differentiated pay in math and science in order to attract high quality applicants for these hard-to-fill positions, to account for student performance in merit pay, and to reward advanced education in the field of specialization rather than compensating advanced teaching certifications.

Many of the elements of the working group proposal have a solid foundation in the education debate for some decades. In the 1990s, Texas started requiring that teachers have degrees in a substantive field, rather than an education degree with a specialization. Numerous states have experimented with, or debated, merit systems of pay and alternative certifications. The opening up of alternatives to the senior year of high school and the desire to see more language instruction reflects an increasingly literate, urbane, and affluent Georgia population. Most interesting for Georgia is the possible reorganization of the technical school and two-year colleges, long protected by rural political interests for reasons other than the educational value of the schools.

CONCLUSION

Education is the most significant policy arena for Georgia government. Nearly every Georgian will come into contact with the education system. The education budget is the single-largest component of the state budget, and educational institutions are among the largest employers in the state.

Education policy in Georgia reflects the evolution of the Empire State of the South. Georgia changed from a rural frontier state built on land speculation, agriculture, and the mill industry to a regional center of transportation and industry and then to a vibrant international destination that is home to the eighth largest urban center in the United States. Education policy has kept pace with the broader needs, requirements, and dominant cultural preferences of Georgia. Advances in civil rights and the changing status of African Americans have been accompanied by changes in the education system. The nature of how Georgia's education system interacts with its African American residents reflected the dominant power structure— Georgia went from a place where it was illegal to instruct a slave to a place where the government funded the instruction of the freedmen, and then to a place where educational institutions were basically denied to blacks based on the ability of the white supremacy ideology to prevail in the broader political structure.

The national battles for integration were fought in Georgia, sometimes for decades. Once Jim Crow had been run from the field by the cannons of federal litigation and federal legislation, the focus of policy in schools shifted from separation to improvement. For nearly three generations, governors of Georgia have made their policy reputations in public education. The evolving emphasis away from a politics of separation and minimal education, designed to serve rural land owners, gave way to an egalitarian desire that schools be good and that teachers be both effective and accountable.

INDEX